U.S. Security Cooperation with Africa

The book is a well-written and timely reminder of the need for the United States to make a greater effort in the areas of diplomacy, development and human security in its security cooperation policy. The author acknowledges the accomplishments of AFRICOM in building military capacity but also incisively criticizes the unintended consequences.

Stephen F. Burgess, *Air War College, USA*

As Africa's strategic importance has increased over the past decade and a half, United States security cooperation with the continent has expanded. The most visible dimension of this increased engagement was the establishment of the U.S. Military Command for Africa (AFRICOM). Some critics are skeptical of AFRICOM's purpose and see the militarization of U.S. Africa policy while others question its effectiveness. Recognizing the link between development and security, AFRICOM represents a departure from the traditional organization of military commands because of its holistic approach and the involvement of the Department of State as well as other U.S. government stakeholders. Nevertheless, AFRICOM's effort to combine security and development faces formidable conceptual and operational challenges in trying to ensure both American and African security interests. The human security perspective's emphasis on issues that go beyond traditional state-centered security to include protecting individuals from threats of hunger, disease, crime, environmental degradation, and political repression as well as focusing on social and economic justice is an important component of security policy. At the same time, the threat of violent extremism heavily influences U.S. security cooperation with Africa.

In this examination of the context of U.S.-African security relations, Robert J. Griffiths outlines the nature of the African state, traces the contours of African conflict, surveys the postindependence history of U.S. involvement on the continent, and discusses policy organization and implementation and the impact of U.S. experiences in Iraq and Afghanistan on the U.S.-Africa security relationship. Africa's continuing geostrategic significance, the influence of China and other emerging markets in the region, and America's other global engagements, especially in light of U.S. fiscal realities, demonstrate the complexity of U.S.-African security cooperation.

Robert J. Griffiths is Associate Professor of Political Science at the University of North Carolina at Greensboro.

Routledge Advances in International Relations and Global Politics

U.S. Security Cooperation with Africa

Political and Policy Challenges

Robert J. Griffiths

NEW YORK AND LONDON

First published 2016
by Routledge
711 Third Avenue, New York, NY 10017

and by Routledge
2 Park Square, Milton Park, Abingdon, Oxon, OX14 4RN

First issued in paperback 2017

Routledge is an imprint of the Taylor & Francis Group, an informa business

Library of Congress Cataloging-in-Publication Data
Names: Griffiths, Robert J., author.
Title: U.S. security cooperation with Africa : political and policy challenges /
    Robert J. Griffiths.
Other titles: United States security cooperation with Africa
Description: New York : Routledge, 2016. | Series: Routledge advances in
    international relations and global politics ; 126 | Includes bibliographical
    references and index.
Identifiers: LCCN 2015042902 | ISBN 9780415532372 (hbk)
Subjects: LCSH: Security, International—Africa. | United States. Africa
    Command. | United States—Military relations—Africa. | Africa—Military
    relations—United States.
Classification: LCC JZ6009.A35 G75 2016 | DDC 355/.0310973096—dc23
LC record available at http://lccn.loc.gov/2015042902

ISBN 13: 978-1-138-48651-5 (pbk)
ISBN 13: 978-0-415-53237-2 (hbk)

Typeset in Times New Roman
by Apex CoVantage, LLC

To Katy for the inspiration and Aaron for the motivation.

Contents

Acknowledgments

Special thanks to Simone Cappati for his invaluable research and bibliographic help. Thanks also to Natalja Mortensen and Lillian Rand at Routledge for their patience and support.

Acronyms

ACIRC	African Capacity for Immediate Response to Crises
ACLED	Armed Conflict Location and Event Data
ACRF	African Crisis Response Force
ACOTA	Africa Contingency Operations Training Assistance
ACRI	African Crisis Response Initiative
ACSS	African Center for Strategic Studies
ADAPT	Africa Deployment Assistance Partnership Team
AFAFRICA	U.S. Air Forces Africa
AFDL	Alliance of Democratic Forces for the Liberation of Congo-Zaire
AFRICOM	United States Military Command for Africa
AGOA	African Growth and Opportunity Act
AMISOM	African Union Mission in Somalia
AMLEP	African Maritime Law Enforcement Partnership
ANC	(Congo) Congolese National Army
ANC	(South Africa) African National Congress
APS	African Partnership Station
APSA	African Peace and Security Architecture
AQIM	Al Qaeda in the Islamic Maghreb
ASF	African Standby Force
AU	African Union
BPC	Building Partner Capacity
BRIC	Brazil, Russia, India, China
CAR	Central African Republic
CEMAC	Economic and Monetary Union of Central Africa
CJTF-HOA	Combined Joint Task Force-Horn of Africa
CNL	Committee of National Liberation (Congo)
CNOOC	China National Offshore Oil Corporation
COCOM	Combatant Command
COIN	Counterinsurgency
COPAX	Council for Peace and Security in Central Africa
CSL	Cooperative Security Location

CSSDCA	Conference on Security, Stability, Development and Cooperation in Africa
DCME	Deputy to the Commander for Civil-Military Engagement (AFRICOM)
DCMO	Deputy Commander for Military Operations (AFRICOM)
DDR	Disarmament, Demobilization and Reintegration
DOD	Department of Defense
DOS	Department of State
DRC	Democratic Republic of Congo
ECCAS	Economic Community of Central African States
ECOMOG	Economic Community of West African States Monitoring Group
ECOWAS	Economic Community of West African States
EEZ	Exclusive Economic Zone
EO	Executive Outcomes
ERM	Early Response Mechanism
FDLR	Democratic Forces for the Liberation of Rwanda
FIB	Force Intervention Brigade
FMF	Foreign Military Financing
FNLA	National Front for the Liberation of Angola
FOCAC	Forum on China-Africa Cooperation
FOMAC	Central African Multinational Force
FOMUC	Force Multinationale en Centrafrique
GAO	Government Accounting Office
GNI	Gross National Income
GSPC	Salafist Group for Preaching and Combat
HAC	Humanitarian and Civic Assistance
ICU	Islamic Courts Union
IDP	Internally Displaced Person
IGAD	Intergovernmental Authority for Development
IMET	International Military Education Training
ISWAP	Islamic State West African Province
JAES	Joint Africa-European Union Strategy
JCET	Joint Combined Exchange Training
JEM	Justice and Equality Movement
LRA	Lord's Resistance Army
LURD	Liberians United for Reconciliation and Development
MAAG	Military Assistance Advisory Group
MARFORF	U.S. Marine Corps Forces Africa
MCA	Millennium Challenge Account
MEND	the Movement for the Emancipation of the Niger Delta
MICROPAX	Mission de Consolidation de la Paix en République Centrafricaine

MINUSCA	Multidimensional Integrated Stabilization Mission in the Central African Republic
MINUSMA	UN Stabilization Mission in Mali
MLC	Mouvement pour la Libération du Congo
MNLA	Azawad National Liberation Movement
MODEL	Movement for Democracy in Liberia
MONUSCO	United Nations Organization Stabilization Mission in the Democratic Republic of Congo
MPLA	Popular Movement for the Liberation of Angola
MUJAO	Movement for Tawhid and Jihad in West Africa
NAVAF	U.S. Naval Forces Africa
NPFL	National Patriotic Front for Liberia
OAU	Organization of African Unity
OEF-TS	Operation Enduring Freedom-Trans-Sahara
OHDCA	Overseas Humanitarian Disaster and Civic Assistance
ONUC	Opération des Nations Unies au Congo
PAGAD	People Against Gangsterism and Drugs
PEPFAR	President's Emergency Program for Aids Relief
PILOT	Partnership for Integrated Logistics Operations and Tactics
PLA	Popular Liberation Army (Congo)
PREACT	Partnership for Regional East African Counterterrorism
PSI	Pan-Sahel Initiative
PSO	Peace Support Operations
QDR	Quadrennial Defense Review
RAF	Regionally Aligned Forces
RCD	Rassemblement Congolais pour la Démocratie
RPF	Rwandan Patriotic Front
RUF	Revolutionary United Front
SADC	Southern Africa Development Community
SALW	Small Arms and Light Weapons
SIPO	Strategic Indicative Plan for the Organ (SADC)
SIPRI	Stockholm International Peace Research Institute
SLA	Sudan Liberation Army
SOCAFRICA	U.S. Special Operations Command Africa
SRF	Sudan Revolutionary Front
SSTR	Security, Stability, Transition, and Reconstruction
SWAPO	Southwest African Peoples' Organization
TFG	Transitional Federal Government
TSC	Theater Security Cooperation
TSCTI	Trans Saharan Counterterrorism Initiative
TSCTP	Trans-Sahara Counter Terrorism Partnership
UCDA	Uppsala Conflict Data Program
UNHCR	United Nations High Commissioner for Refugees

UNAMIR	UN Assistance Mission for Rwanda
UNAMSIL	UN Mission in Sierra Leone
UPA	Union of the Peoples of Angola
UPNA	Union of the Peoples of Northern Angola
USAID	U.S. Agency for International Development
USARAF	U.S. Army Africa

Introduction

Africa's Growing Strategic Importance and the Challenges of Security Cooperation

Africa's vast wealth and its strategic location provided the original motivation for colonialism and continue to account for the continent's importance. Historically, the continent's fortunes have shifted as its strategic importance has waxed and waned. In 2000, *The Economist* described Africa as the "hopeless" continent.[1] By 2013, in a major turnaround, the March 2 issue of *The Economist* special report touted "Emerging Africa" as "a hopeful continent."[2] Clearly much has changed on the continent since that first *Economist* article. Over the past decade and a half, much of Africa has registered strong economic growth, with an aggregate GDP growth rate of 5.8% between 2000 and 2010 and an average growth rate of 4.1% between 2011 and 2013. The World Bank estimates that Africa's growth was 4.5% in 2014 and forecast economic growth rates of 4.6% in 2015, rising to 5.1% in 2017.[3] Growth has been fueled by investments in infrastructure, agricultural production, and an expansion of the service sector, while commodities demand and capital inflows are expected to contribute less to growth.[4] Africa's 2006 total Gross National Income (GNI) of $978 billion put it ahead of India as a total market. In fact, its market was larger than that of all the BRIC (Brazil, Russia, India, China) countries except China. Ranked against countries, Africa's economy would have placed it at number 10 in the world.[5] In 2014, private equity capital raised for investment in Africa was estimated at $4 billion, with more than half of that invested. However, the World Bank estimates that the continent needs an additional $90 billion per year just to improve infrastructure. While investment increases are essential to sustaining recent growth rates, despite these investment increases, only about 1% of global private equity goes to Africa.[6]

Long an economic backwater whose main attraction was its raw materials, Africa has enjoyed recent growth that has made the continent more attractive to investment. Although country growth rates have varied, the continent's vast natural resources, growing middle class, and rapidly expanding population have attracted growing trade and investment and improved the prospects for Africa. Africa's strategic significance goes beyond its vast natural resource wealth and trade potential and also extends to its geographical position astride major sea lanes and growing influence in international forums, where African states make up the largest voting bloc. Of course, Africa's strategic importance is also tied to the threat of radical Islam and the continent's role in the transnational trafficking of drugs, arms, people, and other contraband. These elements of Africa's strategic significance have made Africa a growing U.S. security concern. Most of the commentary on Africa's strategic importance has centered on counterterrorism, access to Africa's natural resources, and the potential for strategic competition, especially between the U.S. and China, but these are not the only strategic factors involved.

Africa has historically been of peripheral interest to American security planners. That has changed as Africa's importance has grown in the past decade and a half. With the continent enjoying the world's second-fastest growing economy, an aggregate GDP of nearly $2 trillion,[7] and progress toward democratic reform, albeit incomplete, uneven, and fitful, Africa's strategic profile has grown as its prospects have improved. Africa's resources drove the exploitation of the colonial era, and the continent's vast energy and mineral resources continue to play a key role in explaining Africa's emergence from economic marginalization. While resource growth continues to be important, growth is also coming from other sectors at the regional and national levels and is less vulnerable to commodity price shocks and less dependent on raw materials exports.

Africa's continued prosperity depends on a secure environment. Yet, stubborn pockets of conflict and instability potentially limit further investment and economic growth in some areas. At the least, instability discourages investment, and, as any examination of the continent's recent security history shows, Africa's conflicts and instability often have broader regional effects. Africa's complex regional security environment includes low levels of development and weak institutions that encourage patronage and identity politics, while its porous borders contribute to the spread of Islamic radicalism, transnational criminal activity, and the potential for spillover from the region's conflict zones.

Although Africa remains a secondary security priority for the United States, its growing strategic importance makes it impossible to neglect the implications of the political, economic, and security climate across the continent. Africa's re-emergence as a strategically important region of the world comes at a time when the U.S. faces strategic challenges from an ascendant China and a resurgent Russia and the U.S. is preoccupied with its efforts to disengage from Afghanistan and Iraq. This, combined with pressure on foreign aid and defense spending and a polarized domestic political environment that led to gridlock and sequestration, makes fitting Africa onto a crowed security agenda a formidable task.

Africa's prosperity has helped increase its confidence, political leverage, and diplomatic clout. Nevertheless, Africa's persistent poverty and low levels of development, entrenched authoritarian rule, military intervention into politics, intrastate conflict, and transnational security threats continue to draw attention to the continent's security environment and its importance to continued growth and prosperity. Demand for resources has helped to improve the economies of many states, but revenues are subject to fluctuation, and the resource curse can increase tensions over the distribution of the revenue from energy and mineral resources. Africa's trade and investment potential, geographical location, and political influence in international forums also highlight concerns about strategic competition for influence on the continent.

Africa's greater strategic importance and the focus on security on the continent prompted the United States to create the U.S. military command for Africa (AFRICOM) as the vehicle for security cooperation with African countries. According to Department of Defense (DOD) Joint Publication 1–02, security cooperation involves DOD interactions to build relationships designed to promote U.S. security, develop allied and friendly military capabilities for self-defense and multinational operations, and provide U.S. forces with peacetime and contingency access to host nations.[8] This development not only raises questions regarding the nature of U.S.-African security cooperation but also comes amid debates over the concept of security in the African context, the nature and scope of Africa's conflicts, state weakness and the persistence of identity politics, and the threat of Islamic radicalism in the region. American security policy toward Africa is also influenced by U.S. wariness about intervening in Africa, especially after the American experience in Somalia in the early 1990s, compounded by a general American weariness after its long involvement in Iraq and Afghanistan, skepticism of U.S. motives in the post-Iraq and Afghanistan era, domestic constraints on American policy, and the diffusion of power in the international system, or what Fareed Zakaria calls the "rise of the rest."[9] These factors create a complex security environment for analysis of American security policy toward Africa.

U.S.-African security policy, particularly the 2007 creation of AFRICOM, has generated substantial controversy regarding deepening U.S. security cooperation with countries across Africa and what some see as the militarization of U.S. Africa policy. U.S. participation in the no-fly zone during the Libyan revolution in 2011, the 2011 decision to deploy a small force of U.S. troops to Central Africa to help fight the Lord's Resistance Army, the growing use of drones for surveillance and intelligence gathering in the fight against Islamic extremism, the dispatch of a small contingent of U.S. troops to assist Nigeria in the battle against Boko Haram, and the dispatch of between three thousand and four thousand troops to West Africa to assist in fighting the Ebola epidemic that erupted in 2014 are among the recent high-profile manifestations of growing U.S. military involvement on the African continent. Beyond these more high-profile activities, the U.S. military is also engaged in a whole range of increasingly routine training and capacity-building operations across Africa.

U.S. security engagement with Africa had been growing since the 2002 United States National Security Strategy focused more sharply on African security and identified Africa as a region of growing importance. By 2004, it was clear that U.S. had recognized "Africa's new strategic significance."[10] The 2006 U.S. National Security Strategy further described the continent as having growing strategic importance for the U.S. and identified Africa as a high priority.[11] The creation of AFRICOM in 2007 and the commencement of its operations in 2008 were the culmination of an increasingly focused U.S. approach to security on the continent. By 2010, the U.S. National Security Strategy specifically noted the complexity and diversity of the continent as well as the challenges and opportunities of engagement. It also highlighted a wide range of U.S. security and development initiatives on the continent.[12]

According to AFRICOM's mission statement, U.S. security cooperation with Africa is driven by several goals: "to deter and defeat transnational threats, prevent future conflicts, support humanitarian and disaster relief, and protect U.S. security interests."[13] In practice, this has included training African troops for peacekeeping, humanitarian intervention, and counterterrorism activities against Islamic radicals and affiliates of al Qaeda and the Islamic State operating in Africa; securing American access to energy and mineral resources; and promoting human rights, development, and democracy. More extensive U.S. engagement with Africa has emphasized not only counterterrorism, peacekeeping, and humanitarian aid but also antipiracy measures, security-sector reform, and an effort to professionalize African armed forces, to both enhance the capacity of partner states and emphasize the importance of a democratic pattern of civil-military relations. It also involves a broader range of activities that involve development-related tasks, capacity building, and civic action activities. These broader activities in particular have fueled the criticism that U.S. Africa policy has become militarized.

While a broad-based approach to U.S. security cooperation with Africa offers the potential to enhance the peacekeeping, counterterrorism, and combat capability of the continent's armed forces and perhaps an opportunity to influence the future role and mission of African armed forces, it also faces substantial obstacles. Recent developments in Sudan, Mali, Nigeria, Somalia, Guinea-Bissau, the Democratic Republic of Congo, the Central African Republic, and Burkina Faso illustrate the wide range of political circumstances, institutional capacity, and security challenges on the continent. The multifaceted security challenge in Africa also draws attention to the conceptual frameworks for analyzing security and politics in Africa, organizational and political constraints on U.S. policy, and global changes that influence security in Africa.

Historically, the United States had relatively limited direct military involvement in Africa. With no colonial history in the region, the U.S., with a few notable exceptions like Ethiopia, Nigeria, Angola, South Africa, and the former Zaire, traditionally viewed Africa as having only peripheral strategic importance. The U.S. was initially content to leave it largely to the European allies to deal with their former colonial possessions. To the extent that the U.S. engaged with Africa during the Cold War, American interests in the region centered on the strategic competition with the Soviet Union; gaining African support for U.S. policies, especially at the UN, where the African countries make up the largest regional voting bloc; maintaining access to Africa's oil and mineral resources; and monitoring the continent's strategically important position astride important sea lanes, particularly those in proximity to the Middle East.[14] Although these remain important strategic considerations, counterterrorism, responses to humanitarian crises and complex emergencies, and concerns about the human dimensions of security are also now part of the security agenda.

America's first post–Cold War humanitarian operation was the ill-fated U.S. intervention in Somalia. The failure of that intervention left the U.S. wary of African entanglements and led to the subsequent failure to intervene to stop the genocide in Rwanda. Somalia and Rwanda not only illustrated Africa's challenging security landscape but also demonstrated the flaws in America's Africa policy. Aside from an unsuccessful effort to create an African Crisis Response Force in 1996, ostensibly to encourage African solutions to African problems, the U.S. reduced its engagement with the continent for much of the 1990s. The bombing of the U.S. embassies in Kenya and Tanzania in 1998 ended America's post–Cold War U.S. neglect of Africa. The embassy attacks were a prelude to the international terrorist threat that escalated with the September 11 attacks on the World Trade Center and the Pentagon. In the aftermath of those attacks, it was not surprising that the 2002 U.S. National Security Strategy focused attention on the threat from weak states and laid the groundwork for increasing U.S. security cooperation with Africa.

A key part of the effort to enhance African security and respond to the terrorist threat begins with the region's armed forces. But African armed forces lack essential capabilities and are themselves often a key source of insecurity. With a history of more than seventy coups since 1956[15] and an often-demonstrated institutional weakness, more professional armed forces are essential to African security. Despite a decline in the frequency of coups, recent military interventions in Mauritania (2008), Niger (2010), Mali (2012), and Guinea-Bissau (2012) demonstrate the continuing need for fully professional armed forces and a democratic pattern of civil-military relations. The use of the armed forces to stifle opposition to unpopular regimes illustrates another dimension of the threat posed by the armed forces. More professional and capable armed forces not only provide greater accountability and discourage the military's political intervention but can help to mitigate conflict, reduce human rights abuses, fight extremism and terrorism, and ensure the stability that contributes to foreign investment and economic growth. The growing emphasis on the connection between security and development also highlights African armed forces' potential role in development-related activities, perhaps leading to changes in the traditional role and mission of the armed forces, especially as the threat of interstate warfare recedes.

More capable, professional, and accountable armed forces alone do not guarantee security in Africa, however. The continent's complex security environment has less to do with traditional threats to the state and more to do with incomplete state building, human security, and regional security challenges. Clearly defining security in the African context, providing appropriate training and equipment, and enhancing the capabilities of the armed forces to deal with a complicated security environment is essential to a successful U.S.-African security partnership.

Adding to the complexity of defining security and implementing effective policy, U.S. security cooperation with Africa takes place in the context of the historical patterns of U.S. relations with Africa. Cold War strategic competition in Africa has led to skepticism over recent U.S. motives. Africa's security environment is further complicated by the range of issues and actors that contribute to conflict and instability. The continent's low levels of development have made it the focus of greater emphasis on human security, which broadens the purview of security tasks.

U.S. security policy toward Africa is also shaped by both the huge disparity between resources available for defense and those marked for diplomacy and development and the American emphasis on counterterrorism. U.S. security cooperation with Africa is also influenced by changes in U.S. military doctrine and strategy as a result of American involvement in Afghanistan and Iraq, particularly an emphasis on counterinsurgency, stabilization operations, and the crucial importance of conflict prevention. Although the emphasis on counterinsurgency and stabilization has declined, elements of these strategies are evident in U.S.-Africa policy.

At the same time, there is an inevitable wariness of overseas military involvement in the aftermath of the withdrawal of U.S. combat troops from Iraq and Afghanistan. The subsequent redeployment of troops to Iraq to counter the Islamic State and the broader tensions in the region, coupled with domestic economic and political constraints on U.S. foreign assistance, the American "pivot to Asia," and the diffusion of global economic and political power will have an impact on how America engages with its African partners.

Nevertheless, Africa has global security and economic dimensions that are impossible for the U.S. to ignore. The continuing threat from extremist groups like Boko Haram, al Shabaab, and al Qaeda in the Islamic Maghreb illustrates Africa's importance in the battle against Islamic extremism. Demand for Africa's energy and raw materials combined with increased African domestic consumption has contributed to recent economic growth trends in the region. In the past, Africa's energy and mineral wealth has been associated with the resource curse, although Africa's movement away from dependence on raw materials export, its growing domestic consumption and expansion of the service sector, and greater emphasis on revenue transparency may help to reduce this problem. Africa's growing importance also helps to strengthen its confidence, particularly given China's increasingly active role on the continent and its role as an alternative to the West and the U.S. in particular.

Security is about more than military assistance, however. Economic growth enhances stability and reduces the chances of conflict. There are growing links between Africa and the world's emerging markets, but U.S. investment in Africa is lagging. The 2014 summit of African leaders in Washington and the reauthorization of the African Growth and Opportunity Act in 2015 represent efforts to reduce this gap. Emphasis on transparency, accountability, and good governance are also essential components of a broad-ranging U.S. policy toward Africa.

U.S. Africa policy must also recognize the contrast between a traditional state-centric approach to security and the influence of the human security perspective. Africa's low levels of development dictate more focus on human security, and African security architecture not only reflects this emphasis on human security but also increasingly involves a regional and subregional focus. There is ample evidence that Africans have adopted a human security perspective in designing their regional and subregional security architecture. Judging from their missions and policy statements, African Union (AU) and subregional organizations aspire to a more integrated regional security approach. Security assistance has to be geared not only toward individual countries but also toward the AU and subregional organizations.

A particular challenge for security cooperation between partners with vastly different capabilities and interests is the management of the security priority mismatch that can result from differing views on the threat of international terrorism. Security cooperation implies that the partners share perspectives on the nature and scope of security threats, but cooperation between actors of vastly different capacities and often differing interests is difficult to coordinate. The U.S. may expect more than African countries are able or willing to provide, and the U.S. may prioritize security challenges differently from its African partners. Lingering perceptions of neocolonialism fuel African concerns that their security will be subordinated to U.S. policy preferences.

U.S. security cooperation with Africa not only involves important policy challenges but also has implications for defining, understanding, and analyzing security in the African context. How security is defined, in whose interest it is pursued, and the perspective from which security cooperation is viewed are all key components that influence the various actors and play a role in the analysis of U.S. security cooperation with Africa.

This book examines the recent evolution of U.S. security policy toward Africa, assesses the implications of growing U.S. involvement on the continent, compares and contrasts the security interests of the U.S. and its African partners, and discusses these developments in the context of the debate over security perspectives and past U.S. involvement with Africa. It traces the development of U.S. security cooperation with Africa, especially since the creation of AFRICOM, and the controversy surrounding the issues and actors involved, ties the evolution of security cooperation to international and regional security challenges, and looks at this collaboration from the standpoint of Africa's politics and the nature of the state, the securitization of African threats, the regional dimension of security, and U.S. power in the post-Iraq, post-Afghanistan era. The objective is to lay out the historical development of U.S.-African security cooperation and examine the challenges of forging a security partnership, using a conceptual framework that takes into account the human security perspective and differences in the capacity and interests of asymmetric partners. American security cooperation with Africa involves a wide range of challenges, including reconciling differences in threat perceptions and security emphasis, recognizing the crucial connection between security and development, and coping with a shifting global order. The effort to forge a U.S. security partnership with Africa takes place in the context of changing definitions of security, reappraisals of the role and mission of the armed forces, and the regional and international distribution of power.

Outline of the Book

Chapter one focuses on the complexity of the African security environment and the array of security challenges in the region, including weak and failing states, the resource curse, transnational criminal activity, piracy, human security, and traditional security challenges such as territorial protection, arms proliferation, and ethnic/regional conflict. It introduces the major security actors and their interests, including states, substate actors such as warlords and militias, and regional and subregional organizations such as the AU and the Southern African Development Community, as well as external actors such a the U.S. and China. It also discusses the conceptual frameworks that are relevant to security cooperation in Africa. A traditional state-centric definition of security largely guides U.S. policy, while a focus on regional institutions and an emphasis on human security are more common in the African context. Constructivism and postcolonial analysis are also relevant given the changing security norms on the continent and the legacy of colonialism. The discussion then turns to the challenge of security cooperation between actors of different capabilities and often divergent security emphases.

Chapter two looks more deeply at conflicts in the Horn, West Africa, and the Sahel region. It examines the diverse causes of conflict and the range of security challenges on the continent and suggests implications for U.S. security cooperation with Africa. It also discusses the regional nature of Africa's conflicts, the development of security architecture of the AU and African subregional organizations, and the influence of the human security focus on those organizations.

Chapter three details U.S. security interaction with Africa from the Cold War to the development of AFRICOM. U.S. policy toward Africa carries the baggage of past American engagement with Africa, driven by the exigencies of the Cold War, which often put the U.S. on the side of autocratic governments. It discusses U.S. engagement with important regional actors such as Nigeria, South Africa, the former Zaire, and Angola, as well as interactions with other states.

Chapter four examines the establishment of the U.S. Military Command for Africa (AFRICOM) and its unique structure, involving a governmental approach in which there is supposed to be cooperation between the Defense Department (DOD) and the State Department (DOS) and other U.S. stakeholders. It assesses this cooperation and the progress toward meeting the goals of connecting security and development by looking at the range of AFRICOM programs and U.S. funding levels. It also looks at African reaction to the creation of AFRICOM, including the responses of individual states, regional organizations, and civil society groups. It also highlights the strengths and weaknesses of the efforts to forge effective security cooperation between the U.S. and Africa and the influence of the American experiences in Iraq and Afghanistan.

Chapter five outlines Africa's strategic importance, including its abundance of oil and other strategic resources, as well as its importance for trade and investment, its geostrategic location, and its political influence in multilateral forums. It defines Africa's place in U.S. policy and more broadly in international affairs and contrasts American priorities and activities on the continent with those of other international actors such as China, India, Russia, Brazil, and other emerging market countries. It also examines the political and economic constraints on U.S. policy toward Africa.

Notes

1 "The Hopeless Continent," *The Economist*, 13 May 2000.
2 "Special Report: Emerging Africa A Hopeful Continent," *The Economist*, 2 March 2013.
3 "Global Economic Prospects, Sub-Saharan Africa," The World Bank, 6 January 2015, available at www.worldbank.org/content/dam/Worldbank/GEP/GEP2015a/pdfs/GEP2015a_chapter2_regionaloutlook_SSA.pdf
4 "Global Economic Prospects, Sub-Saharan Africa," 3.
5 Vijay Mahajan, 2009, *Africa Rising: How 900 Million African Consumers Offer More Than You Think* (Upper Saddle River, NJ: Prentice Hall), 7–8.
6 "A Sub-Saharan Scramble," *The Economist*, 24 January 2015, 55–56.
7 "The Gateway to Africa?," *The Economist*, 2 June 2012.
8 "Security Cooperation," *Joint Publication 1–02, Department of Defense Dictionary of Military and Associated Terms*, 8 November 2010 (as amended through 15 June 2015), 214–215.
9 Fareed Zakaria, 2009, *The Post-American World* (New York: W. W. Norton).
10 Greg Mills, "Africa's New Strategic Significance," *Washington Quarterly*, 27:4 (Autumn 2004), 157–169.
11 See *The National Security Strategy of the United States 2006*, 37, available at www.strategicstudiesinstitute.army.mil/pdffiles/nss.pdf
12 *National Security Strategy of the US*, May 2010, available at www.whitehouse.gov/sites/default/files/rss_viewer/national-security-strategy.pdf
13 AFRICOM Mission Statement, available at www.africom.mil/what-we-do
14 Karl P. Magyar, 2000, "Introduction: Africa's Transitional Role in America's Post-Cold War Era Diplomacy," in Karl P. Magyar, ed., *United States Interests and Policies in Africa* (New York: St. Martin's Press), 5–9.
15 See Jimmy D. Kandeh, 2004, "Civil-Military Relations," figure cited in endnote 4 in Adekeye Adebajo & Ismail Rashid, eds., *West Africa's Security Challenges* (Boulder: Lynne Rienner Publishers), 145–168.

1 The State, Politics, and the African Security Landscape

Africa's economic and demographic growth and its growing strategic importance have focused attention on the continent's security landscape. As the U.S., along with the rest of the world, recognizes Africa's economic, political, and security importance, the implications of the nature of the African state, the sources of conflict and insecurity, and the global dimensions of Africa's security challenges have become more salient.

There is little question that security is a critical state and regional challenge throughout a significant portion of Africa. While fighting ended in several of Africa's long-running wars in the early 2000s, large swaths of the continent continue to face conflict and instability. Africa's recent history has highlighted the challenges of formulating and implementing effective defense and security policy where conflict and instability, uneven economic growth, deep and persistent poverty, and varying levels of state capacity are widespread. Nevertheless, American recognition of Africa's growing strategic importance has led to deeper U.S. involvement on the continent and initiatives to create a partnership between the U.S. and Africa to protect American interests and enhance Africa's security capabilities.

The effort to create a U.S.-African security partnership takes place against a complicated backdrop of regional and global trends. These include political patterns and the nature of the African state, debate over the nature and implications of so-called new wars and fourth-generation warfare, the role of state and nonstate actors in security, the threat of Islamic radicalism, regional approaches to security, the history of U.S. involvement with Africa, economic and political constraints on American policy, and shifting global strategic calculations. Creating an effective security partnership between the U.S. and Africa poses some formidable challenges in defining security in the African context, enhancing the limited capabilities of African armed forces, and formulating policy appropriate to the continent's complex security environment.

The source of valuable raw materials and commodities and a growing market fueled by an expanding middle class, an increasingly important theater in the battle against Islamic extremism, and the site of persistent conflicts and humanitarian crises, Africa has seen its security become a matter of growing concern to the U.S. The former European colonial powers, along with China and emerging markets like India and Brazil, are also increasingly engaged on the continent and provide an additional dimension to any analysis of the continent's security environment.

In the past several years, Africa's natural resources have helped to fuel economic growth on the continent. Although the 2008 global financial crisis caused a dip in Africa's economic growth rates, prospects for increased growth are good. The continent's economy was expected to grow by 4.7% in 2014 and by 5% in 2015. Growth rates in several African countries will be among the strongest in the world. Growth rates vary between regions, with West Africa continuing to have the strongest growth rates and East Africa also performing well. Southern Africa's growth lags a little behind but is also expected to improve, while North Africa is projected to have the weakest growth. Although much of this growth is attributable to demand for African commodities, Africa's resource wealth is a mixed blessing. While it contributes to economic growth, primary production leaves African exporters vulnerable to demand and price fluctuations and has not necessarily boosted job growth.[1]

While the revenue from resource exploitation is essential to growth, it is all too often inequitably distributed. The "resource curse" raises issues of equity, weakens state links with the public, helps privatize the state's economic transactions to the benefit of elites, creates a gap between the state and its citizens, and crowds out investment. Given these drawbacks, it is fortunate that Africa's growth has also been powered by increasing investment from abroad as well as urbanization and domestic consumption.[2]

Africa's role as both producer of raw materials and a growing market for imported goods has drawn the attention of investors from around the world. Africa has now become too strategically and economically important to ignore, not only for its abundance of raw materials and growing internal market but also because of persistent conflict and instability, the threats of Islamic extremism and transnational crime, and geopolitical implications. As the U.S. has become more deeply engaged in Africa, the challenges of security cooperation have become more apparent.

A Brief Overview of the Security Landscape

Peace agreements in Sierra Leone in 2002 and Liberia in 2003 brought an end to brutal conflicts that had raged since the early 1990s. Southern Africa has been largely peaceful since the independence of Namibia in 1990, the end of Mozambique's civil war in the early 1990s, South Africa's 1994 elections that brought an end to apartheid, and the end of the civil war in Angola in 2002. Nevertheless, the ebb and flow of conflict and instability has been a recurrent theme in postindependence Africa, and conflict and instability has stretched across Africa in the postindependence era, from the Mano River region in the west, extending across the Sahel and Sudan and on into the Horn, then bending southwest into the Democratic Republic of Congo (DRC) and the Central African Republic (CAR). Africa's conflict zones have produced some of the world's most brutal wars and worst humanitarian crises in the post–World War II era. From the liberation struggles, to Cold War proxy warfare, to Africa's post–Cold War ethnic and communal struggles, there has been a terrible toll on African societies.

Adding to the list of factors that contribute to Africa's fragile security is the fact that parts of the continent have become a key theater in the battle against Islamic extremism. Although Africa had experienced terrorist incidents in the past, the 1998 bombing of the U.S. embassies in Kenya and Tanzania signaled the broader threat that international Islamic extremism now poses to African security and U.S. interests. The University of Maryland's Global Terrorism Database lists 3,901 terrorist incidents in Africa between 1998 and 2012, most involving armed attacks or bombings. Most attacks were directed against citizens, but government institutions, especially the police and the military, were also heavily targeted. The majority of those attacks were small scale, with 0–10 fatalities. Of the 3,901 attacks, 364 involved between 11 and 101 fatalities. While there was a decline in the number of incidents to fewer than 400 in 2008–2009, since 2010 there has been a dramatic increase. In 2012, almost 1,200 attacks were recorded.[3] Although there is a danger in conflating violence that stems from local conditions and international terrorism,[4] extremist groups such as al Qaeda in the Islamic Maghreb and al Shabaab in Somalia have allied themselves with al Qaeda, while Boko Haram announced its allegiance to the Islamic State in March 2015.

Boko Haram and al Shabaab have both stepped up their activities, with increasingly deadly results. Boko Haram has attacked schools and churches in northeastern Nigeria as well as a police station and UN headquarters in the capital, Abuja. These attacks killed hundreds and forced the Nigerian government to declare a state of emergency in May 2013 in three northeastern states, Borno, Yobe, and Adamawa. Between the declaration and the end of 2013, an additional 1,200 people were killed in Boko Haram attacks.[5] In April 2014, Boko Haram kidnapped more than 200 school girls in Chibok, Bornu state, threatening to sell them off to the group's fighters. The incident sparked national and international outrage and was followed by further attacks and kidnappings. By 2015, some seventeen thousand people had been killed in the Boko Haram insurgency since the beginning of the attacks in 2009. The Nigerian armed forces were criticized as either incompetent or unwilling to confront the militants or both. In some cases where the military did respond, it faced later charges of widespread human rights abuses in its response to attacks. A 2015 report by Amnesty International asserted that some 7,000 young men and boys had died in custody and that there were an additional 1,200 extrajudicial deaths at the hands of the Nigerian armed forces.[6] Friction developed between Nigeria and the U.S. because of human rights abuses by the armed forces. The Nigerian ambassador to the U.S. criticized the American prohibition of arms sales to Nigeria, and in late 2014 the Nigerian government suspended U.S. training of a battalion of Nigerian armed forces that were to be deployed against Boko Haram.[7]

Nigeria's battle against Boko Haram is part of a wider pattern of Islamic radicalism in the region. The roots of this threat go back at least to the Algerian civil war of the early 1990s. The Algerian armed forces annulled the 1992 elections which the Islamic Salvation Front, an Islamist party, was poised to win. The Salafist Group for Preaching and Combat (GSPC) emerged from the civil war and declared itself al Qaeda in the Islamic Maghreb (AQIM) in 2007. In the Sahel, the kidnapping of tourists by groups allied with al Qaeda and the attack on a gas plant in eastern Algeria in January 2013 in which forty workers and thirty-nine attackers were killed highlighted the threat of extremism in the region and demonstrated the complexity of the security threat in the Sahel. The gas plant attack was the work of al Murabitun or the "Signed in Blood Brigade," a splinter group of AQIM led by Mokhtar Belmokhtar, an Islamic radical, veteran of the wars in Afghanistan and Algeria, and cigarette smuggler known as "Mr. Marlboro." His jihadist activities were underwritten by smuggling of not only cigarettes but also drugs, weapons, and illegal immigrants.[8] Belmokhtar was also behind coordinated suicide attacks against a military base and a French nuclear plant in Niger four months after the gas plant attack and threatened further attacks against the French and African countries taking part in the operations against insurgents in Mali.[9] These networks illustrate the intersection of ideology, extremism, and criminal activity, the region's porous borders, and the shifting status of extremist groups.

Concern over the threat of the jihadist movement in the Sahel only grew after extremists seized control in northern Mali after a coup in March 2012 plunged the country into a crisis. Some four thousand French troops, along with troops from Chad, were deployed to oust the jihadists from the towns and cities under their control. Some evidence pointed to cooperation between Boko Haram in Nigeria and the extremists behind the seizure of northern Mali, expanding what many see as an increasingly regional and coordinated radical Islamist threat in the Sahel. In March 2013, in testimony before the Senate Armed Services Committee, General Carter Ham, then Commander of AFRICOM, stated that while al Qaeda in the Islamic Maghreb, Boko Haram, and al Shabaab in Somalia all represented individual threats, the growing collaboration among these groups heightened the extremist threat across the region.[10]

In the Horn, the African Union Mission in Somalia (AMISOM) was established in 2007 with the approval of the UN. Troops from the fledgling Somali government and regional African Union member states succeeded in forcing al Shabaab out of Mogadishu and other strongholds in southern Somalia. The United States has supported these efforts and provided training for AMISOM troops. Ethiopia intervened in Somalia between 2006 and 2009 and then joined AMISOM in early 2014. After initially intervening in Somalia in 2011 after several kidnappings attributed to al Shabaab, Kenya affiliated with AMISOM in 2012. Although it has steadily lost control of territory in the face of AMISOM's success, al Shabaab has demonstrated a willingness and ability to strike regionally. An attack on a bar in Kampala during the World Cup in 2010 killed seventy-four people, and the spectacular Westgate Mall attack in

Nairobi in September 2013 killed more than sixty. These attacks underscored not only the group's deadly capabilities but also its regional reach. Al Shabaab has continued to launch attacks especially against Kenya, including the April 2015 assault on Kenya's Garissa University College that killed 147 and injured another 79. Al Shabaab has also continued to carry out deadly bombings in Mogadishu.

The genocide in Rwanda was the catalyst for Africa's deadliest war. The massive flow of refugees from the 1994 genocide touched off violence in eastern Congo that fueled the rebellion that ousted Mobutu Sese Seko, prompted regional wars that drew in several neighboring countries, gave rise to a volatile and shifting mix of militias and client armies, and resulted in an estimated 5 million war and war-related deaths. The lucrative exploitation of the DRC's rich mineral deposits and land disputes among the region's ethnic groups continue to fuel sporadic violence despite the presence of a large UN force with a peace enforcement mandate. Regional politics continue to influence security and stability across the eastern DRC.

In Uganda, the Lord's Resistance Army (LRA), began its campaign against the government of President Yoweri Museveni in 1986. The LRA was known particularly for its brutality and had a reputation for kidnapping children to serve in its ranks. It was able to sustain itself for more than two decades in part through support from Sudan, which backed the LRA in response to Uganda's support for rebels in South Sudan. With the independence of South Sudan and after a sustained effort by the Ugandan armed forces, the LRA was routed from its northern Ugandan stronghold. Remnants of the LRA have widely dispersed in the border areas of Uganda, South Sudan, DRC, and the CAR. The coup and sectarian violence in the CAR beginning in 2013 have overshadowed the hunt for the LRA and also complicated U.S. cooperation in the effort to finally defeat the LRA and bring its leader, Joseph Kony, to justice.

Africa's conflicts have produced large numbers of refugees and internally displaced peoples across the continent, numbers that have only grown due to continuing sporadic fighting in Darfur; Boko Haram's attacks in Nigeria and neighboring countries; fighting in Mali, Somalia, and the Central African Republic; and the simmering civil war in South Sudan. The office of the United Nations High Commissioner for Refugees (UNHCR) estimated that the agency would have to provide protection and assistance for close to 3.4 million refugees in 2014, compared with 3.1 million in 2012. There are also some 5.4 million internally displaced persons (IDPs), primarily in the DRC, Mali, Somalia, and Sudan. In all, it was expected that around 11 million people would be in need of some assistance in 2014, a figure that included refugees, IDPs, stateless peoples, and those returning to their homes.[11] Africa accounted for 26% of the world's refugees in 2013, a year in which the number of refugees increased for the third consecutive time. Somalia, with more than a million refugees, was second only to Afghanistan as a country of origin. Almost one-third of the UNHCR's population of concern is found in Africa.[12]

The State, Security, and Conflict

If African states were once largely peripheral to global security and insulated from international terrorism, that is no longer true. Although they have often faced internal threats, African countries have rarely been challenged by other nations, primarily because of Africa's remoteness, the indifference of the major powers, and the weakness of other states in the region.[13] Africa is now firmly on the international security agenda, and its conflicts illustrate the complexity of the issues and actors fueling instability and war cross Africa's conflict zones. Africa's conflicts underscore the continuing security challenges posed by weak state institutions, ineffective armed forces, porous borders, ethnic/communal tensions and the competition for resources and public goods, the influence of external actors, and the growing threat of Islamic radicalism. Given the range of issues and actors, a particular challenge to analyzing American security cooperation with the continent is the need to define clearly the components of security in the African context. Security in Africa is shaped by several factors, including the nature of the state in Africa, the capabilities of the armed forces, the characteristics of African conflicts, and the importance of regional and sub-regional organizations to managing security challenges. Differences in state security capabilities, perceptions of security threats, and the roles of nonstate actors are also among the factors that are critical to analysis of regional security and U.S.-Africa security cooperation. These factors cut across the conceptual frameworks that can be used to examine and analyze security and suggest that a traditional approach to security is insufficient to understanding Africa's challenges and formulating policy on security cooperation.

The state remains the primary actor in international affairs as well as the building block for regional and subregional organizations, so the state is critical to analysis of security in Africa. But the African state system inherited from the colonial era comprises many weak states. The Fragile States Index (formerly the Failed States Index) for 2014 lists fifteen sub-Saharan African countries among the top twenty fragile states.[14] Despite being internally weak, African states have generally had a high degree of external security due to international norms regarding state sovereignty and noninterference, which tend to insulate the state from challenges by external actors.[15] Indeed, there have been few cases of interstate war during Africa's postindependence era. Instead, the threats to African states have been primarily internal. Although African states possess the juridical sovereignty that recognition by the international community provides, several states are not able to fully control their territory. Internal threats including ethnic divisions, combined with poverty, low levels of development, criminal activity, and high levels of local violence,[16] reduce the state's ability to provide adequate security for its citizens. Ideally, state authority should be legitimate and capable of providing security for its citizens, ensure a reasonable distribution of public goods, and preside over the administrative apparatus of the state.[17] Too few African states have consistently demonstrated all these capabilities.

Arbitrary drawing of borders during colonialism contributed to serious internal challenges often stemming from the incongruity between colonial-era boundaries and the ethnic and religious make-up of the state. Ineffective or incomplete nation building further contributed to communal/ethnic and tensions, often fueled by the competition for resources and public goods, and increased the prospects for conflict. Several African states continue to exhibit many of the characteristics once ascribed to "third-world" states, particularly a lack of internal cohesion caused by economic and social disparities, major ethnic and regional divisions, a lack of territorial, institutional, and governing legitimacy, and easy permeability of borders.[18]

African state weakness is traceable not only to colonial boundaries but also to the state formation process in the postindependence era. The weakness and fragility of many African states makes them resemble what Robert H. Jackson termed "quasi-states," in which the state has the juridical sovereignty accorded to states in the international system but lacks the internal sovereignty and legitimacy to control the state's territory and provide the state a monopoly on the use of force. Governments of these states often lack the political will, institutional authority, and organized power to protect human rights and provide socioeconomic welfare.[19] Although Clapham argued that over time African quasi-states would have to overcome the obstacles to full sovereignty, many continue to struggle to control their territories and establish effective political systems.[20]

State weakness was the product not only of the external imposition of state boundaries but also of the norm prohibiting alteration of African state borders. The Organization of African Unity decided to reaffirm the colonial era boundaries at the OAU summit in Cairo in 1964, and those boundaries have largely held ever since. There have been only two cases where African borders have been altered, the independence of Eritrea and South Sudan. In both cases these changes came about through extended conflicts in which those favoring independence eventually forced a negotiated split. Unfortunately, in both South Sudan and Eritrea a new round of conflict followed independence. Beginning in 1998, Eritrea and Ethiopia fought a two-year boundary dispute in which thousands died. Tensions remain between the two countries. In the world's newest country, South Sudan, a power struggle between President Salva Kiir and Vice President Riek Machar ignited fighting that has become largely an ethnic struggle between Dinkas and Nuers and resulted in tens of thousands of deaths, the displacement of 2 million more, and the threat of widespread famine. There are also boundary disputes between Sudan and South Sudan. Some rebel groups that fought for independence were left outside the new boundaries and have clashed with Sudan's government forces. Tensions also come from the exploitation of oil resources and disputes between Sudan and South Sudan over the sharing of revenue from oil exploitation.

Africa's conflicts have often been broadly categorized as being the result of greed and grievance. Paul Collier's work points to these factors in explaining Africa's wars. Collier identified weak and stagnant economies, with high poverty levels, that rely heavily on primary production as more prone to civil war. Moreover, there is likely to be a pool of disillusioned young men for whom little opportunity exists and who are easily recruited into militias that promise meager pay and the opportunity for plunder. Although often couched in terms of political grievance, these conflicts are often more about reaping the benefits of resource exploitation.[21] Conflicts over resource exploitation are also more likely to be prolonged by those best described as "doing well out of war,"[22] that is, those enriched by the continuation of conflict.

Africa's ethnic and religious diversity often exacerbates the grievance factor in conflict. A combination of elite competition, backed by supporters often mobilized along ethnic or communal lines, can fuel conflict. Factional conflicts can come about as elites mobilize their supporters in the struggle with other groups over scarce state-controlled resources. Inequitable distribution of these resources, especially along ethnic/religious and regional lines, creates the circumstances conducive to communal conflict.[23] Closely related to this are identity conflicts that challenge the existing power distribution within the state. Although there is some debate as to the role they play, ethnic/religious divisions do not necessarily give rise to these conflicts, but they can do so in conjunction with a colonial legacy that sharpens divisions and political competition. These divisions can be a source of conflict, especially in the context of democratic reforms that politicize differences.[24]

Politics, the Armed Forces, and African Insecurity

African state weakness is reflected in the capabilities of the armed forces. While the security capabilities of African armed forces differ substantially and it is impossible to generalize across the continent, the faults and weaknesses of the security apparatus are evident particularly in Africa's zones of instability. The readiness of African armed forces vary widely; some are capable of protecting the state and responding to crises and may also be able to project power regionally, while some are unable to fully control state territory. The stable and reasonably professional militaries of states like South Africa and Ghana contrast sharply with the militaries of countries like Somalia, Mali, the Democratic Republic of Congo, the Central African Republic, and South Sudan, where the armed forces' capability, cohesion, discipline, and professionalism are limited. Even South Africa's armed forces, which were once considered among the most competent on the continent, have had their reputation tarnished by missteps such as South Africa's interventions in the 1990s in Lesotho. The 2014 *South African Defense Review* found that South Africa's armed forces had been crippled by inadequate funding that eroded the country's peacekeeping capabilities and regional clout.[25] The report found that South Africa had too few personnel, lacked the discipline or ability to rapidly deploy that is necessary for an effective fighting force, had useless or out-of-date equipment and communications, and had severely limited logistics capability.[26]

Nigeria's armed forces, also thought to be competent, were subject to scathing criticism for their response to the threat posed by Boko Haram.

Although they were the backbone of the Economic Community of West African States (ECOWAS) peacekeeping operations in West Africa, Nigeria's military was notably ineffective in responding to the Boko Haram insurgency that began in 2009. A long history of military intervention in Nigeria's politics created mistrust between the military and the state and apprehension about a large standing army. To reduce the possibility of coups, the government cut the size of the armed forces so that Nigeria, with the world's eighth-largest population, has one of the lowest military-personnel-to-population ratios in the world. Troops also lack sufficient counterinsurgency training, are poorly paid, and have low morale. Corruption is widespread in the armed forces, and, because of the military's poor human rights record and incompetence, civilians lack trust in it.[27] The Nigerian armed forces' lack of success against Boko Haram forced them to accept help from Chad, Cameroon, and Niger in the effort to defeat the extremists. The joint effort has made progress in dislodging Boko Haram from many of the towns and villages it controlled, but terrorist attacks continue. Until there is attention to the underlying causes of the insurgency, the threat of violence will remain. Former military ruler Mohammadu Buhari won the 2015 elections and promised to make the defeat of Boko Haram a top priority. He moved the armed forces headquarters from Abuja to Maiduguri, capital of the northeastern state of Bornu, and agreed to the establishment of a regional coalition consisting of troops from Nigeria, Chad, Niger, Cameroon, and Benin, to be headquartered in Chad's capital, N'Djamena, under Nigerian command.[28]

While Africa's armed forces have displayed operational weaknesses, independence-era political patterns have in many cases not only helped weaken the state's overall capacity but also created security concerns centered on the military itself. Africa's politics have often had an impact on the composition and capabilities of the armed forces, making civil-military relations especially important to analysis of African security. Civil-military relations refers to the links and interaction between the armed forces and the society. It involves civilian, democratic control of the armed forces, the organization of defense decision making, legislative oversight, and also the composition of the armed forces, that is, ethnic or communal representation in the officer corps as well as among the rank and file.[29]

A poor record of civil-military relations poses two types of danger to African societies. Personal rule led to several tactics that undermined military professionalism, including recruiting along ethnic lines, allowing or encouraging corruption to enlist the support of the officer corps, creating praetorian guards as a hedge against the regular armed forces, and deploying the armed forces domestically, especially for political reasons.[30] Lack of professionalism contributed to Africa's long history of military intervention in politics. There have been more than 200 coups and coup attempts across the continent since the beginning of the postindependence era. West Africa has been the scene of some 104 of those incidents, followed by 48 in East Africa, 35 in Central Africa, and 16 in Southern Africa. Some 45% of those attempted coups were successful. Of fifty-one states examined in a 2012 Africa Development Bank report, only ten have not experienced any coup or coup attempt. They include Botswana, Cape Verde, Egypt, Eritrea, Malawi, Mauritius, Morocco, Namibia, South Africa, and Tunisia. Of the countries in the study, 80% experienced at least one coup or coup attempt, while 61% experienced more than one.[31]

Civil-military relations has traditionally emphasized the importance of both civilian control of the armed forces and the military's political neutrality. Effective civil-military relations depends on government institutions that are strong enough to provide civilian control of the armed forces and prevent the military's intervention into politics and a military that is disinclined to intervene. The record of coups and coup attempts demonstrates that these characteristics have often been in short supply. Huntington's typology identified three rationales for coups; breakthrough, guardian, and veto.[32] In some cases, the armed forces were among the most progressive forces in country, and the breakthrough coup was an effort to move the country forward. In earlier stages of the independence era, coups were sometimes triggered by elements in the armed forces that wanted to continue or speed up the modernization process or were motivated by ideology; this was the case in Ethiopia in the mid-1970s. The coup in Ethiopia that ousted Haile Selassie and replaced a feudal monarchy with a Marxist military junta had little positive impact on the civilian population.

In a veto coup, the armed forces move against the government to protect their interests, whether they involve the threat of reductions in the military's budget or protection of the military's business or corporate interests. Threats to the armed forces' corporate interests can be risky. Under pressure at home in the late 1990s, President Robert Mugabe found it difficult to extricate Zimbabwe from its involvement in the DRC in part because doing so would have damaged the interests of high-ranking military officers as well as other members of the elite.[33]

Economic mismanagement and corruption have frequently provided the rationale for the armed forces to intervene against incompetent or corrupt leaders. In a guardian coup, corrupt or incompetent civilian regimes may be overthrown by a military that sees itself as intervening to save the country. Several coup leaders have used corruption and incompetence as justifications for intervention. Jerry Rawlings's 1979 coup in Ghana was ostensibly justified by the corruption of previous military and civilian governments. Corruption, combined with ineffective public policy and growing inequality, played a role in several coups prior to the arrival of democracy's third wave in the early 1990s.[34]

Unsuccessful or incomplete nation building coupled with ethnic patterning in the armed forces has also led to some coups. Coups in Uganda in 1971 and in Rwanda in 1973 were both attributed in part to ethnic tensions.[35] During colonial rule, the security forces were often drawn from particular groups, or deployments were guided by a divide-and-conquer strategy that pitted groups against one another. After independence, it was often difficult to overcome the divisions. African armed forces reflected recruitment patterns that mirrored society's ethnic distribution and the influence of dominant groups in society.[36]

Ethnic splits within the officer corps and among the rank and file also added to the tensions. Differences in recruitment patterns and their impact on promotions within the ranks reinforce divisions based on rank, age, and education, particularly where ethnicity is a prime source of identity.[37] Coups may result in the purging of those from the "wrong" ethnic groups. In Uganda, Idi Amin replaced officers with those from groups that were more loyal to him. In Liberia, Samuel Doe relied on those from his Krahn ethnic group.[38] Such ethnic reshuffling of the officer corps undermines the cohesiveness of the armed forces and can lead to countercoups.

There is also the chance that coups and coup attempts stem not only from systemic weakness but also from particularistic, parochial, or idiosyncratic factors. The personal motives of ambitious or dissatisfied officers, less constrained by weak and fragmented political systems, may prompt a coup. In those cases, it is less likely that regional and international condemnation will be sufficient to prevent the military from exercising power.[39] On the other hand, coups may result from a sudden serious challenge to the civilian government that leads to a power vacuum that the military fills. The coup in Mali in 2013 was triggered by the government's inept response to the Tuareg insurgency in the north of the country. Burkina Faso's 2014 slide into military rule resulted from President Blaise Campaore's bid to change the constitution to allow him to run for another term. A popular uprising quickly ousted him after twenty-seven years in power.

Aside from ousting a regime, the military's political role can also deepen corruption. To encourage loyalty, military budgets may be inflated or governments may allow officers to engage in business activities. The appetite for financial gain can also lead military adventurism. Economic opportunity was among the motivations that prompted Zimbabwe to deploy troops in the DRC. Soldiers' avaricious behavior led critics to refer to West Africa's peacekeeping mission ECOMOG (Economic Community of West African States Monitoring Group) as "Every Car or Moving Object Gone."[40] Alternatively, soldiers' pay may be skimmed or payrolls inflated to enrich those higher up the ranks, both creating resentment and offering the incentive for lower ranks to exploit the civilian population for alternative sources of income.[41] Corruption, poor pay, and inferior weaponry led to the refusal of some Nigerian forces to fight Boko Haram.

The trend toward military intervention in African politics has slowed in recent years. Between 2005 and 2012, there were six coups: Mauritania in 2005 and 2008, Guinea in 2008, Niger in 2010, and Mali and Guinea-Bissau in 2012. There were also eight coup attempts: three in Madagascar (2006, 2009, 2010), one in Côte d'Ivoire (2006), one in Chad (2006), and one each in Guinea-Bissau (2010), DRC (2011), and Niger (2011).[42] Burkina Faso had two brief coups, one in 2014 and another in 2015. The slowing of the rate of military coups is attributable in part to international and regional condemnation of the extraconstitutional seizure of power. Article 2, Section 4 of the African Union's African Charter on Democracy, Elections, and Governance prohibits, rejects, and condemns unconstitutional change of government in any Member State as a serious threat to stability, peace, security, and development. Violations result in the suspension of member states that experience coups. The AU's threat of sanctions in the brief military takeover in Burkina Faso after the ouster of President Blaise led the armed forces to agree to a civilian transitional government.[43]

Although the majority of African states have also become more democratic and strengthened institutions that insulate against military intervention in politics, this has not eliminated the threat of coups and coup attempts. In his estimates of the probability of coups, Jay Ulfelder listed the top forty prospects for coups in 2014. Of the countries listed, nine of the top ten were in sub-Saharan Africa, and, overall, twenty-six of the top forty were in the region. According to his model, the African countries at greatest risk were Guinea, Madagascar, Mali, Equatorial Guinea, Niger, Guinea-Bissau, Sudan, Central African Republic, and South Sudan. While inclusion on this list does not mean that there will be a coup, it does suggest that countries on the list face a relatively higher risk than the rest of the world.[44]

Military coups also rarely improve conditions in the countries that experience them. Soldiers are ill suited to running a country, and reliance on an often corrupt or incompetent bureaucracy to carry the day-to-day tasks of governing is unlikely to improve matters. There is also little reason to expect that a military government, particularly one motivated by idiosyncratic motives, will effectively address real security challenges; more often than not, they end up contributing to further insecurity. As the 2012 coup in Mali amply demonstrated, the military takeover did not enhance the armed forces' effectiveness against the Tuareg insurgents and significantly complicated a regional and international response to the crisis. Regional and international pressure led coup leader Colonel Amadou Sonogo to turn over power to a civilian interim president, although Sonogo continued to exert influence after turning over power until he was eventually detained on murder charges, in November 2013. Elections in August 2013 returned the country to civilian rule, but the situation remained tense, with sporadic attacks by insurgents. A small contingent of French troops augmented by a regional force remained in the country to assist the government against insurgents in the north.

Likewise, the 2013 ouster of President Francois Bozize by the Muslim Seleka rebels in the Central African Republic brought widespread chaos and plunged the country into murderous communal conflict. The atrocities carried out by Muslim Seleka rebels led to the formation of a Christian militia, the anti-Balaka. Abuses by both sides threatened communal warfare between Christians and Muslims and have displaced thousands. The Seleka leader Michel Djotodia, who had seized power after Bozize's ouster, was forced to step down at a regional summit in Chad after only a few months in office. Anti-Balaka militia went on a campaign against Muslims in retaliation for abuses carried out during the push to oust Bozize and after Djotodia came to power. Despite the appointment of Catherine Samba-Panza as interim president, attacks by both sides continued, although the anti-Balaka fighters gained the upper hand, displacing hundreds of thousands. Muslim refugees streamed across the border into neighboring Cameroon and Chad, while many remained trapped by the threat of reprisals against fleeing Muslims. With Muslims making up only 15% of the population, there were fears of an impending genocide against the remaining Muslims. The UN announced in March 2014 that it would investigate charges of genocide.[45] In April 2014, the UN authorized the Multidimensional Integrated Stabilization Mission in the Central African Republic (MINUSCA), which took over responsibility from a regional force.

A second potential threat from dysfunctional civil-military relations is the use of the armed forces to protect the regime's power. More concerned with preserving regime power than with bolstering legitimate and accountable armed forces capable of providing state security, some leaders have configured the armed forces to match the regime's ethnic composition.[46] The capability and professionalism of African armed forces have all too often been affected by the exigencies of regime survival, identity politics and ethnic mobilization, and patrimonial relations. The stifling of opposition has involved the use of state forces as the regime seeks to consolidate its control, particularly over those who challenge or oppose it. Because civil war, secession movements, and warlord predation can pose a greater threat than other states,[47] internal conflicts orient the military toward the survival of the government, not the protection of the state. Authoritarian leaders have used the armed forces to put down opposition, shifting the traditional focus of the armed forces to internal rather than external security.

Despite movement toward democracy and accountability in many countries on the continent, the security forces have sometimes continued to be an instrument of government power; in other cases, elements of the armed forces can be a threat to the government. Fears that the regular armed forces might pose a threat to the government led some leaders to organize and equip praetorian guards to insure their power. However, the existence of a presidential guard is no guarantee to the continued exercise of power. Niger's president Ibrahim Bare Mainassara, who came to power in a coup, was reportedly assassinated by members of his presidential guard, and Muammar Qaddafi's mercenary guards were unable to prevent his ouster and death in 2011.

In the face of mounting protests in late 2014 over President Blaise Campaore's effort to prolong his tenure in office, the military, sometimes restive in the past, chose at least not to intervene to save Campaore. The armed forces initially sought to fill the resulting power vacuum, leading to speculation that they were behind the push to oust Campaore.[48] First, General Honore Traore, the head of the armed forces, assumed power after Campaore fled, but his close association with the president provoked further demonstrations and led to the appointment of Colonel Isaac Zida, reputed to be deputy head of the presidential guard, to head a transitional government.[49] Although clearly willing to assume power, the military, after his twenty-seven years in power, was reluctant to back Campaore's effort to amend the constitution to give him another term.

The shift from interstate to intrastate challenges to the state increases the role of the armed forces in internal security, often with far-reaching results. Neopatrimonial systems involve several practices, including personal rule, patronage, little distinction between public and private realms, institutional weakness, a mix of bureaucratic and informal politics, and corruption.[50] These political patterns help entrench leaders in power and make it difficult to dislodge them. Neopatrimonial patronage systems may also extend to the armed forces, providing leaders with military support and officers with the opportunity to enrich themselves. Neopatrimonial politics also promotes inequitable distribution of public goods and repression of ethnic or regional factions who challenge the existing order. Neopatrimonialism and ethnic mobilization can also exacerbate tensions, particularly where the armed forces' recruitment and promotion patterns favor certain groups. Not surprisingly, when opposition to the existing order emerges, the security forces are crucial to regime preservation. While the armed forces may be able to stifle protest in cities, they may be less capable of fully controlling state territory beyond urban areas. Insurgents, militias, and criminals prompt the regime to deploy the armed forces, which too frequently use force in ways that further undermine security and lead to human rights abuses.

A weak security sector compounded by a poor record of civil-military relations, a lack of civilian control and accountability, and human rights abuses not only clearly affects the armed forces' ability to contend with domestic challenges to the state but can prevent cooperation with efforts by the U.S. and other regional actors to work with African militaries. All too frequently, the government's response to regime challenges involves human rights abuses and demonstrates a low levels of military professionalism, discipline, and training in humanitarian law. Militaries with poor human rights records are prohibited by the Leahy Act from receiving U.S. assistance, complicating U.S. efforts to bolster the capabilities of African armed forces. The recent disagreement between Nigeria and the U.S. over military aid and training to battle Boko Haram illustrates the difficulties of counterterrorism cooperation with armed forces that do not respect human rights.

The Nature of Conflicts and the Challenge of Security in Africa

Although some of the continent's brutal civil wars such as those in Angola, Liberia, and Sierra Leone ended between 2002 and 2003, an arc of instability and conflict continues to stretch from West Africa through the Sahel to the Horn and south into central Africa. African security and security cooperation between the U.S. and Africa are shaped by the nature of conflict and the particular challenges of security in this troubled region.

Although terrorism has gotten the most attention from security planners, so-called new wars and fourth-generation warfare represent an additional challenge to African security and the U.S.-Africa security partnership. According to Kaldor, new wars blur the distinction between war and organized crime, involve large-scale violations of human rights, and, despite their local scale, have transnational dimensions. Transnationalism links local conflicts with global and regional actors and trends. New wars are fought by disparate groups that include paramilitary units, local warlords, criminal gangs, police forces, mercenaries, and breakaway elements from regular armies, as well as regular army units. Taking advantage of opportunities in the global economy, these factions finance their operations through plunder of natural resources, hostage taking, and the black market. Some groups are also thought to get external assistance.[51]

The ethnic composition of some African militias highlights another feature of new wars—identity politics. Identity politics is a legacy of the colonial era and the ethnic political patterns that developed in many postcolonial states. The artificial colonial-era boundaries formed the basis for independent states that frequently encompassed or divided ethnic groups that in some cases provided the basis for irredentism and secessionist wars. A lack of political development, inequitable distribution of public goods, and loss of government legitimacy often led political leaders to appeal to communal groups for support, strengthening identity politics. In the struggle for public goods, both supporters and opponents of the government may rally their backers in an effort to capture or retain power and control the allocation of public goods. The struggle for political power can become a contest in which groups vie for the prize of state control and particularly the wealth accumulation that accompanies that control. In predatory regimes like Sudan, Nigeria (particularly under military rule), and the former Zaire, communal factors such as ethnicity and religion were important for access to power and wealth.[52]

The fighting in eastern DRC illustrates this new pattern of conflict. Initially provoked by the genocide in Rwanda, the war in the eastern DRC has subsequently been driven in part by economic interests of both state and nonstate actors who seek to profit from the mining of valuable deposits of coltan, diamonds, copper, cobalt, and gold. A 2001 UN investigation found that exploitation of these resources included confiscation, forced extraction, and price fixing and involved individuals, companies, and neighboring countries. Demand for mineral resources like coltan, used in the manufacture of high-technology goods and consumer electronics such as mobile phones, makes the export of this mineral particularly lucrative. The DRC is one of the world's major producers of the mineral, and demand has helped to fuel the conflict in eastern DRC, where militias use the proceeds from the sale of coltan and other minerals to finance their operations. They are joined in the profiteering by factions of the DRC armed forces. Conflict minerals are mined in small operations and transferred through intermediaries to buyers in urban areas who are connected to rebel groups and militias. International companies then transfer the ore to processors or re-export it through Rwanda and Uganda, whose limited domestic production of coltan does not match their exports. Both Western countries and China are consumers of the coltan exported from the region.[53]

Trade in conflict minerals has provided millions of dollars to groups fighting in the DRC, helped to extend and prolong the fighting in the east of the country, and epitomizes the idea of doing well out of war. Although efforts to curb the trade in conflict minerals have yet to eliminate the problem, the U.S. Dodd-Frank legislation that put in place Wall Street reforms and consumer protections contains provisions that require that U.S. companies disclose their use of conflict minerals in their products and take steps to certify that the minerals used in their products are not sourced from conflict zones. The European Union is also implementing a monitoring scheme. The external dimension of the war was also evident in a 2012 UN report that indicated that Rwanda supported the M-23 rebels, a predominantly Tutsi force many of whom defected in 2012 after having been integrated into the DRC armed forces as a result of a March 2009 agreement. Although the UN report accused Rwanda of supporting the rebels, Rwanda denied the allegations.

Economic stagnation or decline sharpens the conditions for conflict and motivates rebels to take up arms. Governments in Liberia and Sierra Leone struggled with warlords for control of valuable resources. These resources brought economic benefits and opportunities for those previously marginalized while also creating or reinforcing corrupt patronage networks. Profit encouraged the continuation of fighting to ensure the flow of lucrative revenues. This pattern was consistent with Collier's findings that slow or stagnant economic growth and primary production and a large population of disillusioned young men all make countries prone to civil war.[54] Marginalized by economic circumstances, young men acquire weapons on the black market, through looting, or by being recruited into militias led by warlords who may base their power on identity and use the threat of violence or the application of force to stake their claim on resources.[55] Expanded informal and criminal networks create alliances between warlords and external actors, including neighboring states, and business interests in Africa and beyond.[56] The regional networks of informal economic activity that develop around the competition for resources link state and nonstate actors in the region.[57] They illustrate the impact of a dependence on a fluctuating demand for raw materials as well as the global dimension of conflicts in some parts of the continent.

Ending this type of conflict is especially difficult not only because there is an economic incentive to continue fighting but also because alliances and interests may shift as the conflict progresses and the economic, political, and military circumstances change. Nonstate actors become involved in conflicts to further their own interests, and if those interests shift, they may change their allegiances and interactions.[58] The tendency of rebel factions and militias to splinter is also indicative of the shifting contours of African conflicts. As Clapham noted, "Movements also differ markedly in coherence: in their ability to stay united on one hand, or their tendency to split on the other. Splits, indeed, are the key indicators of the way in which a movement is organized: personalist movements are liable to split on personal lines, ethnic movements on ethnic lines, ideological movements on ideological lines."[59] Splintering of rebel groups and transient allegiances also help to account for fighters' drift from conflict to conflict. Political alliances, interests, and positions among and between insurgents can change according to the political, social, economic, and military dimensions of the conflict.[60]

The recruitment of child soldiers also contributes to the problem of drifting fighters and mercenary activity. Combatants recruited as child soldiers may be unable to return to their homes after the fighting ends. Because their skills, education, and prospects are limited, becoming bandits or hired guns allows them to continue to benefit from the plunder that too often accompanies Africa's violent civil wars.[61] The anomie that accompanies this diffuse type of conflict highlights the importance of effective postconflict disarmament, demobilization, and reintegration (DDR) programs as part of any peace process intended to end Africa's wars. The tasks associated with DDR along with the other dimensions of postconflict reconstruction and reconciliation, especially security sector reform, pose a particular challenge in Africa. Ineffective DDR can increase the pool of recruits for extremist groups, militias, and even private military companies.

Executive Outcomes' involvement in Sierra Leone illustrates another dimension of African conflicts: the participation of private military and security companies, providing another connection between localized conflict and the global economy. In Sierra Leone, the Revolutionary United Front (RUF) financed its operations through the sale of "blood diamonds." The lucrative profits provided the rebels ample incentive to fight to maintain control of the mines. Although the RUF was less interested in controlling the government than it was in exploiting the diamonds, the group posed a existential threat to the government. Faced with this threat, the government hired the South African private security firm Executive Outcomes to regain control of diamond exports. Executive Outcomes, along with dozens of other companies, participated in the war in Angola, and operatives from these companies played a variety of roles in the DRC. Private companies also operated in Ethiopia, Sudan, Cote d'Ivoire, Algeria, Kenya, Uganda, and Liberia. Their activities were not restricted to state; there were reports that private companies worked with rebel groups, NGOs, and agencies.[62] Although most of the attention was focused on their participation in combat operations, private contractors can fill an array of functions including guard duty, support and logistics, training, demining, intelligence collection, and advising.[63] Singer makes the useful distinction between military provider companies that provide combat troops, military consultant companies that provide advisory and training services, and military support companies whose main activities are logistics, nonlethal aid, intelligence, and technical support assistance.[64]

Private security operatives have been employed in the fight against Islamic extremists. In March 2015, after the U.S. blocked Israel's sale of attack helicopters to Nigeria, the Nigerians turned to contractors. Retired South African special forces operatives and personnel linked to the now-disbanded Executive Outcomes were reported to be supplying in the use of helicopters provided by

South Africa. There were also reports of involvement by Russian and Eastern European mercenaries as well.[65]

With its growing security cooperation with African militaries, the U.S. employs private companies as well. In 2012, the *New York Times* reported that an American firm, Bancroft Global Development, was contracted indirectly by the U.S. State Department to train African troops to fight al Shabaab in Somalia.[66] A month prior to that, the *Washington Post* reported that the U.S. was employing contractors to conduct intelligence, surveillance, and reconnaissance operations on the continent. The contractors fly and maintain the planes and assist in processing the data.[67] U.S. use of private military contractors is likely to continue due to demand for their services, personnel shortages especially for training missions, and the political advantages that contractors provide.

Private military and security companies are likely to remain a feature of Africa's security landscape. These companies are no longer exclusively instruments of Western countries, as Executive Outcomes illustrates. Security contracting has become a lucrative and global business, and governments have recognized the potential advantages of using these companies.[68]

Global economic forces have affected conditions in Africa's conflict zones in other ways. Neoliberalism's emphasis on economic stabilization, privatization, and deregulation accelerated globalization and contributed to increased levels of unemployment, resource depletion, and disparities of income. A number of African countries that accepted structural adjustment programs as a condition of access to debt relief found that emphasis on the market did not automatically produce legitimate economic enterprises but often rather facilitated corruption and crime. Corrupt businessmen and public officials were often able to make use of their connections and exploit weak state control to enrich themselves. In some cases they did so in conjunction with the manipulation of identity politics and the use of patronage to support their activities. Ties to warlords and an appeal to the alienated and marginalized in society offer the opportunity to mobilize support for capturing or retaining power or exploiting resources.[69] Rural-to-urban migration and migration across borders have helped create networks of corruption and black markets, as well as opportunities for arms and drug trafficking.

Whatever their source, African conflicts have been fueled by the nature of the global arms trade on both the legitimate and the black market for arms. The 2003 Small Arms Survey estimated there were more than 30 million small arms and light weapons (SALW) in circulation throughout sub-Saharan Africa.[70] Military expenditures in sub-Saharan Africa for the period 2003–2009 increased by more than 5% per year. Spending slowed significantly, falling 3.2% between 2009 and 2012, however.[71] Transfers of SALW to sub-Saharan Africa were widespread between 2006 and 2010, with at least thirty-four of the forty-eight countries in the region importing SALW for their armed forces. SALW transfers are difficult to verify fully as some countries do not report their arms transfers.[72]

Although the legal market for small arms in Africa is relatively small and there are no solid numbers on the value of the small-arms market in Africa, by some estimates the value is somewhere between $15 and $30 million annually. A significant portion of the available small arms come from within Africa. After the end of the Cold War substantial arms were transferred to Africa, providing a ready supply of weapons. Sources of small arms and light weapons in Africa include so-called legacy weapons that are recirculated after the end of a conflict, arms from neighboring subregions, arms that were transferred legally to governments but then diverted to the black market by corrupt officials, soldiers, and policemen who sold them to criminals or rebels, and arms transfers conducted by sympathetic governments. As civil wars wound down during the 1990s, arms were recirculated to other conflict zones on the continent. Arms from the civil wars in Liberia and Sierra Leone have continued to show up elsewhere. Arms also filter in from neighboring regions. Weapons have been transferred from the conflicts in Algeria (1992–1998), Chad (1990–2010), Ethiopia (1974–1991), and Sudan (1983–2005). The problem of legacy weapons again highlights the importance of effective postconflict disarmament programs. Corrupt officials are also able to traffic weapons from national arsenals due to poor record keeping regarding the number of weapons the country possesses, and soldiers and police may sell or rent weapons to the people they are supposed to be fighting. Sympathetic governments may also provide arms. For instance, there was evidence that Burkina Faso provided arms to rebels in Côte d'Ivoire in violation of a 2004 UN arms embargo.[73]

Illegal arms transfers, defined as transfers that violate the laws of either suppliers or recipients or both, are a significant contributor to the carnage in Africa. Substantial arms are trafficked illegally into the region through networks of international arms dealers, African middlemen, corrupt officials, and governments in the region.[74] Although these transfers are difficult to track, there is substantial evidence of illegal arms deliveries from 2006 to 2010. The UN concluded that arms were being supplied to rebel groups under arms embargos. The clandestine nature of arms smuggling almost ensures that there are more transfers that go undetected. In some cases these transfers involve small-scale smuggling and may have a greater impact than large transfers from outside the region.[75]

The availability of small arms, especially AK-47s, machine guns, automatic pistols, and rocket-propelled grenade launchers, has fueled the violence and increased the lethal nature of resource wars and communal conflicts. While these weapons may not cause conflict, they make the resort to violence much easier and help to prolong conflicts. Access to SALW also contributes to human rights abuses, war crimes, and violence against women; adds to refugee flows; and helps to militarize refugee camps.[76]

Intraregional weapons flows and their security impact on both regional and international security was clearly illustrated by the influx of weapons into Mali from Libya after the ouster of Muammar Qaddafi in 2011. Tuareg mercenaries employed by the Qaddafi regime returned to Mali after the collapse of the

Qaddafi regime and brought with them weapons looted from Libya's arsenal. Although the size of Qaddafi's arsenal was unclear and the number of weapons available for looting uncertain, using a trafficking rate of 2.5%, the UN Office on Drugs and Crime estimated that some twelve thousand firearms, of which about nine thousand were assault rifles, may have been trafficked from Libya.[77] Although French intervention pushed the rebels into the remote mountains in the border region of Mali, likely depleting the ranks of the insurgents, and seized or destroyed some of their arms, it would not be unreasonable to conclude that many of the weapons may still be hidden, in the hands of rebels and radicals, or on their way to the next market. Africa's conflict zones provide a ready market for the legal and illegal transfer of SALW. The continent's ungoverned spaces such as the vast Sahel smuggling routes make an ideal conduit for trafficking illegal weapons, and gun runners have plenty of potential clients, including groups affiliated with al Qaeda as well as other rebel groups. Arms transfers, resource exploitation, and transborder criminal activity clearly indicate the connections among the state, regional, and international levels of security in the African context.

Spillover, Transnationalism, and Regional Security

The tendency for African conflicts to spill across borders creates broader regional security crises. The most dramatic example of the regional dimension of African security is the DRC, where the influx of refugees from the genocide in Rwanda triggered a massive upheaval in eastern DRC, resulting in two wars and continuing instability in the region. In the first Congo war, Rwanda and Uganda, in conjunction with rebels in eastern Congo, ousted Mobutu Sese Seko, replacing him with Laurent Kabila. The second Congo war, referred to as Africa's world war, involved Rwanda, Uganda, and Burundi, which were seeking to oust Kabila, and Angola, Zimbabwe, Namibia, Sudan, and Chad, which supported Kabila's regime. Although a South Africa–brokered peace agreement brought the war to a formal conclusion in 2003, sporadic fighting and plunder of natural resources at the hands of state and nonstate actors have continued. Since the late 1990s, Congo's wars have claimed the lives of an estimated 5 million people from war and war-related causes. The wars also involved widespread use of rape and sexual abuse as weapons of war and unimaginable suffering among the civilian population.[78]

The spillover of the Liberian upheaval involved state and nonstate actors and contributed to the outbreak of the civil war in Sierra Leone, engulfing the region in a conflict that spawned warlord militias and drew in neighboring countries, including Côte d'Ivoire, Guinea, Nigeria, Burkina Faso, and Togo. The Economic Community of West African States (ECOWAS) deployed peacekeeping troops in an effort to end the conflict.[79] The plunder of natural resources played a significant role in these conflicts and resulted in widespread civilian displacement as well as brutal human rights abuses.

In the Horn, the 1991 collapse of the Siad Barre regime in Somalia plunged the country into furious clan and militia warfare that also eventually spilled across borders. A failed UN and U.S. intervention in the early 1990s led to the withdrawal of U.S. and international forces and essentially abandoned the country to warlords. The rise of the Islamic Courts Union (ICU) prompted Ethiopia, with U.S. assent, to invade Somalia in 2006, setting off more clashes. When the hard-line Islamist group al Shabaab, one of the components of the ICU, emerged as the dominant player, Ethiopia intervened. The Ethiopian intervention was highly unpopular, because of tensions dating back to the Ogaden War in the late 1970s, when Somalia sought to incorporate ethnic Somalis in Ethiopia's Ogaden region. In the face of Somali opposition and allegations of abuse, Ethiopia withdrew its forces from Somalia in 2009. Ethiopian forces re-entered the conflict in Somalia in early 2014, when a contingent of troops joined the African Union's AMISOM mission.

Somalia's long war has also taken on a regional character. Kenya's 2011 incursion into Somalia and its eventual incorporation into AMISOM, behind-the-scenes U.S. efforts to defeat al Shabaab, and the slow progress of the AMISOM peacekeeping mission forced al Shabaab to retreat from its urban strongholds. Demonstrating its continuing relevance and ability to have an impact across the region, al Shabaab began to target neighboring countries. In 2010, al Shabaab took responsibility for bombings in the Ugandan capital, Kampala, during the World Cup soccer tournament. Al Shabaab said the attacks were in retaliation for Uganda's participation in the AMISOM regional peacekeeping force in Somalia. Al Shabaab also took responsibility for the September 2013 attack on the Westgate Mall in Nairobi that killed sixty-seven. According to al Shabaab, that attack was also retaliation for Kenya's 2011 invasion of Somalia and participation in AMISOM. Al Shabaab also stepped up its terrorist attacks inside Somalia. The long-running chaos in Somalia also produced the world's largest refugee camp, Dadaab, on the Kenyan side of the border with Somalia, with some 400,000 residents.

The rebellion in Darfur provides yet another example of conflict spreading across borders. In 2003, after long-standing claims of the region's marginalization, two rebel groups, the Sudan Liberation Army (SLA) and the Justice and Equality Movement (JEM), initiated attacks against the government of Sudan. The government responded by unleashing the janjaweed militia against the civilian population, resulting in another case of massive displacement, refugee flows, and extensive human rights violations. Estimates are that some 300,000 have been killed in the violence and another 2 million displaced. The *New York Times* reported in early 2014 that an additional 400,000 had been displaced by the violence in 2013.[80] The politics of the conflict are further complicated by the factionalization of the rebel movement, the ethnic make-up of the population in the border region of Sudan and Chad, and political tensions between those two countries. Chadian president Idris Deby is from the Zaghawa, one of the ethnic groups that has been involved in the rebellion in Darfur.[81] Both sides accuse the other of supporting rebels. Although Chad's president Deby came to power in a coup against his predecessor, Hissen Habre, with the backing of Sudan, the Sudanese government has supported Chadian rebels who seek to overthrow Deby. According to the Deby government, the rebels that attacked the Chadian capital, N'Djamena, in 2008 had the backing of Sudan. Sudan has also accused Chad of backing the rebels in Darfur.

Additional examples of the spillover effect include Uganda, where the Lord's Resistance Army(LRA) engaged in a decades-long rebellion against the government. Recent successes by government forces, combined with the independence of South Sudan, deprived the LRA of direct support from Sudan, which had backed the LRA in response to Ugandan support for rebels in South Sudan. The LRA has dispersed into the vast border area between Uganda, the DRC, South Sudan, and the Central African Republic (CAR). In the throes of a political upheaval that began in March 2013, the CAR was unable to provide much assistance in this effort. Fighting between the Seleka rebels and the anti-Balaka militia has forced large numbers of refugees to make their way to Chad and Cameroon.

Cameroon has also been dragged into the fighting between Nigeria and the Islamist Boko Haram. Boko Haram radicals have kidnapped foreigners in neighboring Cameroon, and in February 2014 Nigeria closed its border with Cameroon to prevent Boko Haram from using Cameroon as a staging area for attacks.[82] In May 2014, Cameroon was reported to have deployed some one thousand troops to the border with Nigeria to assist in countering Boko Haram's growing threat.[83]

Displacement and refugee flows and the tendency for violence and human rights abuses to cross state borders are not the only manifestations of regionalized conflict in Africa. Weak states facilitate a variety of other interactions across state boundaries between state and nonstate actors. Transnationalism is common in Africa's regional conflicts and links nonstate actors to the global economy and to one another with little state interference.[84] States at the weaker end of the spectrum may face threats of competition among a variety of substate actors seeking their own security or vying for control of the state.[85] Weak states also make it easier for external actors to participate in informal economic and clandestine networks. Regional conflicts feature complex interactions among state security forces, rebels, and perhaps neighboring governments, all with potentially competing interests. Africa's zones of conflict provide state and nonstate actors with the profits of war either by exploiting resources or by providing the guns, ammunition, and supplies that sustain the fighting; their interests may also be otherwise served by a continuation of the conflict.[86] Absent the capacity or will of the international community to deal with the inevitable crises that accompany regional conflicts, the humanitarian costs can be very high.[87] The continent's conflict and instability involve a wide and shifting array of actors and threats. Africa's security challenges are found at the local, national, and regional levels, with a significant degree of interaction across those levels. The complexity of the African security environment shapes the way we understand security in the region and also complicates U.S. policy formulation and implementation.

Perspectives on African Security

Analyzing Africa's insecurity, which is complex on several levels, is a conceptual challenge. The security environment rests at the intersection of several theoretical discussions. Efforts to understand African security must take into account the sources of African conflict and instability and the institutional weaknesses of the African state that contribute to these circumstances, the regional dimensions of security, and the critical connection between security and development. These factors have an influence on national as well as continental efforts to strengthen security and have an impact on the success of a U.S. security partnership with Africa. The region highlights the growing complexity between conceptual frameworks on one hand and the practical challenges of security policy formulation and implementation on the other.

In his seminal work on security, *People, States, and Fear*,[88] Barry Buzan argued that the concept of security bound together individuals, states, and the international system in a way that required a holistic definition of security.[89] The end of the Cold War sharpened the debate over the concept of security, particularly between the neorealist focus on state security and system configuration, the pursuit of power, and the military dimension of security on one side and another perspective that argued for a widening and deepening of the security agenda. Although not without their own internal debates, those who favored the widening and deepening approach argued that the state was not the only referent object of security, that security should extend beyond a purely military focus, and that any concept of security should recognize domestic and transborder threats. Proponents of this approach called for a change in the realist state-centered conflict emphasis of international security.[90]

The identification of security threats reflects the particular conditions in which the threats emerge. Identifying these threats involves the process of securitization, an important component of the analysis of African security. Associated with constructivism and the Copenhagen School, securitization involves identity and societal security and existential threats, as well as the process by which security threats are identified. Threats are securitized through discourse and the actions of authoritative institutions, which has the effect of identifying and acting upon those perceived threats.[91]

At the center of the debate over the international security agenda is the concept of human security, which essentially links security and development. In 1994, the United Nations Development Program's *Human Development Report* drew attention to the dimensions of human security and defined its parameters. Noting that the concept of security had for too long focused on the security of the state, the report stated that for most people, insecurity arose more from worries related to their daily life than from world events. While recognizing a distinction between human security and human development, the HDR defined human security as having two main dimensions: safety from such chronic threats as hunger, disease, and repression and protection from sudden and hurtful disruptions in the patterns of daily life. Broadly, the report defined the two components of human security: freedom from fear and freedom from want. It went on to list the categories of security threats as economic, food, health, environment, personal, and community.[92]

Over the past twenty years, human security has been the subject of considerable debate among security specialists regarding its definition and operationalization.[93] Nevertheless, there is considerable evidence that human security has influenced the establishment of African security architecture. AU documents and those of African subregional organizations reflect the influence of human security concerns. The African Union has integrated the concept into several of its binding agreements, policy documents, treaties, memoranda of understanding, plans of action, mission statements, conventions, and decisions. There is a strong commitment to human security in the decisions, declarations, and protocols adopted by the AU. Unlike its predecessor, the Organization of African Unity (OAU), which explicitly reinforced the primacy of state sovereignty, the AU's recognition of human security also involves an acknowledgment of the potential for humanitarian intervention to protect civilian populations. Of particular importance is the AU's Constitutive Act, Article 4(h), which empowers the AU, with a two-thirds majority vote, to intervene in member states in the event of war crimes, crimes against humanity, and genocide. Intervention does not necessarily require a state's consent to the intervention if the population is at risk.[94] African subregional groups, which have begun to develop their own security apparatus, emulate the AU's emphasis on human security. The basic documents of these subregional organizations not only outline the structure of the peace and security components of the organizations but also make clear reference to human security. This emphasis demonstrates a shift in norms and an effort to formulate policies that more explicitly recognize human security and go beyond traditional state-centric security and the inviolability of sovereignty.[95] Human security has been "securitized" through these documents and the threats that constitute this concept have been identified as requiring a policy response.

The search for African solutions to African problems and the success of the U.S.-Africa security partnership not only hinges on an appropriate conceptualization of security but also has to recognize security's regional dimensions. The overlap of security threats in Africa clearly argues for regional security focus. Africa displays characteristics of Buzan and Waever's definition of a security complex as a group of states or other entities that must possess a degree of security interdependence sufficient both to establish them as a linked set and to differentiate them from surrounding security regions.[96] There is no doubt that for much of Africa, there is a considerable overlap when it comes to security. States in Africa's zones of conflict are linked by cross-border security challenges and the subregional and regional networks that develop around these circumstances. The transborder threat from instability and Islamic radicalism represents a clear regional threat in the Sahel region and the Horn. Much of Africa also faces the challenges of poverty, disease, and environmental degradation, all linked to the development-security nexus and human security.

Africa's multidimensional security environment complicates the American security partnership with Africa. Among the challenges are defining the scope of security, determining the level and emphasis of security threats, overcoming African deficits in operational capability, and negotiating the continent's difficult political environment. The history of American engagement with the continent, U.S. organization for African policy implementation, and domestic political and economic constraints further complicate the security partnership. Africa's struggles with national, subregional, and regional security challenges have implications for international security, but for the U.S. Africa remains a second-tier player in the American global security strategy. Even though Africa's strategic profile has increased in the past decade and a half, the American pivot to Asia, the effort to end U.S. foreign interventions, and the lessons from those engagements will influence American policy. Domestic economic and political constraints will also have an impact on the effectiveness of the security partnership.

The gap between the capabilities of these partners is vast. America's preeminence in military power, reflected in its defense spending and capability, and its worldwide security purview put it in a an unprecedented position. Its security agenda is global, and although regional developments in Africa since the 1998 embassy bombings have put Africa on the U.S. agenda, Africa still represents a secondary, albeit difficult, security terrain, a terrain that has become more threatening with the spread of Islamic extremism. The September 11 attacks prompted the realization that alienation and disillusionment could easily provide fertile ground for radicalism. U.S. experience in Afghanistan and Iraq has also influenced the scope and depth of U.S. involvement in Africa. The U.S. experience in Afghanistan and Iraq created an appreciation of the importance of stability and development to conflict prevention and resolution. The influence of U.S. counterinsurgency doctrine and stability operations in Afghanistan and Iraq are evident in the development of U.S. security assistance to Africa. Although the experience in Iraq and Afghanistan has caused the U.S. to rethink counterinsurgency and stability operations, the fusing of counterinsurgency and stabilization efforts combined with the impact of human security still helps shape U.S. security assistance to Africa.

U.S. security interests tend to focus on the level where state power relative to other states matters and global power projection capability is essential, which explains why U.S. defense spending is equivalent to that of the next fourteen countries combined. The focus on the growing power of China and its increased involvement across the African continent, combined with a heightened threat of global Islamic radicalism, raises questions about how Africa fits into America's security strategy. Efforts to protect America's flank in the global periphery may not always focus on Africa's greatest security threats. A state-centric security emphasis is too narrow to deal effectively with conditions in Africa, where security threats are largely internal, transnational, and regional and the emphasis on enhancing the capability of African countries has less to do with accumulating state power and more to do with enhancing stability and development, addressing the root causes of conflict and instability, and responding to regional challenges. Operating on both international and regional levels requires an integration of U.S. efforts at both the state and the regional levels and includes the adaptation of U.S. expertise in counterinsurgency and stability operations along with recognition of the inextricable links between development and security in Africa and a holistic approach to security.

U.S.-African security cooperation must correspond to the growing regional trend toward security in Africa. The roots of a cooperative, institutionalist approach to African security can be traced back to the 1991 Kampala Document that grew out of the African Leadership Forum. In agreeing to the establishment of the Conference on Security, Stability, Development and Cooperation in Africa (CSSDCA), Article Two of the Principles and Policy Measures of the Document emphasized that the security, stability, and development of every African country were linked and that instability in one country affects the stability of all other African countries. Article Four recognized the interdependence of security, stability, and development of African states and called for a collective solution to these problems.[97] Since then, the reliance on subregional organizations and the African Union for responses to regional security threats has increased. Here, too, the capabilities of the various organizations and their components vary significantly, and, despite the establishment of the CSSDCA at the Thirty-sixth OAU Summit in 2000 and the transformation of the OAU into the AU in 2002, the realization of the lofty goals of a continental approach to security, stability, and development remains elusive, as demonstrated by the slow development of the African Standby Force, a regionally based rapid response force.

Obviously Africa represents an important international security concern. The crucial question is how to understand and analyze security in the African context. As Paul Williams has noted, there are several images of Africa, each reflecting a different set of security concerns.[98] The partnership that the U.S. has proposed through the creation of AFRICOM hinges on congruent views of security threats in the African context. Cooperation further rests on the interaction of actors with sometimes divergent interests, perspectives, and capabilities. Security is a multidimensional challenge in Africa. Weak security institutions, poor civil-military relations, inadequate capability to address the range of issues on an expanded security agenda, and a growing international profile make for a challenging African security environment. Throughout the history of the modern international system, security threats have emanated from strong states, but Africa turns this traditional focus on its head; as the 2002 U.S. National Security Strategy pointed out, it is weak states that pose the greatest challenge in Africa. This calls for a refocusing of perspectives, strategy, and tactics if the U.S.-African partnership is to be successful.

The African security environment and U.S.-African cooperation reflect both the convergence and divergence of security perspectives. On the one hand, the traditional state-centric approach is reflected in the emphasis on the role of the military, but the nature of security threats may require a rethinking of the traditional role and mission of the armed forces, forcing them to develop further expertise in the tasks related to conflict prevention, stability, and development. Analysis and assessment of U.S.-African security cooperation requires the examination of the factors important to evaluating the effectiveness of security cooperation, including the appropriate conceptual frameworks and doctrine to correspond to African security threats and responses, the current global strategic landscape, the history of U.S. engagement with Africa, the organization of American decision making and implementation of policy, and U.S. domestic political constraints. Deeper examination of some of Africa's conflicts illustrates the contours of African insecurity and the challenges of security cooperation.

Notes

1 Mark Tran, "Africa's Economic Growth Failing to Stimulate Development and Jobs," *The Guardian*, 20 January 2014, available at www.theguardian.com/global-development/2014/jan/20/africa-economic-growth-failing-development-jobs
2 For a full discussion of the prospects for Africa's economic growth, see "Africa's Pulse: An Analysis of Issues Shaping Africa's Economic Future," Office of the Chief Economist for the Africa Region, The World Bank, October 2013.
3 Global Terrorism Database, available at www.start.umd.edu/gtd/
4 See, for instance, Wolfram Lacher, 2012, "Organized Crime and Conflict in the Sahel-Sahara Region," The Carnegie Papers, Washington, DC: Carnegie Endowment for International Peace.
5 "UN: Over 1,000 Killed in Boko Haram Attacks," Al Jazeera, 16 December 2013, available at www.aljazeera.com/news/africa/2013/12/un-1224-killed-boko-haram-attacks-20131216175810115265.html
6 See "Stars on Their Shoulders. Blood on Their Hands War Crimes Committed by the Nigerian Military," Amnesty International Report, AFR441657/2015.
7 Sani Tukur, "Nigeria Cancels U.S. Military Training as Relations between Both Nations Worsen," *Premium Times* (Nigeria), 1 December 2014.
8 Jean-Pierre Filiu, 2010, "Could Al-Qaeda Turn African in the Sahel," *Carnegie Papers No. 112*, June 2010, 4.
9 Afua Hirsch, "Niger Suicide Bombings Said to be Work of Mokhtar Belmokhtar," *The Guardian*, 24 May 2013.
10 Statement of General Carter Ham, Commander, United States Africa Command, before the Senate Armed Services Committee, 7 March 2013, 7, available at www.africom.mil.
11 UNHCR, "2014 UNHCR Country Operations Profile-Africa," available at www.unhcr.org/pages/4a02d7fd6.html
12 UNHCR Regional Bureau for Africa, "Fact Sheet October 2013," available at www.unhcr.org/pages/4a02d7fd6.html
13 Quoted in Ken Booth & Peter Vale, 1997, "Critical Security Studies and Regional Insecurity: The Case of Southern Africa," in Keith Krause & Michael C. Williams, eds., *Critical Security Studies* (Minneapolis: University of Minnesota Press), 347.
14 See "Fragile States Index 2014" Fund for Peace, available at http://ffp.statesindex.org/rankings
15 Ken Booth & Peter Vale, 1997, "Critical Security Studies and Regional Insecurity: The Case of Southern Africa," in Keith Krause & Michael C. Williams, eds.,

Critical Security Studies; Concepts and Cases (Minneapolis: University of Minnesota Press), 347.

16 Booth & Vale, "Critical Security Studies and Regional Insecurity," 348.

17 Karin Dokken, 2008, *African Security Politics Redefined* (New York: Palgrave Macmillan), 28.

18 Mohammed Ayoob, 1995, *The Third World Security Predicament: State Making, Regional Conflict, and the International System* (Boulder: Lynne Rienner Publishers), 15.

19 See R. H. Jackson & C. G. Rosberg, 1982, "Why Africa's Weak States Persist: The Empirical and the Juridical in Statehood," *World Politics*, 35:1, 1–24, and Robert H. Jackson, 1990, *Quasi-States: Sovereignty, International Relations, and the Third World* (Cambridge: Cambridge University Press), 21.

20 Christopher Clapham, 1998, "Degrees of Statehood," *Review of International Studies*, 24:2, 144, 146.

21 Paul Collier, 2007, *The Bottom Billion: Why the Poorest Countries Are Failing and What Can Be Done about It* (Oxford: Oxford University Press), 18–20.

22 Paul Collier, 2000, "Doing Well Out of War: An Economic Perspective," in Mats Berdal & David M. Malone, eds., *Greed and Grievance: Economic Agendas in Civil Wars* (Boulder: Lynne Rienner Publishers), 91–111.

23 Naomi Chazan, Peter Lewis, Robert A. Mortimer, Donald Rothchild, & Stephen John Stedman, 1999, *Politics and Society in Contemporary Africa*, 3rd edition (Boulder: Lynne Rienner Publishers), 202.

24 Pierre Englebert & Kevin C. Dunn, 2013, *Inside African Politics* (Boulder: Lynne Rienner Publishers), 292–294.

25 Wendell Roelf, "Exclusive: South African Military in 'Critical Decline' Report Says," *Reuters*, 25 March 2014, available at www.reuters.com/article/2014/03/25/us-safrica-defence-exclusive-idUSBREA2O10U20140325

26 Phillip De Wet, "From Bully Boys to Wimps: The Decline of SA's Military," *Mail and Guardian*, 4 May 2014, available at http://mg.co.za/article/2012–05–04-lack-of-funds-leaves-sa-vulnerable

27 Michael Pizzi, "Nigeria's Undersized, Undertrained Military under Fire," *Al Jazeera, 10* May 2014, available at http://america.aljazeera.com/articles/2014/5/10/nigeria-militaryfailure.html

28 "Nigeria to Lead New Regional Force against Boko Haram, *France 24*, 12 June 2015.

29 The literature on civil-military relations is substantial. Among the best-known theoretical works are: Samuel Huntington, 1957, *The Soldier and the State* (Cambridge, MA: Belknap); Samuel Finer, 1962, *The Man on Horseback* (London: Penguin Books); Amos Perlmutter, 1977, *The Military and Politics in Modern Times* (New Haven: Yale University Press). For detailed discussion of African civil-military relations see: Claude E. Welch, Jr., ed., 1970, *Soldier and State in Africa* (Evanston: Northwestern University Press); Samuel Decalo, 1990, *Coups and Army Rule in Africa*, 2nd edition (New Haven: Yale University Press); Herbert Howe, 2001, *Ambiguous Order: Military Forces in African States* (Boulder: Lynne Rienner Publishers); Mathurin C. Houngnikpo, 2010, *Guarding the Guardians* (Surrey, UK: Ashgate Publishing).

30 Howe, *Ambiguous Order*, 28.

31 Habiba Ben Barka & Mthuli Ncube, 2012, "Political Fragility in Africa: Are Military Coups d'Etat a Never-Ending Phenomena?," African Development Bank, available at www.afdb.org/fileadmin/uploads/afdb/Documents/Publications/Economic%20Brief%20-%20Political%20Fragility%20in%20Africa%20Are%20Military%20Coups%20d%E2%80%99Etat%20a%20Never%20Ending%20Phenomenon.pdf.

32 Samuel P. Huntington, 1968, *Political Order in Changing Societies* (New Haven: Yale University Press).
33 "Scramble for the Congo: Anatomy of an Ugly War," International Crisis Group Africa Report, No. 26, 20 December 2000, 60–65.
34 Ben Barka & Ncube, *Political Fragility*, 7.
35 Chuka Onwumechili, 1998, *African Democratization and Military Coups* (Westport, CT: Praeger), 38.
36 See Cynthis Enloe, 1980, *Ethnic Soldiers: State Security in Divided Societies* (London: Penguin Books)
37 Decalo, *Coups and Army Rule*, 5.
38 Howe, *Ambiguous Order*, 40.
39 Decalo, *Coups and Army Rule*, 13.
40 The ECOMOG Intervention in Liberia, *African Studies Quarterly*, available at asq.africa.ufl.edu/v4/v4i1a1.htm
41 Howe, *Ambiguous Order*, 43–44.
42 Ben Barka & Ncube, *Political Fragility*, 4.
43 Michelle FlorCruz, "Prime Minister of Burkina Faso, Yacouba Isaac Zida Resigns Following RSP Tension," *International Business Times*, 5 July 2015.
44 For a full description of the variables and methodology used, see "Coup Forecasts for 2014" at dartthrowingchimp.wordpress.com
45 David Smith, "Christian Militias Take Bloody Revenge on Muslims in Central African Republic," *The Guardian*, 10 March 2014.
46 See Decalo, *Coups and Army Rule*, 5.
47 Mohammed Ayoob, 1997, "Defining Security: A Subsltern Realist Perspective," in Keith Krause & Michael C. Williams, eds., *Critical Security Studies; Concepts and Cases* (Minneapolis: University of Minnesota Press), 133.
48 Simon Allison, "Burkina Faso: Is the Cure Worse Than the Disease?," *The Daily Maverick* (South Africa), 4 November 2014, available at www.dailymaverick.co.za/article/2014–11–04-burkina-faso-is-the-cure-more-dangerous-than-the-disease/#.VQHk8hb5fGW
49 John Mukum Mbaku, "Has Military Intervention Created a Constitutional Crisis in Burkina Faso?," *Africa in Focus*, The Brookings Institution, November 4, 2014.
50 Englebert & Dunn, *Inside African Politics*, 130.
51 Mary Kaldor, 2006, *New and Old Wars*, 2nd edition (Stanford, CA: Stanford University Press), 2–10.
52 Kaldor, *New and Old Wars*, 81–85.
53 Tiffany Ma, "China and Congo's Coltan Connection," Project 2049 Institute, Futuregram 09–003, available at http://project2049.net/publications.html, 2–3.
54 Collier, *The Bottom Billion*, 20–21.
55 Kaldor, *New and Old Wars*, 87.
56 Mats Berdal, 2003, "How 'New' Are 'New Wars'? Global Economic Change and the Study of Civil War," *Global Governance*, 9, 485.
57 Berdal, "How 'New' Are 'New Wars'," 486, 488.
58 Thomas X. Hammes, 2005, "War Evolves into the Fourth Generation," *Contemporary Security Policy*, 26:2, 209.
59 Christopher Clapham, ed., 1998, *African Guerrillas* (Bloomington: Indiana University Press), 10.
60 Hammes, "War Evolves," 209.
61 On this point, see, for instance, Paul Jackson, 2007, "Are Africa's Wars Part of a Fourth Generation of Warfare?," *Contemporary Security Policy*, 28:2, 275.
62 P. W. Singer, 2003, *Corporate Warriors: The Rise of the Privatized Military Industry* (Ithaca, NY: Cornell University Press), 9–11.
63 Howe, *Ambiguous Order*, 187.

64 Singer, *Corporate Warriors*, 91–97.
65 Siobhan O'Grady & Elis Groll, 2015, "Nigeria Taps South African Mercenaries in Fight against Boko Haram," *Foreign Policy*, 12 March, 2015, available at http://foreignpolicy.com/2015/03/12/nigeria-taps-south-african-mercenaries-in-fight-against-boko-haram/?utm_source=Sailthru&utm_medium=email&utm_term=Flashpoints&utm_campaign=FLASH2015_FlashPoints_PROMO_GMU-RS3%2F12&wp_login_redirect=0
66 Jeffrey Gettleman, Mark Mazzetti, & Eric Schmitt, "U.S. Relies on Contractors in Somalia Conflict," *New York Times*, 10 April 2011.
67 Craig Whitlock, "Contractors Run U.S. Spying Missions in Africa," *Washington Post*, 14 June 2012.
68 "Beyond Blackwater," *The Economist*, 23 November 2013.
69 Kaldor, *New and Old Wars*, 87–88.
70 Cited in Mathurin Houngnikpo, 2011, "Small Arms and Big Trouble," in Terry F. Buss, Joseph Adjaye, Donald Glodstein, & Louis A. Picard, eds., *African Security and the Africa Command* (Sterling, VA: Kumarian Press), 169.
71 "Trends in World Military Expenditure, 2012," SIPRI Fact Sheet, April 2013, available at www.sipri.org/publications
72 Pieter D. Wezeman, Siemon T. Wezeman, & Lucie Beraud-Sudreau, 2011, "Arms Flows to Sub-Saharan Africa," SIPRI Policy Paper No. 30, Stockholm International Peace Research Institute, December 2011, 5.
73 "Firearms Trafficking in West Africa," UN Office on Drugs and Crime, 33, 35–36, available at www.ondoc.org/documents/toc/Reports/TOCTAWest Africa/West-Africa-TOC-Firearms.PDF
74 Houngnikpo, "Small Arms and Big Trouble," 170–171.
75 Wezeman et al., "Arms Flows," 34–35.
76 Houngnikpo, "Small Arms and Big Trouble," 172,175.
77 "Firearms Trafficking in West Africa," 36–37.
78 For a detailed account of the DRC's wars see Gerard Prunier, 2009, *Africa's World War* (Oxford: Oxford University Press), and Jason Stearns, 2011, *Dancing in the Glory of Monsters* (New York: Public Affairs).
79 Dokken, *African Security Politics Redefined*, 50.
80 Rick Gladstone, "Number of Darfur Displaced Surged in 2013," *New York Times*, 23 January 2014, available at www.nytimes.com/2014/01/24/world/africa/number-of-darfurs-displaced-surged-in-2013.html?ref=sudan&_r=0
81 "Defining Sudan-Chad Relations," Voice of America, 27 October 2009, available at www.voanews.com/content/a-13-chad2007–01–14-voa17–66511042/553219.html
82 "Nigeria Seals State Border with Cameroon," *Al Jazeera*, 23 February 2014, available at www.aljazeera.com/news/africa/2014/02/nigeria-seals-state-border-with-cameroon-2014223154723696322.html
83 "Nigeria Violence: Cameroon Boosts Anti-Boko Haram Border Forces," *BBC News Africa*, 24 May 2014, available at www.bbc.com/news/world-africa-27593163
84 Berdal, "How 'New' Are 'New Wars'," 9, 488.
85 Barry Buzan & Ole Waever, 2003, *Regions and Powers: The Structure of International Security* (Cambridge: Cambridge University Press), 22.
86 See Collier, "Doing Well Out of War: An Economic Perspective," 91–111.
87 Dokken, *African Security Politics Redefined*, 48–49.
88 Barry Buzan, 1983, *People, States, and Fear* (Chapel Hill: University of North Carolina Press).
89 Buzan, *People, States, and Fear*, 245.
90 Barry Buzan & Lene Hansen, 2009, *The Evolution of International Security Studies* (Cambridge: Cambridge University Press), 188.

91 Buzan & Hansen, *Evolution*, 212–214.
92 United Nations Development Program, Human Development Report 1994, 22–25, available at http://hdr.undp.org/en/content/human-development-report-1994
93 See, for instance, Shahrbanou Tadjbkhsh & Anuradha M. Chenoy, 2007, *Human Security: Concepts and Implications* (New York: Routledge); Mary Kaldor, 2007, *Human Security* (Malden, MA: Polity Press); Derek S. Reveron & Kathleen A. Mahoney-Norris, 2011, *Human Security in a Borderless World* (Boulder: Westview Press); Roland Paris, 2001, "Human Security: Paradigm Shift or Hot Air?," *International Security*, 26:2, 87–102.
94 Thomas Kwasi Tieku, 2010, "African Union Promotion of Human Security in Africa," *African Security Review*, 16:2, 27, 29.
95 Edward Newman, 2001, "Human Security and Constructivism," *International Studies Perspectives*, 2, 241.
96 Buzan & Waever, *Regions and Powers*, 47–48.
97 "The Kampala Document: Towards a Conference on Security, Stability, Development and Cooperation in Africa, General Principles, Articles 2, 4," available at www.africaleadership.org/rc/the%20kampala%20document.pdf
98 Paul Williams, 2007, "Thinking about Security in Africa," *International Affairs*, 83:6, 1021.

2 An Overview of Africa's Conflict Zones

Conflict and instability have been common in postindependence Africa. While not all countries in the region have experienced these challenges, they have been widespread. Africa's complex security environment currently comprises threats like Islamic extremism, ethnic and communal tensions, and internal challenges to state authority, as well as human security concerns including poverty, disease, and environmental degradation. These threats have not only state and regional impacts but also geopolitical security implications. Although there have been few interstate wars in Africa, large areas of the continent continue to be plagued by conflict and instability. Despite the recent downward trend in warfare globally,[1] the Uppsala Conflict Data Program (UCDP) reported that the greatest increase in conflict between 2010 and 2011 took place in Africa, with the number of armed conflicts increasing by 50%, from ten to fifteen.[2] The UCDP's Nonstate Conflict Database also reported that sub-Saharan Africa had 74% of all nonstate conflict fatalities between 1989 and 2008. A nonstate conflict is defined as fighting between two organized armed groups, neither of which is the government of a state. All but one of the top six countries with the most nonstate fatalities during this period were in sub-Saharan Africa. These countries included Sudan, the Democratic Republic of Congo (DRC), Somalia, Nigeria, and Ethiopia.[3] Deaths from political violence have increased since 2010, and the African countries with the most deaths from political violence in 2014 were Nigeria, South Sudan, Somalia, Sudan, and the Central African Republic (CAR). Those countries accounted for 75.5% of politically related violence in 2014.[4] Adding to the potential for further conflict, the 2014 Fragile States Index shows that fifteen of the top twenty fragile states are in Africa.[5] On top of that, sub-Saharan African countries make up thirty-six of the forty-five countries in the low human development category of the 2014 UNDP Human Development Index.[6]

Poverty, economic stagnation, and a dependence on the export of primary products increase the chances of conflict and insecurity. Moreover, dependence on primary product exports is more likely to result in income inequality.[7] Minerals and fuel exports made up 64% of Africa's exports in 2011, while agricultural products made up another 10% of Africa's exports that year.[8] While some regions of Africa have recently enjoyed rising prosperity, especially those exporting primary products, the 2010 UN Human Development Report showed that sub-Saharan Africa's annual average GDP per capita growth rate for 1970–2008 was 2.7%, and a number of countries showed negative growth rates.[9] Although the global economic crisis of 2008 slowed growth, demand for primary products contributed to Africa's recent economic growth and will continue to play a major role in sustaining Africa's growth for the foreseeable future despite the end of what the World Bank called Africa's "long commodities super cycle."[10]

Africa's population growth provides a potential demographic advantage if growth can be sustained. Africa's fertility rates are double the world average, and the continent's population is likely to almost triple in the next forty years,[11] but if prosperity is not spread more evenly, conflict resulting from a large unemployed/underemployed population of young men will continue to be a strong possibility. Increasingly disillusioned by poverty and low growth rates, unemployed young men make a ready pool of recruits for rebel movements and terrorist organizations.[12]

Africa's socioeconomic indicators and the patterns of politics provide ample motivations for conflict. Ethnic and communal tensions, often centered on either the competition for scarce resources or the avarice spurred by abundant resources,[13] the struggle for political power, and weak and corrupt or inefficient institutions merely compound Africa's problems. In the face of opposition, repressive states often depend on the security forces to maintain their power. Unprofessional and poorly trained soldiers often prey upon their fellow citizens to augment their meager pay or act with callous disregard for human rights. At the same time, as the record of coups and coup attempts shows, the security forces themselves may threaten the government. Military intervention in politics rarely ensures civilians' security or prosperity.

Because conflicts in Africa are rarely restricted by borders and colonial-era boundaries have left African states with multiethnic populations that in many cases straddle those boundaries, the spillover of conflict from one state to another often compounds cross-border threats. Internally, neopatrimonial regimes have helped reinforce ethnic divisions, providing a basis for the struggle for political power. Since independence, Africa has experienced several conflicts with an ethnic identity component. Ethnic diversity alone does not necessarily lead to conflicts, but in many cases it sharpens the competition for public goods and political power. Whether it is greed or grievance that prompts civil war, African conflicts "have a history rooted in the political economy of colonialism, postcolonialism, and neo-liberal globalization; they are as much internal in their causation and scale as they are regional and transnational, involving national, regional and international actors and networks that are simultaneously economic, political, military and social."[14] The recent surge in Islamic radicalism in the Horn and the Sahel has heightened security challenges in those areas. Whatever their cause, large swaths of the continent are affected by conflict, as demonstrated by the UCDP's Georeferenced Event Dataset, which shows a band of conflict from east to west across central Africa between 1989 and 2010.[15] The result of a complicated set of sometimes overlapping factors, conflict has been a consistent theme in several parts of postcolonial Africa.

Major conflicts in sub-Saharan Africa are occurring in Somalia, South Sudan, Nigeria, the Democratic Republic of the Congo, and the Central African Republic. Additionally, Mali continues to face a separatist movement in the north; Niger, Chad, and Cameroon have been drawn into the struggle against Boko Haram; and the Lord's Resistance Army, substantially weakened but still operating in the border region of Uganda, South Sudan, the Central African Republic (CAR) and the DRC, remains a threat. These conflicts feature elements of so-called new wars, characterized by the impact of globalization and the politics of identity.[16] Africa's wars also reflect conditions attributed to "fourth-generation warfare" (4GW), in which the state does not have a monopoly on the use of force and where culture and politics as well as technology and tactics play a role. Fourth-generation warfare links the influence of culture, politics, and technology and also corresponds to the new-wars paradigm and the complex humanitarian emergencies Africa faces.[17]

The Contours of African Conflicts

Africa's conflicts stem from ethnic/communal tensions, competition for public goods, weak government legitimacy and corruption, and ungoverned territory from which regime opponents and insurgents may operate. These wars are fought by a mixture of groups including state security forces, rebels, and militias, as well as Islamic militants who identify with the global aspirations of the jihadist movement. The battle against Islamic extremism has tended to overshadow Africa's other sources of conflict. From the Horn through the Sahel, Islamic extremism poses a significant threat, but other African conflicts have little connection to Islamic extremism. The sources of African conflicts have been many, varied, and sometimes overlapping.

A brief overview of the major conflicts demonstrates the complex circumstances that characterize African conflicts.

Somalia

The prime example of state collapse, Somalia has faced severe security challenges for well over two decades. For much of that time, the chaos has had a regional impact. The 1991 ouster of Mohammed Siad Barre was the beginning of Somalia's state collapse and descent into clan and subclan warlord warfare, Islamic radicalism, sporadic international involvement, breakaway provinces, a weak government, and, until recently, when the focus shifted to the Gulf of Guinea, the world's most lucrative climate for piracy. Ironically, it is not the often-cited scourge of ethnic distinctions that has fueled the fighting. Largely ethnically homogeneous, Somalia is riven by clan and subclan affiliation. Prolonged state collapse hardened these distinctions and facilitated what Zeleza describes as a quintessential war of social banditry and predatory accumulation.[18] Even absent Islamic extremism, the violence might well continue as "spoilers" both internal and external pose an obstacle to any consolidation of government authority.[19]

Barre's reliance on his Marehan clan in the waning years of his rule set the stage for the breakdown of Somali society along clan lines and the warlordism that followed Barre's ouster and led to international intervention. UN peacekeepers were deployed in 1992 to monitor a ceasefire and the George H. W. Bush administration engaged in the first U.S. post–Cold War humanitarian mission, Operation Restore Hope, designed to bring relief supplies to civilians caught between the warring factions. A combination of mission creep and little understanding of the nature of Somali society ultimately led to the failure of the humanitarian operation and provided a costly lesson in the realities of operating in a traditional society and an unfamiliar setting. The downing of a U.S. Black Hawk helicopter in 1993 and the subsequent deaths of eighteen U.S. soldiers in the battle that followed prompted the withdrawal of foreign forces and left Somalia to disintegrate. That experience soured the U.S. and the West on peacekeeping operations and further involvement on the continent, with terrifying consequences for Rwanda.

Once foreign forces withdrew, Somalia drifted further into anarchy. In 2004, under the auspices of the subregional Intergovernmental Authority for Development (IGAD), a Transitional Federal Government (TFG) was formed. Although welcomed by the international community, the establishment of the TFG did little to curb the fighting within Somalia. Criticized as unrepresentative, subclan based, reflecting the influence of Ethiopia, and hostile to Islam, the TFG led to an even more serious crisis. In 2006, fighting broke out between an alliance of Islamists, the Islamic Courts Union (ICU), and a coalition of militias backed by the U.S. The ICU gained control over Mogadishu by mid-2006 and extended that control over most of southern Somalia. Although the ICU brought a measure of order to the areas under its control, an important component of its strength was the hard-line Islamist group al Shabaab. As the ICU strengthened and gained support among Somalis, hardliners gained advantage over more moderate elements, a concern for both the U.S. and Ethiopia. In December 2006, with the support of the U.S., Ethiopia intervened in Somalia and quickly seized Mogadishu. The ICU dissolved, and al Shabaab dispersed into the interior of the country. Ethiopian and Western support created the impression that the TFG was a puppet regime, while al Shabaab portrayed itself as anti-Western, anti-Ethiopian, and a champion of Somali nationalism. Abuses at the hands of the TFG forces combined with the Ethiopian intervention and the escalation of fighting further discredited the TFG's legitimacy and inflamed opposition. Meanwhile, the violence reached new levels, displacing hundreds of thousands. A new transitional government was formed, although it controlled only enclaves in Mogadishu and depended heavily on the African Union Mission in Somalia (AMISOM), created in 2007, to defend what little territory the TFG controlled.[20] Deeply unpopular among

Somalis, the Ethiopians withdrew from Somalia in 2009, despite fears that this would create a dangerous power vacuum. Between 2007 and 2008, al Shabaab forged closer relations with al Qaeda, and it announced formal links with al Qaeda in 2012. U.S. support for Ethiopian intervention resulted in exactly what the U.S. and Ethiopia had feared in the first place—greater sympathy for al Shabaab and greater radical Islamist influence in Somalia.[21]

As AMISOM increased its capability, al Shabaab was forced to withdraw from many of its strongholds. To demonstrate its relevance and capability, al Shabaab not only continued to attack targets within Somalia but began to strike beyond Somalia's borders. In July 2010, al Shabaab claimed responsibility for bomb blasts in the Ugandan capital of Kampala that killed some seventy-four fans watching the World Cup soccer matches. Uganda was reportedly targeted because it had become the primary provider of the AMISOM forces deployed to bolster the TFG in Somalia. By August 2011, al Shabaab withdrew from Mogadishu, having become unpopular due to its strict rule and its failure to contend with drought and famine in areas it controlled. In late 2011, Kenya, increasingly concerned by the chaos in Somalia and its spillover into Kenyan territory, began a military operation, Linda Nchi (Protect the Nation), to defeat al Shabaab. Weakened by internal divisions, facing an increasingly strong AU force that included Kenyan forces, incorporated in 2012, and Ethiopian troops, included in 2014, and targeted by U.S. drone strikes as well, al Shabaab turned to guerrilla tactics and suicide bombings. The deadly al Shabaab attack on Nairobi's Westgate Mall in September 2013 and attacks against a mining operation and a bus in northern Kenya in late 2014, as well as an attack on Garissa University in April 2015 that targeted non-Muslims, demonstrates al Shabaab's continuing threat. AMISOM's modest success has weakened al Shabaab, and the death of its leader, Ahmed Abdi Godane, in a U.S. airstrike in September 2014 left a leadership vacuum and led to speculation that the group was in decline, but al Shabaab's external operations combined with continuing attacks within Somalia indicate its resilience.

Gains by AMISOM forces against al Shabaab offered some hope that Somalia's long-running anarchy might be ending. AMISOM has provided a measure of security in the Somali capital, Mogadishu, and parts of the surrounding territory and afforded some room for optimism and societal reconstruction.[22] Nevertheless, any optimism should be tempered by the enormous long-term challenge of postconflict recovery and reconstruction, particularly after more than two decades of state failure and deep clan and political divisions. Even should the Somali government elected in the 2012 elections manage to further extend its control, the questions of what to do about the self-declared although unrecognized independence of Somaliland in the northwest and how to reintegrate the autonomous region of Puntland, which straddles the Horn and was once the hub of pirate activity, remain significant potential obstacles to unity. Moreover, the new Somali government is still well short of establishing effective control over the south of the country and remains heavily dependent on foreign assistance.

Rwanda and the DRC

The genocide in Rwanda is frequently portrayed as an ethnic conflict, a particularly brutal example of what was regarded as an age-old hatred and unavoidable clash of ethnic groups. The roots of this murderous rampage are traceable to the colonial era. During colonialism, the Belgians favored the Tutsi, about 14% of the population, over the Hutu, who make up 84% of the population. Independence in 1962 brought the Hutu to power, and they began a systematic program to settle old scores with the Tutsi. Many Tutsi went into exile in neighboring countries, eventually forming the core of the Rwandan Patriotic Front (RPF), whose offensive brought an end to the genocide and brought the RPF to power in the aftermath of the 1994 genocide.

In the run-up to the genocide, Hutu extremists became increasingly hostile to the Tutsi minority, referring to them as "cockroaches" who had to be exterminated. In the face of mounting pressure from the RPF, a power-sharing deal was reached in Arusha, Tanzania, between the rebels and the Hutu-dominated Habyarimana government in 1993. Hutu extremists deeply opposed the agreement, and when Rwandan president Habyarimana's plane was shot down, in early April 1994, it triggered the genocide that claimed the lives of an estimated 800,000 Tutsi and Hutu moderates. Influenced by the failure of intervention in Somalia, the West and particularly the U.S. were reluctant to intervene. In fact, the UN failed to bolster the peacekeeping operation that was deployed to oversee the Arusha Accords despite pleas by the commander of the UN Assistance Mission for Rwanda (UNAMIR) to augment the mission. Instead, the force was reduced in size after the deaths of ten Belgian peacekeepers who were protecting the moderate Hutu prime minister. The failure to intervene is now recognized as an appalling breakdown on the part of the international community.

By July 1994, the RPF had taken the capital, Kigali, and brought an end to the genocide, but the RPF victory sent some 2 million Hutus into exile in neighboring Zaire, now the Democratic Republic of Congo (DRC). The result was particularly devastating, provoking two wars, the involvement of several countries in the conflict, and massive casualties and displacement.[23] The reverberations of these events continue to be felt in the eastern DRC.

The influx of refugees from the Rwandan genocide triggered the eventual ouster of the notorious Mobutu Sese Seko, who had come to power in a U.S.-sanctioned military coup in 1965. For over three decades, Mobutu ruled the country he renamed Zaire with a combination of guile and an iron fist. With the complicity of the West, which valued his anticommunism, he plundered the country's resources and spent the proceeds on a lavish lifestyle that regularly had him ranked as one of the world's richest individuals despite the fact that he ruled a country that ranked among the world's poorest.[24]

The camps established in eastern Congo to accommodate the refugees fleeing the Rwandan genocide became a haven for Hutu extremists from the Interahamwe ("those who work together") militia, which had perpetrated the genocide. Congolese Tutsi, known as Banyamulenge, who had been living in eastern Congo since their migration to escape earlier ethnic violence in Rwanda, began an effort to oust the Hutu extremists, prompting Mobutu to crack down on the Banyamulenge. The RPF and its Ugandan allies organized the Alliance of Democratic Forces for the Liberation of Congo-Zaire (AFDL) and installed Laurent Kabila as the leader. By May 1997, these forces reached the capital, Kinshasa, and succeeded in overthrowing Mobutu, who by then had been largely abandoned by the West and was dying of cancer. Kabila became president of Zaire in December 1997 and renamed the country the Democratic Republic of Congo.

The second Congo war, sometimes referred to as Africa's first world war, started in July 1998. Kabila sought to oust Rwandan troops that had helped the AFDL, but this provoked a mutiny among DRC troops in the east that morphed into a rebellion against Kabila. This new group, the Rassemblement Congolais pour la Démocratie (RCD), was joined by forces from Rwanda and Uganda that invaded North and South Kivu provinces. Rwandan troops also tried to take control of Kinshasa but were thwarted by Angolan troops that intervened on behalf of Kabila. Namibia and Zimbabwe also sided with Kabila, preventing the rebels from taking control of the country. The rebels then concentrated their efforts in the eastern DRC, occupied large areas, and advanced toward Kasai. A new insurgency, the Mouvement pour la Libération du Congo (MLC), emerged in the north, backed by Uganda.[25]

The 1999 Lusaka Accords, signed by all the major players in the conflict, brought a ceasefire and an agreement on holding a national dialogue. Violence continued, and the Inter Congolese Dialogue, formed after the Luska Accords, failed to accommodate the interests of various factions in the DRC.[26] In 2000, former allies Rwanda and Uganda clashed in Kisangani over their interests in eastern DRC, and a splintering of factions operating in the region further complicated the situation. Kabila was assassinated in 2001 and his son, Joseph, came to power. An agreement was reached in 2002 that provided for a transition government and elections, originally scheduled for 2005. The elections were subsequently pushed back until 2006. Violence continued in the eastern DRC, where an estimated 80% of the population of the provinces of Orientale and North and South Kivu were displaced at some time during the fighting. Estimates vary, but some suggest that 4 to 5 million people died of war and war-related causes.[27]

Despite the presence of the UN Organization Stabilization Mission in the DRC (MONUSCO), sporadic violence continued when mutinous troops from the DRC armed forces formed yet another faction, the M23 Movement. Consisting of Tutsis who continued to fight against Hutu militias operating in the region, the group took its name from a March 23, 2009, agreement ending a Tutsi rebellion in North Kivu. Soldiers integrated into the DRC army as a result of that agreement mutinied and formed M-23, claiming that the terms of the agreement had not been fully implemented. The group was headed by a notorious former DRC general, Bosco Ntaganda, who, after a power struggle within

M-23, surrendered in Rwanda. He was transferred to the custody of the International Criminal Court where his trial for war crimes began in September 2015. The UN charged that Rwanda had supported the rebels, a charge Rwanda has denied. At their height in 2012, the rebels threatened the city of Goma, capital of North Kivu province.[28] M-23 and the DRC government signed a peace deal in late 2013, but the region continues to suffer from sporadic violence.

In March 2013, the UN deployed the Force Intervention Brigade (FIB), an additional three thousand troops to MONUSCO, with a more robust mandate to protect civilians and defeat and disarm rebel groups. Combined with greater effectiveness of the Congolese forces, this led to a string of military defeats that led to the defeat of M-23. UN forces attacked the rebels with helicopter gunships and the fighting produced yet another round of displacement among the civilian population.[29] However, there are an estimated forty militias and rebel groups still operating in Congo,[30] including the Democratic Forces for the Liberation of Rwanda (FDLR), made up of Hutu extremists who participated in the genocide in Rwanda. FDLR troops were supposed to surrender in January of 2015 but failed to do so. A DRC offensive against the rebels was announced in February 2015. Subsequent retraction of MONUSCO support for the government's offensive because of a dispute over leadership of the operation raised questions about the government's ability to defeat the rebels.[31] Momentum after the February 2013 signing of the Peace, Security, and Cooperation framework stalled, crippling progress on dismantling militias and promoting government reform in the DRC.[32] The sheer number of militias indicates a sizable pool of recruits as well as the potential for combatants to join other rebel groups. Despite agreements to end the fighting, order and the rule of law have been elusive, and the region's riches are a powerful draw that continues to fuel violence. The interests of the DRC's neighbors, particularly Rwanda, also undermine peace efforts.

Sudan

The DRC is not Africa's only complicated, multifaceted conflict. Riven by ethnic and religious divisions, Sudan has been engaged in conflict since a series of civil wars began shortly after independence in 1956. The country is "characterized by cultural diversity, social organization of the various ethnic groups, and enormous variations of the physical environment, all of which affect the daily lives of its inhabitants. The interaction among these factors leads to the multiple complexity"[33] that has contributed to Sudan's long history of conflict. Sudan's conflicts have had national, regional, and international dimensions and feature ethnic divisions, competition for public goods and resources, and a glimpse of the looming impact of climate change on competition for increasingly scarce land and water resources.

Sudan's long history of conflict started just prior to independence, in 1956. A peace agreement in 1972 halted the fighting, but living conditions deteriorated in the South and a power struggle combined with ethnic mobilization and the imposition of Islamic law led to renewed fighting in 1983. A brutal civil war between the Arab-dominated North and the South, made up of an ethnically and religiously distinct population, lasted for twenty years and resulted in an estimated 2 million casualties and 4 million internally displaced Sudanese.[34] The 2005 Comprehensive Peace Agreement included provision for a referendum for independence in the South, which was overwhelmingly approved in January 2011. South Sudan became independent on July 9, 2011. Almost immediately, disputes between Sudan and South Sudan occurred over the division of oil revenues and the demarcation of the boundary between the two countries. The tense relations between Sudan and South Sudan over the distribution of oil revenue and border demarcation sparked fighting in the Abyei region, particularly over the oil town of Heglig. South Sudan briefly seized the town in April 2012 before coming under international pressure to withdraw. Although the permanent Court of Arbitration ruled in 2009 that Heglig was not a part of the Abyei region, the border between Sudan and South Sudan remains ill defined and is also tied to issues of identity and belonging.[35] The oil dispute is unlikely to disappear, however. When South Sudan became independent, it got 75% of Sudan's oil. But the South needs Sudan's pipelines to get its oil to the market. South Sudan depends on oil for 98% of its export earnings[36] and 60% of its GDP, making it the most oil-dependent country in the world.[37] South Sudan has explored the possibility of an alternative pipeline to avoid reliance on Sudan, but that could further destabilize relations. Both sides have also accused each other of supporting rebels across the disputed border, further adding to tensions.

The tensions between Sudan and South Sudan over oil have been overshadowed by the civil war in South Sudan. A political struggle between President Salva Kiir and his vice president, Riek Machar, led to Machar's ouster. Fighting between rebels aligned with Machar and government forces controlled by Kiir began in December 2013 and has killed tens of thousands and displaced an estimated 2 million, creating a massive humanitarian crisis. A May 2014 ceasefire agreement failed to end the fighting, which has taken on a largely ethnic character. Kiir's forces are largely Dinka, while those backing Machar are Nuer. This ethnic split has historical precedent going back to 1991, during the North-South civil war when Machar split from the SPLA. Troops under Machar's command then killed hundreds of Dinka, settling off ethnic clashes.[38] Kiir and Machar came together after the 2005 Comprehensive Peace Agreement, but fighting broke out in late 2013, after Kiir accused Machar of planning a coup and ousted him from the vice presidency.

As the country marked its fourth anniversary of independence in 2015, the war raged on. It has caused tremendous suffering, threatens widespread food insecurity, and has a record of horrific atrocities committed by both sides. Just prior to the anniversary, the UN Security Council issued a statement deploring the violence, calling the situation a manmade catastrophe, and charging that Kiir and Machar had put personal ambition above the welfare of South Sudan's citizens.[39] Prospects for peace appear dim. A day before the anniversary, Machar said the war would go on as long as Kiir remained in power. That might be at least another three years since parliament voted in March 2015 to extend Kiir's term for three years, scrapping plans for elections in 2015.[40]

Tensions between Sudan and South Sudan and the civil war in South Sudan are part of the larger conflict dynamic. In 2003, rebels in the Darfur region of western Sudan destroyed several Sudanese air force planes in an attack on an airbase in North Darfur. The attack signaled the beginning of a rebellion against what its supporters claimed was a pattern of marginalization by the government in Khartoum. In response to the rebel threat, Sudan's government organized militia called janjaweed and set them loose to commit atrocities primarily against the Fur, Zaghawa, and Masalit populations across the region. Tensions had existed for decades between Arabs and non-Arabs in the region. Climate change intensified the struggle for increasingly scarce resources between the largely Arab pastoralists and non-Arab farmers. A breakdown in traditional methods of resolving disputes, the introduction of modern weaponry, and severe drought contributed to the conflict. The two rebel groups that initially emerged, the Sudan Liberation Army/Movement (SLA) and the Justice and Equality Movement (JEM) signed a ceasefire agreement with the government in 2004 that also resulted in the deployment of the African Union Mission in Sudan. In 2005, the SLA splintered, and only one rebel faction, the SLA/Minawi, signed the Darfur Peace Agreement. Tensions between Sudan and Chad, which each backed rebels against the other's government, threatened to expand the fighting.[41] In 2009, Chad and Sudan began an effort to normalize relations in which they pledged to stop supporting each other's rebels. Chad expelled the JEM from its territory while Sudan forced Chadian rebels away from the border.[42]

Fighting in the region erupted again in July 2012, when Sudanese government forces clashed with JEM rebels. The fighting took place in the disputed region of South Kordofan just over the border from East Darfur. An earlier agreement between the JEM and two factions of the Sudan Liberation Army that, along with Sudan Peoples Liberation-North rebels, opposed Kahartoum's rule in Sudan's southern Kordofan and Blue Nile provinces created a loose alliance, the Sudan Revolutionary Front (SRF). Although the intensity of the violence declined, tensions continued despite the 2011 Doha Document for Peace in Darfur, which attracted only limited support among the rebels. In June 2014, the Enough Project reported that the government of Sudan had reconstituted the janjaweed militia and merged them into the armed forces. Sudan denied the report's claims.[43]

The partition of Sudan reignited fighting between North and South over boundaries and oil revenues, spawned a civil war in South Sudan, encouraged proliferation of armed groups, and spilled over into neighboring countries. After the 2005 Comprehensive Peace Agreement, Khartoum maintained ties with government opponents in the South. In 2011, SPLA units left in the North after partition, in loose coalition with rebel forces from Darfur, formed the Sudan Revolutionary Front and, with support from South Sudan, began fighting in the border states of Blue Nile and South Kordofan. Once the civil war broke out in South Sudan in 2013, Uganda sent troops to bolster Kiir's forces, which worsened relations between Uganda and Sudan, both of which had been supporting armed groups across their borders for years. Rebels fighting the government in Khartoum sided with Kiir's forces in hopes of retaining bases in the South. The fighting has created more splits particularly among the combatants in the ironically named Unity State, where there has been intra-ethnic conflict among Nuers, fighting between Dinka and Nuer, and battles between Nuers and Darfurians. A focus only on the fighting between Kiir's and Machar's forces neglects the proliferation of armed groups that operate across the Sudan–South Sudan border and may be beyond the control of the main antagonists.[44]

The war reflects the multilevel nature of African conflicts. On the local level groups fight over resources, while at the national level rebels challenge the national governments. Meanwhile, at the international level Sudan's neighbors and the major powers react to the conflict on the basis of their own interests.[45] Similar patterns are evident in the DRC and the Sahel. While a diplomatic solution to the multifaceted conflict in the region is the only way to ensure peace, the factionalization of combatants and the intransigence of the government, combined with the region's low level of development, political marginalization, and a declining resource base, in addition to internecine warfare and the competing interests of regional players, make such an outcome difficult to achieve.

The indictment by the International Criminal Court of Sudanese president Omar al-Bashir for war crimes in Darfur adds another layer of complication and illustrates an additional link between the regional and international levels. To date, the ICC's caseload has focused on Africa, and this has prompted an African backlash against the Court. The failure of the cases against Kenyan president Uhuru Kenyatta and the refusal of other African states to arrest Sudan's al-Bashir are not only a test of Africa's commitment to international law but a test of the global effort to hold human rights abusers accountable. Efforts to resolve differences and bring an end to the fighting in the region face an even steeper uphill battle when participants are under either indictment for humanitarian law violations or suspected of human rights abuses.

West Africa

West Africa has also had a complicated security environment. Although the conflicts in Sierra Leone and Liberia wound down in 2002–2003, while they were raging these conflicts demonstrated the deadly threats of arms-trading networks, illicit resource extraction and smuggling, extensive human rights violations, and the spillover of conflict into neighboring countries. In Liberia's 1980 coup, Master Sergeant Samuel Doe came to power, overthrowing the Americo-Liberian elite that had ruled the country since the country's founding by freed American slaves in the nineteenth century. Doe relied heavily on his own ethnic group, the Krahn, and the corrupt patronage system did little to improve conditions for Liberians. A reported coup attempt by army commander Thomas Quiwonkpa in 1983 led Doe to weaken the armed forces in favor of more loyal paramilitary units, a strategy that became costly when he was confronted with challenges to his power.[46]

In 1989, the National Patriotic Front for Liberia (NPFL), led by Charles Taylor, invaded Liberia with support from Libya and Burkina Faso.[47] In August 1990, forces from the Economic Community of West African States Monitoring Group (ECOMOG) prevented Taylor from taking Monrovia, dividing the country among forces loyal to Doe, Taylor's militia, and ECOMOG troops. Later that year, a breakaway faction, the Independent National Patriotic Front of Liberia under Prince Johnson, captured and executed Doe. The war raged on until a peace deal paved the way for elections in 1997, in which Taylor was elected president. By 1999, he faced opposition from two rebel groups, Liberians United for Reconciliation and Development (LURD), backed by Guinea, and the Movement for Democracy in Liberia (MODEL), backed by Côte d'Ivoire. Taylor was forced to step down in 2003 and went into exile in Nigeria.

The wars in Liberia and Sierra Leone became closely intertwined when the civil war began in neighboring Sierra Leone in 1991. Taylor had moved forces to the border area of Sierra Leone in hopes of capturing control of the cross-border commerce. Initially, the NPFL and officials of the Sierra Leone government cooperated in the clandestine trading networks. This deprived the Liberian government of revenue, weakening it, while helping to arm the NPLF. When fighting broke out in Sierra Leone in 1991, the NPFL aided rebels from Foday Sankoh's Revolutionary United Front (RUF), who engaged in a brutal campaign against the government and its citizens. Dissatisfied Sierra Leone troops led by Captain Valentine Strasser launched a coup against President Joseph Momah in 1992. The military's temporary gains in 1992 and 1993 stalled, and increasingly undisciplined soldiers took to staging attacks that looked like those of the rebels, earning them the reputation of soldier/rebels or "sobels." Both soldiers and the rebels engaged in illicit mining, depriving the government of badly needed revenues. By 1995, the military was consuming 75% of the national budget but was still unable to control the rebels. The government then hired Executive Outcomes (EO), a South African private security company, to help in the fight against the RUF in return for a share of the profits from resource extraction. EO played a crucial role in pushing the rebels back from the capital, attacked their operations in the mines, and engaged in combat operations. Strasser's second-in-command, Brigadier Julius Maada Bio, using his ties to EO, carried out a coup against Strasser in early 1996. Elections brought Ahmed Tejan Kabbah to power. Kabbah failed to extend EO's contract, and the company ceased its Sierra Leone operations in February 1997. Kabbah was overthrown in May 1997 in a coup led by Johnny Koroma.[48] In February 1998, ECOMOG forces ousted Koroma and restored Kabbah to power, and the UN authorized an observer mission for Sierra Leone. Fighting continued, with rebels holding half the country. In December, rebels briefly took control of Freetown before they were ousted by ECOMOG. The UN authorized a more robust peacekeeping force, eventually leading to an end to the civil war in 2002.[49] Indicted by the Special Court for Sierra Leone in 2003 as a result of his activities during Sierra Leone's civil war, Taylor was convicted of war crimes in 2012 and sentenced to fifty years in prison.

Instability was not confined to just Liberia and Sierra Leone. Taylor also provided refuge in Liberia for a former Guinean minister who tried to mount a 1996 coup against then-Guinean president Lansana Conte. In return, Conte allowed the anti-Taylor rebel group, Liberians United for Reconciliation and Democracy (LURD), to use Guinea as a base of operations when fighting resumed in Liberia in 1999. Cross-border political ties and rivalries among rebels and governments in neighboring countries encouraged the fighting. Support for insurgencies in the region became a part of the political strategy used by Taylor and other leaders in the region as well as Western governments.[50]

A 1999 coup in Côte d'Ivoire triggered instability in what had been one of Africa's most stable and economically prosperous countries. The country has become polarized over issues related to identity and prone to violence. A 2002 mutiny led to fighting that mostly ended by 2004 but left the country divided between north and south. After several delays, elections were held in 2010 but the loser, Laurent Gbagbo, refused to relinquish power until forces loyal to the winner, Allasane Ouattara, with the help of the French, ousted Gbagbo in 2011. Instability persists in Côte d'Ivoire in the aftermath of the violence that followed the 2010 elections, especially in the country's western region. Fertile land has attracted migrants from within Côte d'Ivoire and from neighboring countries. Competition for land, exacerbated by political manipulation, is a continuing source of conflict between the indigenous population and migrants. Control of the western regions, a major cocoa-producing area and the key to the transport of raw materials to export markets, provides control of the main source of foreign exchange. Making matters worse, mercenaries from neighboring Liberia engage in brutality and take advantage of the weakness of the Liberian and Ivorian armed forces.[51]

Guinea also has a history of instability. After the 2008 death of President Lansana Conte, who came to power in a 1984 coup, the military again seized power. Captain Moussa Dadis Camara emerged as the head of a military government. In September 2009, soldiers fired upon protesters, killing some 157 and sparking international condemnation. Camara was shot by a former aide in December 2009 and left the country for treatment. A transition government oversaw the return to civilian rule and presidential elections. After a runoff in 2010, Alpha Conde was declared the winner of the country's first democratic elections. The presidential residence was attacked in July 2011, and the former head of the army was subsequently arrested. Parliamentary elections originally scheduled for late 2011 were further delayed to July 8, 2012.[52] The elections were finally held in September 2013, and President Alpha Conde's party won the majority of seats. Ethnic divisions lay below the surface of the elections. The 2010 presidential elections were contested by representatives of two of Guinea's largest ethnic groups, Alpha Conde, a Malinke, and his rival, Cellou Dahein Diallo, a

Peulh. The opposition sees Conde as promoting the interests of the Malinke at the expense of other groups.[53] Although the armed forces have returned to the barracks, they are riven by ethnic and generational cleavages. There have been some reforms, but the extent to which the army has embraced democratic reforms remains unclear.[54]

Nigeria

Nigeria has Africa's largest population and the continent's biggest economy, and it plays an important regional role in West Africa. Those factors make the difficult security challenges Nigeria faces on several fronts a matter of particular concern. After independence in 1960, Nigeria's first coup took place in 1966. With the exception of four years of civilian rule from 1979 to 1983, the country was ruled by the military from 1966 until the return of civilian rule in 1999. Nigeria experienced a civil war from 1967 to 1970, when the eastern region, home of the Igbo, one of the dominant ethnic groups in the country, unsuccessfully attempted to break away and form the independent country of Biafra. Nigeria is home to hundreds of ethnic groups but the three major groups are the Hausa-Fulani, Yoruba, and Igbo. The country is also roughly divided between a Muslim north and a Christian and animist south. Ethnic and religious relations have always been contentious, and that trend continues.

Several of northern Nigeria's states adopted Sharia law beginning in 1999, raising concerns that Africa's most populous country could become fertile ground for Islamic radicals. There was some pro–al Qaeda sentiment in the north, and the states that adopted Islamic law became increasingly intolerant.[55] Fears of Islamic radicalization increased with the arrest of the so-called underwear bomber, the Nigerian national Umar Farouk Abdulmutallab, in the attempted bombing of a U.S. airliner on Christmas in 2009. Concern mounted further when the UN reported in 2005 that al Qaeda had established bases in Nigeria,[56] although connections between Nigeria's Muslims and the international jihadist movement appeared to be limited.[57]

The emergence of Boko Haram further escalated fears of Islamic radicalism in Nigeria. Founded in 2002 by a radical Muslim cleric, Mohammad Yusuf, Boko Haram aims to establish an Islamic state. When Yusuf was killed by security forces during an armed uprising in 2009, he was succeeded by Abubakar Shekau, who has led the group in increasingly violent attacks. Although concentrated largely in the group's strongholds, the attacks have also taken place in the capital, Abuja, including the bombing of police headquarters in June 2011 and an attack on the UN headquarters in August that year. Undeterred by the state of emergency enacted in May 2013, Boko Haram stepped up its campaign of bombings, violence, and abductions and began to take control of territory in northeastern Nigeria. In April 2014, Boko Haram kidnapped more than two hundred girls from a school in the northeast state of Borno. International outcry against this led to Western offers of help in freeing the captives. The U.S. deployed a team of military law enforcement, intelligence, and development personnel to Nigeria and began reconnaissance flights over Nigerian territory but pulled U.S. personnel out in late 2014.[58] Boko Haram has killed thousands since 2009. In 2014 alone, the Armed Conflict Location and Event Location Project reported that fighting related to Boko Haram had killed 6,347 people.[59] Human rights abuses have been attributed to both Boko Haram and government forces. The violence has displaced hundreds of hundreds of thousands, destroyed infrastructure, disrupted the economy in one of Nigeria's poorest regions, and demonstrated the Nigerian armed forces' troubling inability to control the situation. A regional military coalition consisting of troops from Nigeria, Chad, Cameroon, and Niger began to have some success against the militants in 2015, forcing them to relinquish territory, but, in response, Boko Haram has escalated its terror attacks.

Boko Haram is evolving into more of a regional challenge. The group used bases in Cameroon and Niger to stage attacks, and it was thought that it also had links with al Qaeda in the Islamic Maghreb (AQIM) and Somalia's al Shabaab movement.[60] In 2015, however, Boko Haram announced its allegiance to the Islamic State, proclaiming the territory it controlled the Islamic State West Africa Province (ISWAP). While Boko Haram is focused on Nigeria, a splinter group, Ansaru, is thought to be more inclined toward global jihadist goals and may represent a threat beyond the local focus of the violence.

Religious violence between Christians and Muslims flared after Nigeria's return to civilian rule in 1999. By 2002, some six thousand had been killed in the religious violence, and clashes between Christians and Muslims produced thousands of dead in north central Nigeria.[61] Economic, religious, and ethnic differences, largely along a north-south divide through Nigeria's Middle Belt, have long been a source of friction in Nigeria. Boko Haram's violence against Christians has further encouraged religious reprisals, while economic competition and Nigeria's state residency laws also contribute to tensions.[62]

Apart from the religious conflict, there has been a history of violence in the oil-producing Niger Delta region of Nigeria. Between 2005 and mid-2009, attacks against Nigeria's oil installations reduced oil exports by 25% to 40%.[63] These attacks were the product of organized resistance to the way the oil revenues are allocated as well as expanded criminal opportunity. Nigeria's oil-producing regions have long complained that the revenues from extraction have not been used to build essential infrastructure or to clean up the effects of oil production. Negotiations between the rebels and the government produced an amnesty in 2009. Some twenty-six thousand participated in the program designed to persuade rebels to relinquish their weapons and disavow violence. Although attacks declined after the amnesty, there are indications that some of those who benefited from the amnesty have taken up arms again and that the program has merely pushed the attacks offshore to ships and oil platforms. An August 2012 attack on an oil barge off the Nigerian coast in which two Nigerians were killed and four foreign workers were kidnapped was indicative of that threat. Critics of the amnesty have also charged that the Nigerian government is simply buying peace and that this program is unsustainable.[64] Criminal gangs, using the umbrella of opposition to mask their intent, have also engaged in kidnapping, oil theft, and piracy, which have added to growing threats in the Gulf of Guinea region.

Mali

Mali's 2012 security crisis illustrates the breadth of security threats in the Sahel region. The nomadic Tuareg people of Mali have long complained of marginalization by the central government. For decades they have engaged in a struggle for at least autonomy, if not independence. Their cause got a boost when Tuareg fighters, who had served in Libya's armed forces, returned to Mali after the ouster of Muammar Qaddafi in 2011, bringing heavy weapons looted from Qaddafi's arsenals with them. They quickly overwhelmed Malian armed forces in the north, leading to a coup that ended what had been regarded as a democratic regime since the country's first multiparty elections in 1992. Soldiers, upset that the government had not provided sufficient resources to fight the rebellion in the north, overthrew the government of President Amadou Toumani Toure. Not only did the coup fail to stop the Tuareg rebels; it also plunged the country into a serious crisis. The coup was roundly condemned by the international community, while the coup leaders appeared particularly inept. The motivation for the coup was to secure additional resources for a more effective fight against the rebellion in the north, but the military government then called for peace talks; put forth a new constitution, then withdrew it; and called for a national conference and then canceled it when opponents refused to attend.[65] Pressure from the international community and regional neighbors forced the military to appoint a civilian president, Dioncounda Traore. However, Traore was physically attacked by supporters of the military government and forced to seek treatment abroad, which only deepened the political crisis. In the meantime, the disarray let rebels consolidate their hold on the northern part of the country.

The Azawad National Liberation Movement (MNLA) proclaimed an independent state in northern Mali in April 2012 in conjunction with the Islamist guerrilla group Ansar al-Dine al-Salafiya, which is connected to al Qaeda in the Islamic Maghreb (AQIM). The Islamist guerrillas quickly gained the upper hand over their nationalist counterparts, who had run short of money and lost recruits.[66] The north came under the control of Ansar al-Dine, which imposed a strict version of Islam on the population, leading to the displacement of many as well as the destruction of culturally important sites that the Islamists regarded as offensive. A regional and international force was proposed to protect the capital and prevent the takeover of the country but was to take several months to deploy. After gains by the Islamists, fears that the region would become a staging ground for Islamic extremism prompted the French to intervene before the force could be deployed. Although the French intervention routed the rebels from the major towns, the rebels retreated into the mountains and still represent a threat. Despite the establishment of the UN Stabilization Mission in Mali

(MINUSMA) in April 2013, northern Mali continued to experience banditry, jihadi attacks, intercommunal violence, clashes between the armed forces and armed groups, and attacks against UN peacekeepers. The violence prevented the distribution of relief supplies, and delivery of government services, never extensive, was further crippled, leading to greater criticism of the government. The UN High Commissioner for Refugees, citing the displacement of hundreds of thousands into neighboring countries that are grappling with food shortages, warned that the crisis would have effects across the region.[67]

Extremism and the Threat of Islamic Radicalism

Sectarian violence in Nigeria and Mali, the growing influence of radical Islam throughout the Sahel, and developing connections between extremist groups have heightened international and regional concerns about the threat of violence and terrorism. With the notable exception of the hijacking of an Israeli airliner to Uganda in July 1976, Africa remained on the periphery of international terrorism until the bombing of the U.S. embassies in Kenya and Tanzania in August 1998. Since then, the continent has become an important focus in the efforts to combat terrorism. The U.S. invasion of Afghanistan after the September 11 attacks raised the possibility that al Qaeda fighters would seek to establish bases in Somalia and prompted the U.S. to create the Combined Joint Task Force-Horn of Africa (CJTF-HOA) to increase the American presence in East Africa and its coastal waters. Up to four thousand U.S. civilian and military personnel are based at Camp Lemonnier in Djibouti, which remains the only permanent U.S. installation on the continent. It serves as a base for U.S. drone operations, training, and intelligence gathering and as a conduit for humanitarian assistance, all designed to combat extremism. It is part of a network of drone and intelligence-gathering bases around the continent geared toward counterterrorism.[68] Terrorism poses an expanding security challenge to Africa, but it is important to understand the nature of the threat and to put it into perspective with other security threats to African security.

The August 1998 bombing of the U.S. embassies in Kenya and Tanzania clearly demonstrated international terrorism's threat to both Africa and America's interests. Terrorists connected to al Qaeda simultaneously detonated bombs, destroying the U.S. embassy in Nairobi and damaging the U.S. embassy in Dar-es-Salaam. Two hundred ninety-one people, including eleven Americans, were killed and about five thousand were injured in Nairobi. The death toll in Dar-es-Salaam was ten, including three Americans, with seventy-seven wounded. The attacks signaled a new front in radical Islam's war with the U.S.

In retaliation for these attacks, the Clinton administration ordered cruise missile attacks on terrorist training bases in Afghanistan and a pharmaceutical manufacturing facility in Sudan suspected of developing chemical weapons. In the early 1990s Osama bin Laden operated businesses in Sudan and was said to be connected to the pharmaceutical factory. He had been expelled from Sudan in 1996 and had made his way back to Afghanistan. Although the attack on Sudan was controversial because the evidence that the factory was producing chemicals for weapons was inconclusive, it signaled a more robust U.S. approach to Islamic terrorism and the threat to American interests on the continent.

Further underscoring the terrorist threat, al Qaeda took responsibility for the simultaneous November 2002 attack on an Israeli-owned hotel in Mombasa, Kenya, and a failed effort to bring down an Israeli airliner during takeoff from Mombasa's airport. Somalia was identified both as the probable source of the missiles used in the airliner attack and the point of entry into Kenya for the hotel's suicide bombers.[69] A subsequent UN report confirmed that Somalia played a key role in the attacks and warned that substantial quantities of arms continued to be smuggled into the country.[70] Since the emergence of al Shabaab in 2006, Somalia has been a major focus of U.S. efforts to combat extremism. Long thought to be cooperating, in 2012 al Shabaab announced its allegiance to al Qaeda. Since being forced out of its strongholds in parts of southern Somalia by AMISOM forces, al Shabaab has claimed responsibility for a string of terrorist attacks throughout the region. Al Shabaab militants have targeted Uganda, Djibouti, and Kenya for their participation in the AU's AMISOM mission in Somalia. The militants have also carried out bombings in Mogadishu.

Al Qaeda was also active in West Africa during the region's civil wars. Evidence surfaced that al Qaeda had become involved in the region's conflict diamond trade in order to circumvent efforts to cut off the organization's funding. A Belgian newspaper reported that al Qaeda had converted $10 million into diamonds prior to September 11. Subsequent evidence indicated that the trade ultimately yielded twice that amount, making it possible for al Qaeda to finance its operations in spite of international efforts to deny the organization funding.[71] Al Qaeda's purchase of some $20 million in diamonds said to be mined by Sierra Leone's Revolutionary United Front (RUF) was reportedly aided by the cooperation of the governments of Liberia and Burkina Faso.[72] An April 2003 report by Global Witness noted that al Qaeda used diamonds to raise funds for terrorist cells, protect assets targeted by financial sanctions, launder profits from criminal activity, and convert cash into a valuable and easily transferable commodity. The report details al Qaeda's trade in diamonds and other precious commodities across Africa from its entry into this trade in Kenya and Tanzania in the early to mid-1990s to its involvement in Sierra Leone and Liberia in 2000–2001.[73] These events provide a clear example of the transnational dimensions of African security threats and their links to the global economy.

There are several extremist groups operating in the Sahel region. Al Qaeda in the Islamic Maghreb (AQIM), until 2007 known as the Salafist Group for Preaching and Combat (GSPC), was an outgrowth of Algeria's 1991 elections. On the verge of an Islamist victory, the Algerian armed forces annulled the elections, sparking a bloody insurgency. The GSPC affiliated with al Qaeda and renamed itself AQIM in 2007. AQIM has a record of violence and extremism, including kidnapping foreigners, launching attacks in the Sahel and Maghreb, and assisting militant groups in the region. Its major focus has been on forging links with other Sahel extremists in one of the least governed areas of the world, where criminal activity, corruption, and poverty are rampant. Of particular concern are AQIM's links to groups like Ansar al-Dine and the Movement for Tawhid and Jihad in West Africa (MUJAO), which are operating in northern Mali. Despite the French intervention in northern Mali, these groups remain a threat. AQIM was also thought to have links to Boko Haram, providing training and instruction on tactics, but in 2015 Boko Haram announced its allegiance to the Islamic State. Although AQIM's links to these groups are fluid and depend on the circumstances, they represent a dangerous and perhaps contagious threat. Beyond the rhetoric of global jihad, there is little evidence that AQIM has the intent or capability to attack outside the region. AQIM maintains the ability to destabilize the region and may aspire to attack Europe and the U.S., but it has not done so yet.[74]

Although extremism has been largely absent in southern Africa, South Africa had a brush with radical Islam. The country's financial networks, open society, well-developed infrastructure, and abundant natural resources apparently drew some terrorist activity. Evidence came to light that al Qaeda had used South Africa as a haven to launder money and plan attacks. An al Qaeda operative was also known to have entered South Africa shortly after the East African embassy bombings in 1998.[75] Ronnie Kasrils, a former South Africa minister of national intelligence, reportedly confirmed an al Qaeda presence in the country.[76] There may also have been connections between al Qaeda and two groups that operated in the Cape Flats outside Cape Town, People against Gangsterism and Drugs (PAGAD) and Qibla.[77] PAGAD was involved in bombings in Cape Town, most notably the 1998 bombing of the Planet Hollywood at the Victoria and Alfred Waterfront tourist area. South African authorities have since curtailed the group's activities through a vigorous law enforcement effort.[78]

Several factors help to account for Africa's emergence as a theater in the battle against radical Islam. Islam's influence has rapidly expanded on the continent. Since the beginning of the twentieth century, the number of Muslims in sub-Saharan Africa increased from an estimated 11 million in 1900 to some 234 million in 2010. On the continent as a whole, Islam and Christianity both have between 400 and 500 million followers.[79] Twenty-two members of the Organization of the Islamic Conference are African nations.[80] Within Africa's increasingly large Muslim population there are clearly some who are attracted to radical Islam's message. Low levels of development, poor state service delivery, marginalization, and a lack of government legitimacy make the extremist message more attractive.

Not only might conditions be conducive to the recruitment of terrorists, but the security environment in parts of Africa also makes it easier for terrorists to operate. The ungoverned spaces that characterize weak regimes and fragile states facilitate terrorist activity. The region's porous borders, weak law enforcement, and ineffective and sometimes corrupt security sector can also permit terrorist groups to move personnel, money, and weapons around the region.[81] When combined with additional factors such as a weak judicial system and low wages for security and immigration officials, these conditions create a climate where corruption can also facilitate terrorist activity.[82] Refugee flows related to regional conflict, the widespread availability of weapons, and weak security around public buildings also contribute to a favorable climate for terrorist activity.[83]

The Influence of Nontraditional Security Perspectives

The attention focused on terrorism and the brutality of Africa's conflicts sometimes overshadows the underlying factors that all too frequently affect many on the continent. While Africa's wars affect millions, many millions more are subject to grinding poverty, disease, food insecurity, and environmental degradation.

Despite its recent economic growth, Africa is still the world's poorest continent. Sub-Saharan African countries regularly make up the vast majority of those countries ranking in the low human development category of the UNDP's Human Development Index, and the data from the HDI provide ample evidence of the continent's low levels of development. Prospects in these poor countries are not promising. Large numbers of citizens are poor, and many are disaffected, lack educational opportunities, have little or no influence on decision makers, and lack much hope for immediate improvement. Although there is some debate over whether poverty is a direct cause of conflict, instability, and terrorism, low levels of development can produce a substantial pool of disillusioned and angry individuals from which combatants may easily be recruited.[84]

Although it is at odds with the traditional national security emphasis on state security, the introduction of the human security concept draws particular attention to the intersection of development and security in Africa. Human security accentuates the importance of peace, justice, order, and economics as the foundations of security,[85] while also emphasizing the food, health, environmental, personal, and community dimensions of security.[86] If there is any place that exemplifies the importance of the connection between security and development, it is Africa. Both the continent's record of conflict and its low levels of development suggest that human security may represent a more relevant framework for addressing Africa's security and development challenges than the traditional view that emphasizes state security. Although critics of human security argue that the expansion of the security agenda to include such a wide variety of threats makes the concept of security meaningless, there is no avoiding the fact that a comprehensive approach to security, exemplified by the term "human security," is essential to addressing the roots of Africa's security challenges and should be a component of U.S.-African security cooperation. It is evident that this perspective has had an influence on thinking about security in Africa.

The best effort to redefine security and reorient defense policy in this way can be found in South Africa's 1996 Defense White Paper and the subsequent Defense Review.[87] The 1996 White Paper states:

> In the new South Africa national security is no longer viewed as a predominantly military and police problem. It has been broadened to incorporate political, economic, social and environmental matters. At the heart of this new approach is a paramount concern with the security of people. Security is an all-encompassing condition in which individual citizens live in freedom, peace and safety; participate fully in the process of governance; enjoy the protection of fundamental rights; have access to resources and the basic necessities of life; and inhabit an environment which is not detrimental to their health and well-being.[88]

The AU has also integrated human security into its agenda. Many AU agreements, policy documents, treaties, memorandums, statements, and decisions have a strong human security emphasis.[89]

Among the issues subsumed by human security are health, including HIV/AIDS, malaria, and deadly communicable diseases such as Ebola. Africa's HIV/AIDS rates make it the world's most seriously affected region. An estimated 24.7 million of the 35 million persons living with HIV/AIDS in 2013 were in sub-Saharan Africa, representing 70% of global HIV cases.[90] Eastern and southern Africa are the most seriously affected regions in sub-Saharan Africa, with 34% of all those living with HIV found in the ten countries of those region. HIV/AIDS prevalence in Western and central Africa, estimated at 2% or lower in twelve countries in the region in 2009, remains comparatively low.[91] The implications of this epidemic are enormous, particularly with respect to development. The loss of skilled workers, teachers, civil servants, and other professionals undermines development efforts. The loss of agricultural workers affects food production, and the situation is compounded by the lost labor of family members who must care for the sick.

The impact of the disease also has specific consequences for security. AIDS is the leading cause of deaths in African militaries,[92] and by some estimates, somewhere between 40% and 80% of military personnel in the region may be HIV positive.[93] AIDS affects the armed forces in several ways. It undermines their effectiveness, reduces the pool of able-bodied recruits, depletes the leadership ranks, and can be spread either intentionally or unintentionally during deployment in conflict zones.[94] At a time when there is an increasing need for African peacekeeping forces, HIV/AIDS threatens to reduce the personnel available, while the deployment of HIV positive peacekeepers also increases the chances of spreading the disease.

Recently, the prospects for controlling the disease have improved. The number of newly infected persons fell from 2.2 million in 2001 to 1.8 million in 2009. In twenty-two countries in sub-Saharan Africa, the HIV incidence rate fell by 25% between 2001 and 2009 and AIDS-related deaths fell by 20%

between 2004 and 2009. In southern Africa, the number of children under the age of fifteen newly infected by the disease fell by 32% between 2004 and 2009. By 2009, almost 37% of medically eligible children and adults received antiretroviral treatment for AIDS, up from only 2% seven years earlier.[95] While U.S. funding through the President's Emergency Program for Aids Relief (PEP-FAR) has substantially contributed to the reduction in those infected and to the availability of extended care for victims, the repercussions of the epidemic will continue to have an impact on security and development for years to come.

The Ebola epidemic in West Africa beginning in 2014 infected more than twenty-seven thousand and killed more than eleven thousand, primarily in Liberia, Sierra Leone, and Guinea, by March 2015.[96] It created a global health scare, prompted an international response, and had a serious economic impact on a region that is still recovering from civil war and instability. The epidemic was estimated to cost the affected countries more than $1 billion, with sub-Saharan Africa as whole incurring up to $6 billion in lost consumer confidence, cross-border trade, and travel.[97]

The impact of climate change on Africa also looms large as a potential security threat. Although there is a debate over whether environmental degradation should be considered a security threat, climate change will increase the prospects for conflict and instability. Although Africa has contributed little to the greenhouse gas emissions that are driving climate change, the continent is more vulnerable to its impact and is likely to feel its effects sooner and more dramatically than developed regions of the world. Climate change will alter the availability of water, affect food security, contribute to the spread of disease, lead to greater displacement of the population, and increase the risk of conflict as climate change exacerbates threats such as water scarcity, a reduction in agricultural crop yields leading to higher prices and increased food insecurity, higher sea levels with consequences for coastal areas, more frequent natural disasters, and the degrading of agricultural land. It is difficult to imagine that the cumulative impact of these conditions will not contribute to conflict and instability.[98] The fighting in Darfur has already illustrated the impact of growing population, migration, and competition for scarce resources.

Rural-to-urban migration is also increasing the population of many cities on the continent. Many new residents are forced to live in slums that are prone to insecurity. Rising urban populations increase demand for water, food, and energy and increase pollution.[99] Conflict-generated population displacement also contributes to environmental degradation. Land is also lost to refugee camps, and the surrounding area faces more rapid deforestation.[100] The deterioration of the environment due to resource exploitation also contributes to activism. One of the issues triggering tension in the Niger Delta has been the destruction of the environment from oil production.

Organizing for Regional Security in Africa

The regionalism that characterizes African security challenges highlights the importance of the African Union and subregional organizations' role in addressing those challenges. Although regional organizations do not necessarily indicate the existence of a regional security complex,[101] a nascent African security architecture exists at both the regional and subregional levels. The AU has shared responsibility for peacekeeping with the UN at the regional level and acted independently with UN Security Council approval. Africa's framework for a security architecture at the regional and subregional level dates to the 1991 Kampala Document, which recognized the links among security, stability, development, and cooperation. Subsequently, the Twenty-ninth OAU Session in 1993 adopted the Mechanism for Conflict Prevention, Management, and Resolution. Since then, there has been a broader effort to construct a regional security architecture. The transition from the OAU to the African Union in 2002 brought the establishment of the African Peace and Security Council in 2003. In 2004, the AU adopted the Common African Defense and Security Policy, followed by the Non-Aggression and Common Defense Pact in 2005. There is also a Continental Early Warning System, a Panel of the Wise, and a Peace Fund. While the framework for regional security exists, most of the building out remains to be done. For instance, the African Standby Force (ASF), which is a key component of the AU's African Peace and Security Architecture, calls for the development of regional brigades to be contributed to the Force for deployment in crisis situations. The ASF was supposed to be established by 2010, but by 2014 it had yet to become a reality. The target date was pushed back to 2015 with the ASF finally holding its first training exercises, Amani Africa II, in South Africa in October, 2015. Because of the delays in the readiness of the ASF, at the AU conference in 2013 South African president Jacob Zuma proposed the African Capacity for Immediate Response to Crises (ACIRC), a temporary force to be created in light of the crises in the CAR and South Sudan and Africa's lack of an effective response. Funding for the program was uncertain, and there were questions about whether participants could meet the demands of rotational deployment.[102] Although the ACIRC participated in the Amani Africa II exercise, there are questions about its compatibility with the ASF, whether the two forces will continue to function, or if the ACIRC will be integrated with the ASF.[103]

The subregional organizations' peace and security measures have varied in capability. ECOWAS, SADC, and IGAD, in keeping with the UN Charter's Chapter VIII, Article 52 provisions regarding regional security operations, have authorized peacekeeping efforts at the subregional level. ECOWAS was in the forefront of a subregional approach to security. Deployment to Liberia and Sierra Leone in the 1990s, whatever its flaws, established a precedent for subregional action.

The IGAD peacekeeping mission to Somalia in 2006 had difficulty getting off the ground and was superseded by the AU's AMISOM mission in 2007. AMISOM is an AU peacekeeping force of more than twenty thousand troops authorized by the UN and made up of soldiers from Uganda, Burundi, Djibouti, Kenya, and Ethiopia. Its mandate was due to expire in November 2015, but success against al Shabaab prompted the UN Security Council to extend the mission until May of 2016. The original IGAD mission was hampered by a lack of resources and a stipulation that none of the troops deployed could be from Somali's neighbors.[104] IGAD has also struggled to come up with a response to the violence that began in 2013 in South Sudan.

In central Africa, two regional economic organizations, the Economic Community of Central African States (ECCAS) and the Economic and Monetary Union of Central Africa (CEMAC) have also developed security components. CEMAC deployed a peacekeeping force, Force Multinationale en Centrafrique (FOMUC) to the CAR from 2002 to 2008, at which time ECCAS, which had been developing security architecture, took over responsibility with the Mission de Consolidation de la Paix en République Centrafricaine (MICROPAX). ECCAS has a Council for Peace and Security in Central Africa (COPAX), made up of a Commission for Peace and Security (CDS), an early-warning mechanism (MARAC), and a Central African Multinational Force (FOMAC). Insufficiently funded and with relatively few troops,[105] FOMUC was an ineffective deterrent to violence in the CAR. The advance of the Seleka rebels from the north to take over the capital in March 2013 and the subsequent fighting between the largely Muslim rebels and the anti-Balaka Christian militia resulted in the UN Security Council's authorization of the AU's International Support Mission to the Central African Republic (MISCA). French troops were also deployed to restore order, and the EU was scheduled to send an additional thousand troops.[106] MISCA transitioned to the UN Multidimensional Stabilization Mission in the CAR (MINUSCA) in September 2014.

The Southern Africa Development Community (SADC) has a substantial peace and security component. In 2001, SADC passed the Protocol on Politics, Defense and Security Cooperation, which provides the legal framework for the Organ on Politics, Defense, and Security Cooperation. The SADC Treaty, the Protocol on Politics, Defense, and Security Cooperation, and the Strategic Indicative Plan for the Organ (SIPO) guide the activities of the Organ.[107] This arrangement connects defense and security to development and demonstrates a more explicit focus on human security.

SADC's peacekeeping efforts got off to a rocky start, however. In 1998, Namibia, Angola, and Zimbabwe sent troops to the DRC under SADC auspices to help keep Laurent Kabila in power. That same year, South Africa and Botswana sent troops to Lesotho, also under SADC auspices. Unrest surrounding the 1998 elections in Lesotho led to the deployment of some six hundred South African troops and two hundred troops from the Botswana Defence Force. Even though the troops were invited by the Lesotho government, the operation met resistance from elements of Lesotho's army and was widely criticized as a failure. This was actually the second intervention in Lesotho. In 1994, South Africa, Botswana, and Zimbabwe intervened to restore order after the military ousted the Basotholand Congress Party, which had won the 1993 elections.[108]

The African security architecture suggests a clear direction, although capability lags behind the ideal. Resources to carry out regional security tasks are always tight and require the cooperation and contributions of African countries and the U.S. and its Western allies. The question is whether the U.S. can provide the appropriate security assistance to develop the skills African armed forces will need to confront complex twenty-first-century challenges without sacrificing African interests to U.S. global security strategy. Given the history of U.S. intervention in Africa, there is some skepticism that these goals can be accomplished.

Notes

1   See Joshua S. Goldstein, 2011, *Winning the War on War: The Decline of Armed Conflict Worldwide* (New York: Dutton).
2   "The Number of Conflicts Increased Strongly in 2011," Press Release, Uppsala Conflict Data Program, 13 July 2012, available at www.uu.se/en/media/news/articl e/?id=1724&area=2,3,16&typ=pm&na=&lang=en
3   Ralph Sundberg, Kristine Eck, & Joakim Kreutz, 2012, "Introducing the UCDP Non-State Conflict Database," *Journal of Peace Research*, 49:2, 352–353, 357.
4   John Bugnacki, "Critical Issues Facing Africa: Terrorism, War, and Political Violence," American Security Project, 17 January 2015, available at www.americansecurity project.org/critical-issues-facing-africa-terrorism-war-and-political-violence/
5   "Fragile States Index 2014," Fund for Peace, available at http://ffp.statesindex.org/
6   UNDP Human Development Index 2014, available at http://hdr.undp.org/en/
7   See Paul Collier, 2007, *The Bottom Billion: Why the Poorest Countries Are Failing and What Can Be Done about It* (Oxford: Oxford University Press), 18–35, 81.
8   Merchandise Trade, tables 11.3, 11.4, *World Trade Organization, International Trade Statistics 2012*, 63, available at www.wto.org/english/res_e/statis_e/ its2012_e/its12_merch_trade_product_e.pdf
9   United Nations Human Development Report 2010 Statistical Tables, Table 16, Sustaining Environment: Economy and Infrastructure, 210, available at www.hdr.undp. org/en/media/HDR2010_en_tables_reprint.pdf
10 "Despite the End of the Commodities Boom, African Countries Can Sustain Their Economic Rise," *News, The World Bank*, 21 April 2015, available at www. worldbank.org/en/news/feature/2015/04/21/despite-the-end-of-the-commodity-boom-african-countries-can-sustain-their-economic-rise
11 "Fertility Treatment," *The Economist*, 8 March 2014, available at www.economist. com/news/leaders/21598648-birth-rates-are-not-falling-africa-fast-they-did-asia-more-contraception-would
12 Collier, *The Bottom Billion*, 20–21.
13 See, for instance, Indra de Soysa, 2000, "The Resource Curse: Are Civil Wars Driven by Rapacity or Paucity?," in Mats Berdal & David M. Malone, eds., *Greed and Grievance: Economic Agendas in Civil Wars* (Boulder and London: Lynne Rienner Publishers), 113–135.
14 Paul Tiyambe Zeleza, 2008, "Introduction: The Causes and Costs of War in Africa from Liberation Struggles to the 'War on Terror,'" in Alfred Nhema & Paul Tiyambe Zeleza, eds., *The Roots of African Conflicts: The Causes and Costs* (Athens: Ohio University Press in conjunction with OSSREA), 15.
15 UCDP Georeferenced Event Dataset, available at www.ucdp.uu.se/ged/

16 Mary Kaldor, 2006, *New and Old Wars: Organized Violence in a Global Era*, 2nd edition (Stanford: Stanford University Press), 7–8.

17 Paul Jackson, 2007, "Are Africa's Wars Part of a Fourth Generation of Warfare?," *Contemporary Security Policy*, 28:2, 268–271.

18 Zeleza, 2008, "Introduction: The Causes and Costs of War in Africa," 8.

19 See Ken Menkhaus, "Somalia: What Went Wrong?," *RUSI Journal*, August 2009, 11.

20 Menkhaus, "Somalia," 7–8.

21 Menkhaus, "Somalia," 7–8.

22 "Surprising Somalia: Nice Beaches & Good Shopping," *The Economist*, 16 June 2012, 58–59.

23 For a detailed account, see Gerard Prunier, 2009, *Africa's World War* (Oxford: Oxford University Press).

24 For a fascinating account of Mobutu's reign, see Michela Wrong, 2001, *In the Footsteps of Mr. Kurtz* (New York: HarperCollins).

25 Denis M. Tull, 2007, "The Democratic Republic of Congo: Militarized Politics in a 'Failed State,'" in Morten Boas & Kevin C. Dunn, eds., *African Guerrillas: Raging against the Machine* (Boulder: Lynne Rienner Publishers), 115.

26 Macharia Munene, 2005, "Mayi Mayi and Interahamwe Militias: Threats to Peace and Security in the Great Lakes Region," in David J. Francis, ed., *Civil Militia: Africa's Intractable Security Menace?* (Burlington: Ashgate Publishing), 246.

27 Tull, "Militarized Politics," 116.

28 "Congo's M23 Rebels Threaten to Take Goma," *AlJazeera Online*, available at www.aljazeera.com/news/africa/2012/07/2012711172138525791.html

29 "DR Congos's M23 Rebels Attacked by UN Forces," *BBC News Africa*, 25 July 2012, available at www.bbc.co.uk/news/world-africa-18983159

30 Sudarsan Raghavan, "Congo's M-23 Rebel Group Ends Its Insurgency," *Washington Post*, 5 November 2013, available at www.washingtonpost.com/world/africa/congos-m23-rebel-group-ends-its-insurgency/2013/11/05/fdbbf56e-462a-11e3-bf0c-cebf37c6f484_story.html

31 "DR Congo Launches Offensive against FDLR Rebels," *Al Jazeera*, 26 February 2015.

32 "Overview, Congo: Ending the Status Quo," *Africa Briefing No. 107, International Crisis Group*, 17 December 2014, 1.

33 Abdel Ghaffar M. Ahmed, 2008, "Multiple Complexity & Prospects for Reconciliation and Unity: Sudan," in Alfred Nhema & Paul Tiyambe Zeleza, eds., *The Roots of African Conflicts: The Causes and Costs* (Athens: Ohio University Press in conjunction with OSSREA), 75.

34 Ahmed, "Multiple Complexity," 71.

35 Nacasius Achu Check & Thabani Mdlongwa, "The Hegleg Oil Conflict: An Exercise of Sovereignty or an Act of Aggression?," *Policy Brief No. 78*, August 2012, Africa Institute of South Africa, 4.

36 James Copnall, "Sudan Mobilizes Army over Seizure of Oilfield by South Sudan," *The Guardian*, 11 April 2012.

37 "South Sudan Overview," The World Bank, 2015, available at www.worldbank.org/en/country/southsudan/overview

38 Marc Santora, "As South Sudan Crisis Worsens, 'There Is No More Country,'" *New York Times*, 22 June 2015.

39 "Leaders' Personal Rivalry Has Undermined South Sudan's Hard-Won Independence—Security Council," *UN News Centre*, 9 July 2015.

40 "Rebel Leader Gives Ultimatum to South Sudan President," *Al Jazeera*, 8 July 2015.

41 "Darfur 2007: Chaos by Design Peacekeeping Challenges for AMIS and UNAMID," Human Rights Watch, 20 September 2007, available at www.hrw.org/node/10678/section/5

42 "The Sudan-Chad Proxy War," Human Security Baseline Assessment for Sudan and South Sudan, available at www.smallarmssurveysudan.org/facts-figures/sudan/darfur/sudan-chad-proxy-war-historical.html

43 Jeffrey Gettleman, "Sudan Said to Revive Notorious Militias," *New York Times*, 25 June 2014, A5.

44 "Executive Summary, Sudan and South Sudan's Merging Conflicts," Africa Report No. 223, International Crisis Group, 29 January 2015.

45 James Copnall, "Darfur Conflict: Sudan's Bloody Stalemate," *BBC Africa*, 29 April 2013.

46 William Reno, 1999, *Warlord Politics and African States* (Boulder: Lynne Rienner Publishers), 85–91.

47 William S. Reno, 2007, "Liberia: The LURDS of the New Church," in Morten Boas & Kevin C. Dunn, eds., *African Guerrillas: Raging against the Machine* (Boulder: Lynne Rienner Publishers), 69.

48 Reno, *Warlord Politics*, 123–138.

49 "Sierra Leone-UNMAMSIL-Background," available at www.un.org/en/peacekeeping/missions/past/unamsil/background.html

50 Reno, "Liberia," 70, 73.

51 International Crisis Group, "Cote d'Ivoire's Great West: Key to Reconciliation," Executive Summary and Recommendations Africa Report No. 212, 28 January 2014, available at www.crisisgroup.org/en/regions/africa/west-africa/cote-divoire/212-cote-divoire-s-great-west-key-to-reconciliation.aspx

52 "Guinea Profile Timeline," available at www.bbc.co.uk/news/world-africa13443183

53 "Guinea: Deadlock over Parliamentary Elections," *IRIN News*, 29 August 2012.

54 International Crisis Group, "Guinea: Reforming the Army," Executive Summary and Recommendations, Africa Report No. 164, 23 September 2010.

55 See Statement of J. Stephen Morrison before the U.S. House of Representatives, Subcommittee on Africa, Hearing on Africa and the War on Global Terrorism, 107th Congress, 1st Session, 15 November 2001 (hereafter House Subcommittee on Africa Hearing), 19, and "The Next Hotbed of Islamic Radicalism?," *Washington Post*, 8 October 2002.

56 "Africa's Second Front," *Foreign Policy*, September/October 2005, 22.

57 Princeton Lyman, 2013, "The War on Terrorism in Africa," in John W. Harbeson & Donald Rothchild, eds., *Africa in World Politics: Engaging a Changing Global Order* (Boulder: Westview Press), 295.

58 Armin Rosen, "Almost a Year after #BringBackOurGirls, They're Still Missing but the U.S. Has Pulled Its 80 Troops Looking for Boko Haram," *Business Insider*, 11 March 2015.

59 "Nigeria Suffers Highest Number of Deaths in African War Zones," *The Guardian*, 23 January 2015.

60 Andre LeSage, "Africa's Irregular Security Threats," *Strategic Forum*, 4. See also Toni Johnson, "Boko Haram," Council on Foreign Relations Backgrounder, available at www.cfr.org/Africa/boko-haram/P25739

61 See for instance, "Curbing Violence in Nigeria (II): The Boko Haram Insurgency," International Crisis Group, 3 April 2014, available at www.crisisgroup.org

62 John Campbell & Asch Harwood, "Why a Terrifying Religious Conflict Is Raging in Nigeria," *Atlantic*, 10 July 2013.

63 Cyrl I. Obi, 2010, "Oil Extraction, Dispossession, and Conflict in Nigeria's Oil-Rich Niger Delta," *Canadian Journal of Development Studies*, 30:1–2, 2.

64 See "Nigeria Gunmen Storm Oil Ship—Two Dead, Four Kidnapped," *BBC News Africa*, 4 August 2012, available at www.bbc.co.uk/news/world-africa-19127704, and "Nigeria's Precarious Oil Amnesty," *BBC News Africa*, 1 August 2012, available at www.bbc.co.uk/news/world-africa-19067711

65 Gregory Mann, "Foreign Policy: The Mess in Mali," *National Public Radio* 10 April 2012, available at www.npr.org/2012/04/10/150343027
66 Edward Cody, "In Mali, an Islamist Extremist Haven Takes Shape," *Washington Post*, 7 June 2012, available at www.washingtonpost.com/world/africa/in-mali-an-islamic-extremist-haven-takes-shape
67 "UNHCR: Mali Humanitarian Crisis 'Threatens Whole Region,'" *Euronews*, 3 August 2012, available at www.euronews.com/2012/08/03/unhcr-mali-humanitarian-crisis-threatens-whole-region/
68 Craig Whitlock, "Remote U.S. Base at Core of Secret Operations," *Washington Post*, 25 October 2012, available at www.washingtonpost.com/world/national-security/remote-us-base-at-core-of-secret-operations/2012/10/25/a26a9392–197a–11e2-bd10–5ff056538b7c_story.html
69 "Somali SAMS?," *Africa Research Bulletin*, December 2002, 15134.
70 "UN Warns of Somalia Terror Link," *BBC News World Edition*, 4 November 2003, available at http://news.bbc.co.uk.11/1–30/02, 15093
71 "Bin Laden's $20m African Blood Diamond Deals," *Africa Research Bulletin*, November 2002, 15093.
72 For a detailed account of al Qaeda's activities in the region see Douglas Farah, 2004, *Blood from Stones: The Secret Financial Network of Terror* (New York: Broadway Books). See also Douglas Farah, "Report Says Africans Harbored Al Qaeda," *Washington Post*, 29 December 2002, and the Global Witness report "For a Few Dollars More: How al Qaeda Moved into the Diamond Trade," available at www.globalwitness.org/reports
73 "For a Few Dollars More: How al Qaeda Moved into the Diamond Trade," available at www.globalwitness.org/reports
74 Christopher S. Chivvis & Andrew Liepman, 2013, "North Africa's Menace: AQIM's Evolution and the U.S. Policy Response," Rand Corporation Research Report 415-OSD, 2–13.
75 "Spreading Influence: In South Africa, Mounting Evidence of al Qaeda Links," *Wall Street Journal*, 12 October 2002.
76 "Al Qaeda Presence in South Africa?," *African Terrorism Bulletin*, December 2004, Institute for Security Studies, available at www.iss.co.za/Pubs/Newsletters/Terrorism/0104.htm
77 See Statement of Morrison, House Subcommittee on Africa Hearing, 19.
78 "Patterns of Global Terrorism 2002," Office of the Coordinator for Counterterrorism, United States State Department, available at www.state.gov/s/ct/rls/pgtpt/2002/html/19981.htm
79 "Tolerance and Tension: Islam and Christianity in Sub-Saharan Africa," Pew Research Center on Religion and Public Life, 15 April 2010, available at www.pewforum.org/2010/04/15/executive-summary-islam-and-christianity-in-sub-saharan-africa/
80 "Stoking Fires: Muslims in Africa," *The Economist*, 22 September 2001.
81 Statement of Susan E. Rice, U.S. House of Representatives, Subcommittee on Africa, Hearing on Africa and the War on Global Terrorism, 107th Congress, 1st Session, 15 November 2001 (hereafter House Subcommittee on Africa Hearing), 23.
82 David H. Shinn, "Fighting Terrorism in East Africa and the Horn," *Foreign Service Journal*, September 2004, 38.
83 Mike Hough, "International Terrorism: Contemporary Manifestations in Africa," *Strategic Review for Southern Africa*, 23:2 (November 2001), available at www.infotrac.galegroup.com
84 Statement of Susan E. Rice, House Subcommittee on Africa Hearing, 23.
85 See Agostinho Zacharias, 2003, "Redefining Security," in Mwesiga Baregu & Christopher Landsberg, eds., *From Cape to Congo: Southern Africa's Evolving Security Challenges* (Boulder: Lynne Rienner Publishers), 31–51.

86 Roland Paris, 2001, "Human Security: Paradigm Shift or Hot Air?" *International Security*, 26:2 (Fall 2001), 87–102.
87 See "Defense in a Democracy: White Paper on National Defense for the Republic of South Africa," May 1996, and "South African Defense Review," available at www.mil.za/secretariat/defense
88 "Defense in a Democracy: The Challenge of Transformation" National Defense White Paper, Republic of South Africa, 1996, available at www.gov.za/documents/national-defence-white-paper
89 For a full description of the AU's human security focus, see Thomas Kwasi Tieku, 2007, "African Union Promotion of Human Security in Africa," *African Security Review*, 16:2 (June 2007), 26–37.
90 "Global Statistics: The Global HIV/AIDS Epidemic," available at www.aids.gov/hiv-aids-basics/hiv-aids-101/global-statistics/
91 "Fact Sheet UNAIDS, 2010," available at www.unaids.org/en/regionsandcountries/regions/easternandsouthernafrica/
92 Lindy Heinecken, 2009, "The Potential Impact of HIV/AIDS on the South African Armed Forces: Some Evidence from Outside and Within," *African Security Review*, 18:1, 62.
93 Lindy Heinecken, 2001, "HIV/AIDS, the Military, and the Impact on National and International Security," *Society in Transition* 32:1, 121–122.
94 Jeremy Youde, 2010, "Confronting Africa's Health Challenges," in Jack Mangala, ed., *New Security Threats and Crises in Africa* (New York: Palgrave Macmillan), 136.
95 "Fact Sheet UNAIDS 2010."
96 "The Toll of a Tragedy," *The Economist*, 8 July 2013.
97 "Ebola: Most African Countries Avoid Major Economic Cost but Impact on Guinea, Liberia, and Sierra Leone Remains Crippling," World Bank Press Release, 20 January 2015, available at www.worldbank.org/en/news/press-release/2015/01/20/ebola-most-african-countries-avoid-major-economic-loss-but-impact-on-guinea-liberia-sierra-leone-remains-crippling
98 Oli Brown & Alec Crawford, 2009, *Climate Change and Security in Africa* (Winnipeg, Canada: International Institute for Sustainable Development), 89.
99 Paul Williams, 2007, "Thinking about Security In Africa," *International Affairs*, 83:6, 1026.
100 Williams, "Thinking," 1033.
101 Barry Buzan & Ole Waever, 2003, *Regions and Powers: The Structure of International Security* (Cambridge: Cambridge University Press), 233.
102 Liesl Louw-Vaudran, "Africa: Who Will Foot the Bill for Africa's New Intervention Force?," *Institute for Security Studies*, 7 July 2014.
103 See Jason Warner, 2015, "Complements or Competitors: The African Standby Force, the African Capacity for Immediate Response to Crises, and the Future of Rapid Reaction Forces in Africa," *African Security*, 8: 56–73.
104 Daveed Gartenstein-Ross & Seungwon Chung, 2010, "The African Union's Beleaguered Somalia Mission," *The Long War Journal*, available at www.longwarjournal.org/archives/2010/07/the_african_unions_b.php
105 For an account of the efforts to establish a Central African security arrangements, see: Angela Meyer, 2011, "Peace and Security Cooperation in Central Africa," Discussion Paper 56, Uppsala: Nordic Africa Institute, available at www.diva-portal.org/smash/get/diva2:442741/FULLTEXT01.pdf?
106 Nick Cumming-Bruce, "UN Warns of Anti-Muslim Violence in Central African Republic," *New York Times*, 20 March 2014, available at www.nytimes.com/2014/03/21/world/africa/un-central-african-republic.html

107 "Organ on Politics Defense and Security," Southern Africa Development Community, available at www.sadc.int/sadc-secretariat/directorates/office-executive-secretary/organ-politics-defense-and-security/
108 Karin Dokken, 2008, *African Security Politics Redefined* (New York: Palgrave Macmillan), 104–105.

3   American Engagement with Africa

Since decolonization, Africa has been on the periphery of U.S. security interests. America's lack of a colonial history on the continent meant that the U.S.
was content to leave its European allies, the former colonial powers, to deal
with African countries. After the continent gained its independence in the post–
World War II era, its strategic importance was tied to the Cold War. Although
not a priority, Africa was a pawn in the ideological struggle between the West
and the former Soviet Union and a region whose resources had to be denied to
the communists. The end of the Cold War initially marginalized Africa further
in U.S. policymaking. The 1990 National Security Strategy of the United States
devoted less than a page to Africa, briefly recognizing Africa's importance as
a source of strategic raw materials and the continent's human potential. It also
emphasized American support for economic reforms and negotiated settlement
of the region's conflicts.[1] The 1994 National Security Strategy noted that Africa
was one of the greatest challenges for the strategy of engagement and enlargement outlined in that document. It went on to say that the U.S. sought to "help
support democracy, sustainable economic development, and the resolution of
conflicts through negotiation, diplomacy, and peacekeeping." While it noted
the U.S. humanitarian intervention in Somalia, it stated that, "in the end, however, such efforts by the U.S. and the international community must be limited
in duration and designed to give the people of a nation the means and opportunity to put their own house in order."[2]

By 1998, there was an indication of the strategic importance that Africa had
come to represent. The 1998 National Security Strategy stated that "serious
transnational security threats emanate from pockets of Africa, including state-
sponsored terrorism, narcotics trafficking, international crime, environmental
damage and disease. These threats can only be addressed through effective,
sustained engagement in Africa."[3] Subsequent National Security Strategy
papers have continued to upgrade Africa's significance. As Africa's importance
has grown, it is useful to examine the historical pattern of U.S. security cooperation with the continent. During the Cold War, the U.S. played a role in many
of the continent's high-profile crises. Briefly surveying U.S. security policy
toward Africa during the independence era, this chapter examines the thrust of

U.S. security cooperation with Africa and the factors that drove Washington's policy toward the continent.

The U.S. and Africa during the Cold War

Although Africa was never a priority for American policy, security has always been at the center of U.S. relations with the continent. As Claude Ake observed, "The considerable attention that Africa enjoyed in the 1960s and 1970s owed much to the cold war. Africa, like every other region of the developing world, was courted for diplomatic support. Even those parts of Africa with limited strategic, political, and economic attraction were courted as each side in the Cold War tried to limit the influence of the other side and to expand its own."[4] Ake's observation highlights the fact that Africa's strategic importance has rarely been valued on its own. Rather, U.S. policy has consistently treated Africa as an adjunct of some other security interest. To a significant degree, this continues to be the case.

In the aftermath of World War II, U.S. opposition to colonialism was tempered by the desire to maintain close relations with European allies and the recognition that European recovery was dependent on maintaining economic links with African colonies. As a result, deference to Europe and the exigencies of the Cold War trumped African demands for rapid decolonization and a faster pace of socioeconomic and political progress.[5]

Because American involvement in Africa was limited prior to the continent's independence, the U.S. was content to defer to the European powers on decolonization. European skepticism about if not outright opposition to granting independence caused the U.S. to mute its support for decolonization. European reluctance, combined with concern about rising nationalism after the 1955 Bandung Conference, which led to the formation of the Non-Aligned Movement, and the convening of the All African Peoples' Conference in Accra in 1958 further encouraged U.S. caution in advocating independence, leading American officials instead to support the status quo and hope for a slow, managed transition. Eisenhower was cautious about decolonization, discouraging the independence of African states for fear of communist influence. He was skeptical of African nationalism and believed that African colonial territories were incapable of governing themselves.[6]

Decolonization was secondary to ensuring access to strategic minerals and concerns about the European ability to recover from the war and resist Soviet encroachment. Africa's raw materials and European trade opportunities with the continent were seen as essential to that goal. Africa's strategic location astride important sea lanes made establishing bases from which to monitor the Soviets a major U.S. policy goal. The wish to cultivate friendly states that could provide such bases and the hope of encouraging them to resist Soviet influence were among the primary motivations for U.S. policy.[7] By the 1960s the U.S. was drawn into Africa more directly.

The Congo Crisis

Even though it was considered a "foreign policy backwater,"[8] Africa was thrust onto the U.S. foreign policy agenda by the first Congo crisis, between 1960 and 1964. The crisis surrounding the independence of the Belgian Congo on June 30, 1960, resulted in the first U.S. involvement in postindependence Africa.[9] Sensitive to Belgian economic concerns and wary of the prospect of Soviet influence in the resource-rich Congo, the U.S. was a participant in the intrigue surrounding the ouster and assassination of the Congo's uncompromising nationalist and pan-Africanist prime minister, Patrice Lumumba.

Lumumba became prime minister after his MNC-L party won the majority of seats in the lower house of parliament in the pre-independence elections.[10] Only days after independence, in June 1960, a mutiny in the Force Publique plunged the Congo into a deep and complicated crisis. The chaos resulted in Belgian troops re-entering the Congo, ostensibly to restore order and protect Belgian nationals. A day later, with Belgian complicity, mineral-rich Katanga province announced its secession further complicating a volatile situation.

Responding to the chaos, the UN authorized Opération des Nations Unies au Congo (ONUC), a peacekeeping force, to try to restore order in the country. Because the UN failed to take action against the Belgian troops in Katanga, Lumumba threatened to turn to the Soviet Union for assistance in ousting the Belgians. This confirmed the fear within the Eisenhower administration that even if Lumumba himself was not a communist, his behavior and what they saw as the growing influence of "radical" advisers made the Congo vulnerable to communist influence.[11] On August 12, Albert Kalonji, a Lumumba rival, announced the secession of South Kasai. The secession coincided with a push through South Kasai by the Congolese National Army (ANC) toward Katanga. In the course of this military action, the army committed atrocities against civilians. In a U.S. National Security Council meeting on August 18, the consensus emerged that Lumumba had to be removed.[12]

The CIA formulated a covert plan to assassinate Lumumba, but in the end Lumumba's Belgian and Congolese opponents captured and executed him. According to Thomas Kanza, the first Congo representative to the UN, Andrew Cordier, a U.S. official with ONUC, "arranged things in favor of Kasavubu and the interests of the West."[13] On September 5, 1960, President Kasavubu announced that Lumumba had been dismissed as prime minister. Lumumba then responded that he was replacing Kasavubu, setting off even more confusion that came to an end when Joseph Mobutu, who had been appointed army chief of staff by Lumumba, stepped in and installed a college of commissioners headed by Foreign Minister Justin Bomboko to run the country. In October, in response to fears that Lumumba would be able to rally his supporters, he was put under house arrest. On November 27, Lumumba escaped and fled Kinshasa but was captured on December 1, 1960, as he tried to make his way to his supporters' stronghold in Kisangani. He was transferred to the hands of his opponents in Katanga in January 1961. Beaten by his captors during the flight to Katanga and again after his arrival in Elisabethville, he was executed by a firing squad shortly thereafter.[14]

The chaos continued after Lumumba's death. However, the Kennedy administration took a different approach, supporting the withdrawal of Belgian troops and backing the reconvening of parliament. This reflected the Kennedy administration's view that moderate nationalist forces could hold radical elements in check and prevent Soviet influence. Kennedy also favored a more forceful approach against the Katangan leader Moise Tshombe, but this was opposed by both European allies and conservative domestic critics who saw Tshombe as strongly anticommunist.[15]

By early 1963, UN efforts prevented the secession of Katanga. The U.S. began a training program for Congolese armed forces in order to be able to secure the country after UN forces withdrew. In September 1963, President Kasavubu dismissed parliament, which led to the formation of the opposition Committee of National Liberation (CNL), under the leadership of Christopher Gibenye, former minister of the interior. Shortly thereafter the Popular Liberation Army (PLA) was created as the CNL's military wing. Another guerrilla army was organized by Pierre Mulele, a Lumumbist and former minister of education. Fearing the collapse of Congo's coalition government, the CIA became more deeply involved in the efforts to prop up the government. In October 1963, the U.S. supported a military-backed government reorganization that led to the resignation of Prime Minister Adoula and the appointment of Tshombe as prime minister. Tshombe's control of mercenary forces and his anticommunist credentials were attractive to U.S. and Belgian hard-liners. After Kennedy's assassination, the Johnson administration adopted a more conservative and active policy stance toward the Congo.[16]

The CIA-sponsored effort against the growing insurgency included Cuban exile pilots, CIA front organizations, and mercenary forces under the leadership of Mike Hoare, a former British officer and ex-Katanga mercenary.[17] As the insurgency gained strength, the CIA played an even larger role in combating the insurgents, including air strikes against the PLA. With the Belgians willing to take a larger role in the fight against the insurgents, when the PLA began to take expatriates hostage, the U.S. authorized Operation Red Dragon on November 24, 1964. Planes flown by U.S. pilots dropped Belgian paratroopers into Kisangani to rescue the hostages. A second attack, Operation Black Dragon, took place two days later and freed more hostages. The insurgency collapsed shortly thereafter. These paramilitary operations contributed to political instability in the Congo. Tshombe organized his own national political party in February 1965, threatening Kasavubu's political future. Kasavubu took steps to thwart Tshombe's plans, creating a political struggle that ended when Mobutu ousted the civilian regime on November 24, 1965.[18] Initially promising to hold power for five years, after which elections would be held, Mobutu clung to power, with American help, for thirty-two years, plundering the resources of the country he renamed Zaire and presiding over a particularly corrupt and brutal regime. Mobutu's anticommunism was solid insurance against U.S. reaction to the abuses of his regime. Mobutu was especially valuable as a conduit for support for rebels in Angola, which also became a battleground in the Cold War struggle.

Angola and South Africa

Angola's struggle against Portuguese colonialism dates to the 1950s. The Popular Movement for the Liberation of Angola (MPLA), formed in 1956, drew its support from Luanda and the surrounding areas. The MPLA sought aid from the U.S. but was refused by the Eisenhower administration because of concern about the impact on U.S. access to a base in the Portuguese Azores. The Union of the Peoples of Northern Angola (UPNA) was founded in 1954, under the leadership of Holden Roberto. In 1958, the UPNA became the Union of the Peoples of Angola (UPA). Originally a movement in support of unifying Bakongo peoples divided by colonial boundaries, the UPA broadened its leadership in 1961 to include non-Bakongo. Among those recruited was Jonas Savimbi, an Ovimbundu. The UPA identified itself as a party of oppressed Angolans while portraying the MPLA as the party of the privileged. In 1962, the UPA became the National Front for the Liberation of Angola (FNLA) and obtained support from the U.S. The FNLA also had the support of the government in the capital, Leopoldville, in neighboring Congo. While the Kennedy administration was more amenable to contacts with nationalist groups, fear of losing access to the Azores forced the administration to reduce those contacts.[19] Mobutu's 1965 coup solidified Congolese support for the FNLA.[20] The MPLA received the backing of the Organization of African Unity's (OAU) Liberation Committee in 1964, while the FNLA eventually lost OAU financial support in 1968. The two Angolan parties took different stances, with the MPLA espousing a more revolutionary position and the FNLA taking the position of a nationalist and anti-Soviet party.[21]

With the end of military rule in Portugal, in 1975, the Alvor Agreement was supposed to lead Angola to a transitional government followed by elections. The Portuguese left Angola without effecting a formal power transition, igniting a civil war between the three contenders for power in postindependence Angola. The FNLA and the MPLA fought for control of Luanda while UNITA, without external support, was sidelined. As the MPLA gained ground, the U.S. began to fund UNITA as well. The Ford administration covertly supported the FNLA and UNITA, recruiting mercenaries to fight against the MPLA and providing reconnaissance and supplies. The U.S. also cooperated with South Africa to provide U.S. military support through Zaire for the FNLA and UNITA.[22] South Africa intervened on behalf of the anti-MPLA forces, while Cuba supported the MPLA. The combination of Cuban involvement and U.S. congressional approval of the Tunney Amendment restricting funding to the Angolan rebels caused the South Africans to withdraw, leaving the MPLA in control of Luanda. Following clashes with UNITA, the FNLA ceased to be a factor in the struggle for power. UNITA withdrew into its stronghold in the southeast but later benefited from support given to anticommunist rebels under the Reagan Doctrine.[23]

Reagan administration policy had a significant impact on southern Africa. The administration's strategy included renewal of U.S.–South African military contacts suspended in the 1960s and adoption of "constructive engagement," which was supposed to moderate South African regional behavior. The U.S. also encouraged South African, Moroccan, Israeli, Saudi Arabian, and Zairean material support for UNITA and linked the normalization of U.S. relations with Angola and Namibian independence to the withdrawal of Cuban troops from Angola.[24]

The 1984 Lusaka Accords called for the establishment of a joint South African–Angolan Commission to monitor the withdrawal of South African troops from Angola in return for Angola's denying sanctuary for the anti–South African Southwest African Peoples' Organization (SWAPO). The Accords established a status quo that even Chester Crocker, the U.S. assistant secretary of state for Africa, described as "an alternative context for prosecuting the underlying conflict."[25]

The 1985 repeal of the Clark Amendment, originally passed in 1976, which had extended the Tunney Amendment's ban on covert support for rebels in Angola, was part of the Reagan Doctrine's effort to roll back communist influence. Fighting between the MPLA and UNITA escalated during 1987–1988.[26] Rejuvenated by the influx of support with the repeal of the Clark Amendment, UNITA resumed its activities and plunged Angola back into a war of attrition that had a devastating impact on the civilian population.[27] By 1987–1988, South Africa had also become more deeply involved in Angola and beginning in November 1987 came into direct contact with Angolan and Cuban forces in the area around Cuito Cuanavale, in southeastern Angola. For several months Cuban and MPLA troops clashed with troops from South African and UNITA. The South Africans faced effective Cuban anti-aircraft weapons that negated South African air superiority. Stung by its failure to prevail, South Africa entered into talks with Cuba and Angola. A U.S.-mediated agreement that included a timetable for Namibian independence, withdrawal of Cuban troops from Angola and an end to South African aid to UNITA, and the departure of ANC officials from Angola was reached in December 1988.[28]

The George H. W. Bush administration continued to support Savimbi and UNITA. A peace plan negotiated in Gbadolite, Zaire, in 1989 collapsed when Savimbi, with the backing of the Bush administration, rejected it, putting forth his own plan for a transitional government.[29] Fighting for control of Angola continued until the Bicesse Accords in May 1991 established the dates for elections in 1992. However, Savimbi refused to accept the MPLA electoral victory and returned UNITA to war. The MPLA had renounced Marxism in 1990, and under the Clinton administration the U.S. recognized the MPLA government and ended support for UNITA. The war finally ended with Savimbi's death in an Angolan government offensive in 2002.

South Africa's involvement in Angola complicated U.S. policy but also provided the rationale for the policy that linked Angola to independence for Namibia. South Africa continued to illegally administer Namibia after the 1966 UN revocation of the mandate granted to South Africa by the League of Nations in the aftermath of World War I. Although the U.S. linkage policy eventually led to the independence of Namibia, it also reduced the pressure on South Africa to disengage with Angola and Namibia until Cuban troops left Angola.[30]

The U.S. security relationship with South Africa was inextricably tied up with both race and ideology. As the U.S. slowly began to embrace racial justice in the post–World War II era, a widening gap emerged between the U.S. and the unreconstructed racist South African regime. Nevertheless, South Africa's participation on the Allied side during World War II and its staunch anticommunism made a strong case for cooperation between Washington and Pretoria. It became much more difficult to cooperate with South Africa as the National Party government cracked down harder and harder on the opposition to apartheid. The March 1960 Sharpeville massacre, during which the South African security forces opened fire, killing sixty-nine demonstrators protesting the pass laws, clearly demonstrated the South African government's willingness to use violence against anti-apartheid protestors. Nevertheless, the exigencies of the Cold War too often overshadowed human rights concerns as the global opposition to apartheid strengthened and the U.S. sought to walk a fine line between condemning the institutionalized racism of apartheid and retaining a strategic relationship with South Africa. This strategic relationship involved secure access to South African minerals, especially uranium, and a desire to maintain relations in order to benefit from South Africa's position astride the Cape sea route and the critical monitoring opportunities that relationship provided.

The fine line that the U.S. sought to navigate was evident in the Kennedy administration's August 2, 1963, decision to impose a unilateral arms embargo on South Africa. A voluntary UN arms embargo under UN Security Council Resolution 181 was passed on August 7, 1963. The administration announced that as of the end of the year, it would no longer sell military equipment to South Africa. Reflecting both disagreement within the administration regarding the strategic importance of South Africa and the desire to have it both ways, the administration sought to distinguish between goods that could be used to enforce apartheid and those that were for national defense. Although not of vital importance, several missile tracking stations in South Africa were up for lease renewal in the early 1960s, and the Kennedy administration had committed to selling South Africa submarines in early 1963. Hoping to retain these tracking stations as well as cooperation with South African intelligence and cognizant of a role for South Africa in countering Soviet influence, Kennedy approved the sale of the submarines under an exemption that permitted the sale of items deemed important to international security.[31] Under the Johnson administration, despite some pressure to provide military aid to South Africa under the strategic exemption provision of the arms embargo, the administration's policy was to reject sales under the exemption and also prohibit sales of dual-use equipment. The administration also banned U.S. naval visits after an incident in which U.S. sailors were subject to apartheid laws during a visit by the aircraft carrier USS *Franklin D. Roosevelt*.[32]

The Nixon administration undertook a wide review of foreign policy. National Security Study Memorandum 39 dealt with southern Africa and U.S. relations with South Africa. It laid out five options ranging from closer cooperation with South Africa to U.S. avoidance of the conflicts in the region. The U.S. opted for option two, which called for adapting past policy and advocated closer ties with both black and white regimes in the region. Based on the assumption that the white-minority regimes were unlikely to go away anytime soon, policy was geared toward trying to encourage the South Africans towards reform by easing some of the restrictions on U.S. relations with South Africa. The administration allowed the sale of grey-area products as well as dual-use goods, as long as they did not have combat or internal security uses.[33] NSSM 39 also allowed for resumption of U.S.–South African military contacts, continued U.S. access to the tracking stations, and nuclear cooperation.[34] The NSSM 39 policy, dubbed "a policy of communication" by the Nixon administration,[35] was the forerunner of the Reagan administration's constructive-engagement policy.

The Carter administration's emphasis on human rights prompted a shift away from the more accommodating policies of the Nixon and Ford administrations. In the wake of the 1976 Soweto uprisings, the administration supported the mandatory arms embargo established by UN Security Council Resolution 418, passed unanimously on November 4, 1977. The U.S. also withdrew its naval attaché from Pretoria, closed the grey-area exemptions on military goods in place under the Nixon and Ford administrations, restricted the sale of light aircraft and computer equipment with military application, tightened visa requirements for South African military personnel, and strengthened export regulations on nuclear technology.[36]

Cold War considerations again became the primary focus and dictated U.S. policy toward South Africa under the Reagan administration that came to power in the 1980 elections. The constructive-engagement policy adopted by the administration harked back to the "communication" policy that followed from NSSM 39 during the Nixon administration. Constructive engagement was a renewed effort to encourage South Africa toward reform by engaging with Pretoria. Indeed, the architect of the policy, Chester Crocker, the assistant secretary of state for Africa, emphasized that he "did not propose a dramatic departure from the last twenty years of American policy toward South Africa. Under constructive engagement, we would continue our adherence to the arms embargo, our refusal to make use of South African defense facilities, our categorical rejection of apartheid policies and institutions—as well as our rejection of trade and investment sanctions and all forms of economic warfare against South Africa."[37] He went on to describe the policy as one designed to assert American leadership and as an effort to work with all countries in the region to enhance U.S. credibility as a regional partner in peacemaking. Crocker claimed that critics misinterpreted and distorted the policy, seeing it as directed only toward South Africa and equating it with opposition to sanctions and failure to adequately pressure Pretoria, which opponents saw as coddling the apartheid regime. Instead, he claimed that the policy was an effort to dissuade countries in the region from pursuing their goals militarily, push South Africa towards reform, and end the regional cycle of violence that had followed from the collapse of Portuguese colonialism.[38]

If ending the violence in the region was the goal, it is hard to see how the repeal of the Clark Amendment prohibiting aid to rebels in Angola fit in with that goal. Passed in 1976, after the collapse of Portuguese colonialism and the beginning of the civil war in Angola, the law prohibited aid to rebels fighting in Angola. The Reagan administration successfully pushed for the repeal of the amendment in 1985, allowing aid to UNITA. The Reagan administration's effort to roll back communism fit well with the "total onslaught" narrative that South Africa had been peddling since the independence of Angola and Mozambique. MPLA control in Luanda and Frelimo's emergence in Mozambique, combined with the South African view that it was under siege at home by the communist, terrorist African National Congress (ANC), shaped this narrative. Instead of reducing the violence, repeal of the Clark Amendment and U.S. collaboration with South Africa only increased violence in Angola. It also allowed the South Africans to believe that the threat of communist influence in the region would trump U.S. opposition to apartheid. By 1986, growing outrage against South Africa's refusal to make any meaningful reforms resulted in the passage of the Comprehensive Anti-Apartheid Act over the veto of the Reagan administration. Over the next four years, the combination of international pressure and growing internal opposition led to the end of apartheid and normalization of U.S.-South African relations under the George H. W. Bush administration.

East Africa

Dating back to the World War II era, the Horn of Africa has also been a focus of U.S. security policy, ensuring that it would continue to be important during the Cold War. The strategic value of the region was too great for it not to become a security concern. Ethiopia was identified as an important component of a U.S. global communications network, and an agreement with Ethiopia that provided the U.S. with communications facilities was signed. The U.S. also supported the federation between Ethiopia and Eritrea in 1952 and raised no objection when Ethiopia incorporated Eritrea in 1962. Ethiopia's value as a communications asset was only one dimension of its strategic value during the Cold War. Nasser's rise to power and Egypt's involvement in Yemen as well as fears of links between the Eritrean Liberation Front and Arab nationalists further highlighted Ethiopia's critical importance.[39] Between 1969 and 1973, the U.S. provided an average of $12 million a year to Ethiopia. This included money for military modernization and additional jet fighters. Ethiopia came to account for some 80% of all security assistance to Africa and had the largest military assistance advisory group (MAAG) on the continent.[40] Emperor Haile Selassie was a reliable ally until his ouster in the 1974 Ethiopian Revolution that brought a military committee called the Derg to power, with Mengistu Haile Mariam as chairman. A 1976 decision to provide the Derg, despite its revolutionary rhetoric, with F-5E fighter planes demonstrated how important Ethiopia was considered to be to U.S. security interests.[41] By 1977, deterioration of human rights under the Derg led to an end to U.S. military aid and the closing of the communication facility at Kagnew. In April 1977, Ethiopia expelled U.S. personnel associated with the MAAG and ended a mutual defense pact, and in response the Carter administration suspended all U.S. military aid, including equipment for which the Ethiopians had already paid.[42]

The split between the U.S. and Ethiopia widened further when Somalia invaded the Ogaden in 1977. Under Mohammed Siad Barre, who came to power in a 1969 coup, Somalia saw the political upheaval in Ethiopia as an opportunity to push Somali irrendentist claims over the region. The Ogaden War prompted a regional realignment when the Soviet Union shifted its support firmly behind Ethiopia. Soviet aid to the Derg, combined with the arrival of some twenty-five thousand Cuban troops to bolster the Ethiopians' defense, offset initial Somali gains, turned the tide in favor of Ethiopia, and eventually forced the Somalis to withdraw from the Ogaden. Global geostrategic interests led the U.S., despite the opposition of Africa experts in the foreign policy bureaucracy, to closer ties with Somalia. The Carter administration had approved military aid to Somalia just prior to the Ogaden invasion, and, although there was significant concern over the potential fallout from backing the clear aggressor in this case, Carter pushed for stronger ties, especially after the decisive Soviet and Cuban support for Ethiopia. Once the Somalis withdrew from the Ogaden after being soundly defeated by a joint Cuban-Ethiopian offensive, it became somewhat easier to justify closer ties with Somalia as an effort to prevent the expansion of Soviet influence in Africa. The 1979 Iranian Revolution and the Soviet invasion of Afghanistan that same year tilted U.S. policy further in the direction of Somalia, access to whose port facilities was deemed important to counter the growing Soviet regional threats in the Persian Gulf, southwest Asia, and the Horn.[43]

The ouster of Said Barre in 1991 resulted in the collapse of the Somali state and more than two decades of chaos. In 1992, the George H. W. Bush administration launched the first American post–Cold War intervention, Operation Provide Relief. The deployment began as a humanitarian effort to ensure an end to raids on the delivery of food supplies to Somalia. Despite having little familiarity with Somalia, the first Bush administration chose to ignore the warning of the U.S. ambassador to Kenya, Smith Hempstone, that "if you liked Beirut, you'll love Mogadishu" and that the U.S. should "think once, twice, and three times before you embrace the Somali tarbaby."[44] Without fully appreciating the complexity of Somalia's clan and cultural landscape, the U.S. allowed mission creep to lead to the October 1993 operation to try to capture Mohammed Farah Aideed, the warlord believed to be behind the killing of twenty-three Pakistani U.N. peacekeeping troops. An intense battle resulted in the deaths of eighteen U.S. servicemen as well as many more Somalis and not only soured the U.S. on the Somali humanitarian intervention but also influenced U.S. thinking on security and intervention for the next decade and a half. The withdrawal of U.S. troops and UN peacekeepers by late 1995 left Somalia to complete state collapse from which it has only recently and tentatively begun to emerge.

The American experience in Somalia had a decisive impact on U.S. willingness to become involved in other African operations, especially in conjunction with the UN. The growing cost of UN peacekeeping in the post–Cold War era, combined with the cost and outcome of the Somalia operation, was unpopular with conservative Republicans who were skeptical of the UN and critical of humanitarian operations that did not involve vital U.S. interests.[45] Burned by the Somalia experience and wary of multilateral interventions and with no strategic interests at stake, the U.S. voted to reduce the UN presence in Rwanda, contributing to the catastrophic genocide in Rwanda. Moreover, even after learning of the magnitude of the killing, the U.S. resisted labeling the rampage "genocide"[46] since doing so would have required a response under the Genocide Convention.

East Africa has grown into a major focus for American interests in the region since the bombing of the U.S. embassies in Kenya and Tanzania. Terrorists connected to al Qaeda simultaneously detonated bombs that destroyed the U.S. embassy in Nairobi and damaged the U.S. embassy in Dar-es-Salaam in August 1998. In retaliation for these attacks, the Clinton administration ordered cruise missile attacks on terrorist bases in Afghanistan and on a manufacturing facility in Sudan suspected of developing chemical weapons. The factory was alleged to be connected with Osama bin Laden, who had been expelled from Sudan two years before. Although the attack on Sudan was controversial because the evidence that the factory was producing chemicals for weapons was inconclusive, it foreshadowed a more robust U.S. approach to counterterrorism on the continent.

Not only was Sudan suspected of supporting terrorism, but the country's civil wars had produced a widespread humanitarian crisis, prompting U.S. efforts to mediate the civil war. British colonialism had left a deep rift between the north and south of the country. The Anyanya rebellion from 1963 to 1972 resulted in an agreement that consolidated three southern provinces into one, incorporated Anyanya fighters into the armed forces, and opened positions in the Sudanese government to southerners.[47] Fighting between the north and the south resumed after the Nimeiri government introduced Sharia law in 1983. The U.S. initially supported the government of Sudan in a further effort to isolate Libya's Colonel Qaddafi, who supported the rebels in the south.[48] Nimeiri was overthrown in a coup while he was visiting the U.S., and the increasingly Islamist regime worried the U.S. The second Sudan civil war raged until the signing of the Comprehensive Peace Agreement in 2005, which provided for a referendum on the future of the south. Although the war was regarded primarily as a struggle between the Islamic north and the Christian and animist south, the U.S. became involved in trying to broker an agreement in what was actually a much more complicated conflict than was widely understood, prompted in part by concerns in the U.S. Congress that Christians were being targeted by the Sudanese government. After the January 2011 vote in which the south overwhelmingly supported independence, South Sudan gained independence in July 2011.

African Solutions to African Problems?

Because there was little likelihood of large-scale direct American involvement after the failed intervention in Somalia in the early 1990s, the development of an indigenous peacekeeping/intervention capability became a key component of U.S. security policy toward Africa. Presidential Decision Directive 25, signed on May 3, 1994, laid out U.S. policy on peacekeeping. In that document, the U.S. stated its support for efforts to improve the capabilities of regional organizations. In the aftermath of the disaster in Somalia and the genocide in Rwanda and with rising ethnic tensions in Burundi in 1996, the influence of PDD-25 was evident when then U.S. secretary of state Warren Christopher proposed the creation of an African Crisis Response Force (ACRF). Under this plan African troops were to be trained and equipped by the U.S. for deployment into crisis situations such as the threat of another round of ethnic fighting that was unfolding in Burundi at the time. A coup in Burundi sidetracked the plan, and the ACRF was never created.[49] It is doubtful that this initiative would have been successful anyway. African countries were particularly suspect about ACRF because the U.S. did not seek sufficient consultation about its formation. The U.S. offer of peacekeeping training also raised questions about both American intentions and ACRF's effect on peacekeeping efforts initiated by African regional organizations.[50] Critics charged that ACRF reflected a neo-colonialist approach to peacekeeping in which African armed forces would be used to achieve American goals.[51] Although the skeptical African response to ACRF helped to derail the original idea, it did not prevent subsequent efforts to create an indigenous peacekeeping capability and promote African military professionalism.[52] Not surprisingly, concerns about American intentions did not subside with subsequent efforts.

In 1997, the ACRF concept reemerged as the African Crisis Response Initiative (ACRI), with a broad emphasis on leadership; communications; logistics and equipment maintenance; and specific peacekeeping skills such as checkpoint procedures, coordination with NGOs and the press, vehicle searches, and basic marksmanship.[53] ACRI also emphasized a common peacekeeping doctrine and provided communications equipment that would allow the various national contingents to communicate during deployments. The goal was to train twelve thousand troops contributed by the participating states. These troops could then be deployed to trouble spots either as national units or collectively as a multinational peacekeeping force. Participating governments included Benin, Ghana, Malawi, Mali, Senegal, and Uganda, and more than 5,500 troops trained under this program. Mali and Ghana deployed ACRI forces to Sierra Leone as part of the ECOWAS peacekeeping force. Benin sent ACRI-trained troops to Guinea-Bissau, and Senegal participated in a mission in the Central African Republic.[54] Related to but exceeding the parameters of ACRI, Operation Focus Relief provided training for Nigerian, Ghanian, and Senegalese troops in the use of force and supplied lethal weapons in response to the May 2000 hostage-taking incident in Sierra Leone involving UN troops participating in the UN Mission in Sierra Leone (UNAMSIL).[55] In 2004, the George W. Bush administration renamed ACRI the Africa Contingency Operations Training Assistance (ACOTA) program. Among the features that distinguished it from the previous program were its emphasis in its training efforts on addressing specific circumstances, the implementation of a "training-the-trainer" approach to address concerns about loss of trained troops and unit cohesiveness, and the introduction of a peace-enforcement dimension along with the necessary equipment to carry out such a mission.[56] Between 1997 and 2012, ACOTA trained some 215,000 African peacekeepers from the twenty-five partner states. Those troops participated in peacekeeping missions throughout the region.[57]

The September 11 Attacks and U.S. Security Policy toward Africa

In the aftermath of the September 11 attacks, U.S. national security focused even more intently on the threat of terrorism. The 2002 U.S. National Security Strategy stated that the U.S. was less threatened by conquering states than by failing ones and emphasized the threat of global terrorism. It juxtaposed Africa's promise and opportunity with its rampant poverty, disease, and conflict and emphasized the threat this contradiction posed to America's core value of promoting human dignity and its strategic priority of defeating terrorism.[58] U.S. attention to the region has grown significantly since then; the American military presence in the Horn has increased, and Africa has become a major component of U.S. counterterrorism policy. In October 2002, U.S. forces at Camp Lemonnier in Djibouti were increased by 400 to about 1,200 troops. Troop levels have since climbed to 4,000. The troops conducted training missions and took up positions from which to stage attacks against al Qaeda forces believed to be in the region.[59] These troops were involved in aerial reconnaissance missions along the East African coast and in marine interdiction efforts designed to prevent al Qaeda members escaping Afghanistan from going to East Africa.[60] The Combined Joint Task Force-Horn of Africa (CJTF-HOA), established in 2002 and headquartered in Djibouti, coordinates regional military action against terrorists, including operations across the Bab al Mandaab in Yemen.[61] It also participated in antipiracy efforts in the waters off the Horn. In addition to monitoring movements in the region and serving as a staging area for attacks against terrorists, Djibouti has also been used to train U.S. forces for desert warfare. The CIA Predator drone that killed al Qaeda suspects in 2002 in Yemen was launched from Djibouti.[62] CJTF-HOA has also added development initiatives to its military training mission.[63] Task force personnel have been involved in civic affairs, including building schools, clinics, and hospitals and drilling wells.[64]

The simultaneous November 2002 attack on an Israeli-owned hotel in Mombasa, Kenya, and a failed effort to bring down an Israeli airliner during takeoff from Mombasa's airport, both attributed to al Qaeda, further heightened regional security concerns. Somalia was identified both as the probable source of the missiles used in the airliner attack and as the point of entry into Kenya for the suicide bombers of the hotel.[65] In an effort to prevent further attacks, President Bush announced the East African Regional Security Initiative in 2003. The program was designed to bring together several agencies to strengthen border security, immigration control, aviation security, and regional intelligence sharing. The initiative also included social and economic development programs as a way to prevent radicalization.[66] The program became the Partnership for Regional East African Counterterrorism (PREACT) in 2009 and became part of Operation Enduring Freedom, the global war on terrorism.

The threat of Islamic radicalism across the Sahel had prompted the U.S. to create the Pan-Sahel Initiative (PSI) in 2002. This program offered training as well as vehicles, radios, and other equipment to help countries improve security and border surveillance.[67] Initial participants in this program included Chad, Mauritania, Niger, and Mali. In March 2004, Chadian troops engaged in a battle along the border with Niger with elements of the Algerian Salafist Group for Preaching and Combat (GSPC), now known as al Qaeda in the Islamic Maghreb (AQIM). Reports that United States had provided logistics and command and control for the operation indicated a more active role for the U.S.[68] The PSI was replaced by the Trans Saharan Counterterrorism Initiative (TSCTI), inaugurated in June 2005 with Exercise Flintlock. The TSCTI (now the Trans-Sahara Counter Terrorism Partnership, or TSCTP) is aimed at strengthening regional counterterrorism capabilities, enhancing cooperation among the region's armed forces, promoting democratic governance, and reinforcing links between the U.S. military and armed forces in the region.[69] The program was expanded beyond the original four participants to include Nigeria, Senegal, Algeria, Morocco, and Tunisia. In conjunction with the TSCTP, USAID was to initiate education programs while the State Department worked on airport security and the Treasury Department focused on tightening financial controls.[70]

The U.S. became more deeply involved behind the scene as fighting broke out in Somalia in 2006 between the forces of a loose coalition of U.S.-backed militias and what became the Islamic Courts Union (ICU), a coalition of various Islamic factions. Among the forces making up the ICU included al Shabaab, based among former al-Ittihad fighters whose goal was the establishment of a pan-Somali Salafist regime. The ICU defeated the U.S.-supported forces and extended its control, bringing some semblance of order to the chaos while gaining support among the population. The hard-line al Shabaab drew support from across clan lines, was more nationalist, and supported Somali irredentist claims. The ascendance of al Shabaab worried the U.S. and its ally Ethiopia.[71] In December 2006, with backing from the U.S., Ethiopia invaded Somalia and occupied Mogadishu. The violence worsened, provoking outrage against Ethiopia, further radicalizing the population, ultimately strengthening al Shabaab, and deepening the links between al Shabaab and al Qaeda.[72] Replacing the Inter-Governmental Authority on Development (IGAD) Peace Support Mission authorized by the AU in 2006, the African Union created the AU Mission in Somalia (AMISOM) in 2007. Ethiopian troops withdrew from Somalia in 2009, but the chaos continued. Concern about the spillover from Somalia intensified after al Shabaab took responsibility for the June 2010 attacks in Uganda in which more than seventy people were killed. Although al Shabaab withdrew its forces from Mogadishu in the face of increasingly effective AMISOM forces in August 2011 and although the famine in the region has undermined its support and divided its leadership, al Shabaab remains a threat to the fledgling Somali government.[73] Beginning in 2007, the U.S. carried out targeted attacks against al Shabaab personnel and training camps, including a U.S. cruise missile attack that killed al Shabaab's top military commander, Aden Hashi Ayro, and several deputies in May 2008.[74] Al Shbaab's leader, Ahmed Abdi Godane was killed in U.S. airstrike in 2014.

Although counterterrorism and enhancement of African military capability were at the top of the list of U.S. security concerns, there was also growing recognition that Africa's low levels of development also represented a security challenge. The Bush administration was surprisingly active toward Africa, particularly on health issues. The devastation caused by the AIDS epidemic, the cost to development in the future, and the recognition of the connection to security focused attention on Africa, the region most seriously affected by the epidemic. In 2003, the Bush administration announced the President's Emergency Plan for AIDS Relief (PEPFAR), a five-year $15 billion initiative to provide funding for AIDS education and treatment. PEPFAR was reauthorized in 2008. By 2012, PEPFAR had provided treatment to more than 5.1 million people and care for an additional 15 million, including 4.5 million orphans and vulnerable children. The program also provided antiretroviral medication to some 750,000 HIV-positive pregnant women, resulting in the births of some 230,000 HIV-free children.[75] In 2004, the Bush administration also created the Millennium Challenge Account (MCA), designed to provide grants to countries that meet requirements related to governance, economic freedom, and good macroeconomic policy. African countries accounted for ten of the eighteen compacts signed by 2008. Nine additional countries qualified for help in gaining access to the MCA. Under the African Growth and Opportunity Act (AGOA), originally passed by the Clinton administration, the Bush administration also expanded the range of African products that can enter the U.S. duty-free.[76]

Once the backwater of American foreign policy, Africa has come to occupy a much more important role in U.S. security policy, especially since the

September 11 attacks. As the U.S. has become more engaged with the continent since then, past policies have continued to have an influence on the substance of U.S. policy and on perceptions of its intent. Although Africa's strategic importance has increased, African security is still to a significant degree secondary to U.S. security interests, while U.S. priorities continue to influence the nature of security cooperation with Africa. During the Cold War, Africa's importance was always in the context of the East-West struggle. Now, U.S. policy toward African security is closely tied to U.S. efforts to defeat violent Islamic extremism. During the Cold War, the U.S. put expedience ahead of human rights, propping up the likes of Mobutu in the former Zaire and cooperating with South Africa in Angola. More recently, U.S. support for the Ethiopian intervention in Somalia again raised questions of whether the U.S. is willing to overlook a questionable human rights record in pursuit of its larger security goals.

U.S. policy toward Africa is still prone to overlook the importance of local factors as explanations for conflict and instability. The tendency to focus on international terrorism leads to a failure to adequately appreciate the importance of poverty, lagging development, frustration, and disillusionment in contributing to conflicts in places like Somalia, northern Mali, and northern Nigeria. This is reminiscent of the U.S. approach during the Cold War, when American policy equated nationalism with communism in the Congo and failed to recognize ethnicity and competition for resources and political power as important factors in the Angolan civil war. As the U.S. embarked on a restructuring of security policy toward Africa with the establishment of the U.S. military command for Africa in 2007, past U.S. policy provided context for the debate on the future of U.S.- Africa security policy.

Notes

1 *The National Security Strategy of the United States*, March 1990, 13–14, available at http://bushlibrary.tamu.edu/research/pdfs/national_security_strategy_90.pdf

2 *A National Security Strategy of Engagement and Enlargement*, July 1994, 26, available at http://nssarchive.us/NSSR/1994.pdf

3 *A National Security Strategy for a New Century*, October 1998, 32, available at http://nssarchive.us/?page_id=66

4 Claude Ake, 1996, *Democracy and Development in Africa* (Washington, DC: The Brookings Institute), 98, available at www.scribd.com/doc/26036536/Democracy-and-Development-in-Africa

5 See John Kent, 2000, "The United States and the Decolonization of Black Africa, 1945–63," in David Ryan & Victor Pungong, eds., *The United States and Decolonization: Power and Freedom* (New York: St. Martin's Press), 168–187.

6 Mitch Lerner, 2011, "Climbing Off the Back Burner: Lyndon Johnson's Soft Power Approach to Africa," *Diplomacy and Statecraft*, 22:4, 580.

7 Alan P. Dobson & Steve Marsh, 2006, *U.S. Foreign Policy since 1945*, 2nd edition (New York: Routledge), 111–112.

8 Peter J. Schraeder, 1994, *United States Foreign Policy toward Africa: Incrementalism, Crisis and Change* (Cambridge: Cambridge University Press), 2–3.

9 F. Ugboaja Ohaegbulam, 2004, *U.S. Policy in Postcolonial Africa: Four Case Studies in Conflict Resolution* (New York: Peter Lang Publishing), 59.
10 Georges Nzongola-Ntalaja, 2002, *The Congo from Leopold to Kabila: A People's History* (New York: Zed Books), 94.
11 Schraeder, *United States Foreign Policy toward Africa*, 55.
12 Nzongola-Ntalaja, *The Congo from Leopold to Kabila*, 105–107.
13 Quoted in Nzongola-Ntalaja, *The Congo from Leopold to Kabila*, 108.
14 For a detailed account of Lumumba's assassination see Ludo De Witte, 2001, *The Assassination of Lumumba* (London and New York: Verso).
15 Schraeder, *United States Foreign Policy toward Africa*, 61–63.
16 Schraeder, *United States Foreign Policy toward Africa*, 66–69.
17 For a more detailed description of the CIA's involvement, see Jeffrey H. Michaels, 2012, "Breaking the Rules: The CIA and Counterinsurgency in the Congo 1964–1965," *International Journal of Intelligence and Counterintelligence*, 25:1, 130–159.
18 Schraeder, *United States Foreign Policy toward Africa*, 73–76.
19 Luis Nuno Rodrigues, 2004, "Today's Terrorist Is Tomorrow's Statesman: The United States and Angolan Nationalism in the Early 1960s," *Portuguese Journal of Social Science*, 4:2, 136.
20 Paul Nugent, 2012, *Africa since Independence*, 2nd edition (New York: Palgrave Macmillan), 266–268.
21 Nugent, *Africa since Independence*, 269.
22 Ohaegbulam, *U.S. Policy in Postcolonial Africa*, 178.
23 Nugent, *Africa since Independence*, 291.
24 Ohaegbulam, *U.S. Policy in Postcolonial Africa*, 181–182.
25 Chester A. Crocker, 1993, *High Noon in Southern Africa: Making Peace in a Rough Neighborhood* (New York: W. W. Norton), 199.
26 Ohaegbulam, *U.S. Policy in Postcolonial Africa*, 157.
27 Nugent, *Africa since Independence*, 293.
28 For a full discussion of these events, see Crocker, *High Noon in Southern Africa*.
29 Ohaegbulam, *U.S. Policy in Postcolonial Africa*, 184.
30 Nugent, *Africa since Independence*, 326.
31 Alex Thomson, 2008, *U.S. Foreign Policy towards South Africa, 1948–1994: Conflict of Interests* (New York: Palgrave MacMillan), 35–44.
32 Schraeder, *United States Foreign Policy toward Africa*, 205.
33 Thomson, *U.S. Foreign Policy towards South Africa, 1948–1994*, 75. See also Schraeder, *United States Foreign Policy toward Africa*, 206–209.
34 Thomson, *U.S. Foreign Policy towards South Africa, 1948–1994*, 76.
35 Schraeder, *United States Foreign Policy toward Africa*, 209.
36 Thomson, *U.S. Foreign Policy towards South Africa, 1948–1994*, 100.
37 Crocker, *High Noon in Southern Africa*, 77.
38 Crocker, *High Noon in Southern Africa*, 77–79.
39 Peter Woodward, 2006, *U.S. Foreign Policy and the Horn of Africa* (Hampton, UK, and Burlington VT: Ashgate), 18–19.
40 Schraeder, *United States Foreign Policy toward Africa*, 135.
41 Schraeder, *United States Foreign Policy toward Africa*, 139.
42 Schraeder, *United States Foreign Policy toward Africa*, 140–141.
43 See, for instance, Schraeder, *United States Foreign Policy toward Africa*, 142–152; Woodward, *U.S. Foreign Policy and the Horn of Africa*, 22–27.
44 Quoted in Paul Alexander, 2013, "Fallout from Somalia Still Haunts U.S. Policy 20 Years Later," *Stars and Stripes*, 3 October 2013.
45 Brian J. Hesse, 2005, "Celebrate or Hold Suspect? Bill Clinton and George W. Bush in Africa," *Journal of Contemporary African Studies*, 23:3 (September), 327–344.

46 For a fuller account of the effort to avoid American involvement, see Samantha Power, 2002, *A Problem from Hell: America and the Age of Genocide* (New York: HarperCollins).
47 Nugent, *Africa since Independence*, 86.
48 Nugent, *Africa since Independence*, 459.
49 See Eric G. Berman, 2004, "Recent Developments in US Peacekeeping Policy and Assistance to Africa," *African Security Review*, 13:2, available at www.iss.co.za
50 Russell J. Handy, 2003, "African Contingency Operations Training Assistance: Developing Training Partnerships for the Future of Africa," *Air & Space Power Journal*, available at www.airpower.maxwell.af.mil/airchronicles/apj/apj03/fal03/handy.html
51 See Herbert M. Howe, 2001, *Ambiguous Order: Military Forces in African States* (Boulder: Lynne Rienner Publishers), 250.
52 Howe, *Ambiguous Order*, 251.
53 Howe, *Ambiguous Order*, 252.
54 See "Africa Crisis Response Initiative, African Contingency Operations Training and Assistance," available at www.globalsecurity.org/military/agency/dod/acri.htm
55 See Berman, 2004, "Recent Developments," and Kay Whiteman & Douglas Yates, "France, Britain, and the United States," in Adekeye Adebajo & Ismail Rashid, eds., *West Africa's Security Challenges* (Boulder: Lynne Rienner Publishers), 373–374.
56 See Handy, "African Contingency Operations Training."
57 See "African Contingency Training Operations and Assistance," U.S. Africa Command Fact Sheet, available at www.africom.mil/Doc/9836
58 "The National Security Strategy of the United States, September, 2002," The White House, 1, 10.
59 "US to Add Forces in Horn of Africa," *New York Times*, 30 October 2002.
60 "About 1,000 More Americans Headed to Hunt for al Qaeda in and around Horn of Africa," Associated Press, 8 November 2002.
61 "Pentagon Creating New Military Command in Djibouti to Monitor Terrorists in the Horn of Africa," Associated Press, 4 November 2002.
62 "Threats and Responses: US Turns Horn of Africa into a Military Hub," *New York Times*, 17 November 2002.
63 See Robert G. Berschinski, "AFRICOM's Dilemma: The Global War on Terrorism, Capacity Building, Humanitarianism, and the Future of U.S. Security Policy in Africa," Strategic Studies Institute, available at www.strategicstudiesinstitute.army.mil
64 "CJTF-HOA Factsheet" available at www.hoa.africom.mil
65 "Somali SAMS?," *Africa Research Bulletin*, 1–31 December 2002, 15134.
66 Jendayi E. Frazer, 2010, "Reflections on U.S. Policy in Africa, 2001–2009," *Fletcher Forum of World Affairs*, 34:1 (Winter 2010), 104.
67 "US Targets Sahara Militant Threat," *BBC News World Edition*, 14 January 2004, available at http://news.bbc.co.uk/2/hi/africa/3397001.stm
68 See Stephen Ellis, 2004, "Briefing: The Pan-Sahel Initiative," *African Affairs*, 103:412, 459–464; Giles Tremlett, "US Sends Special Forces into North Africa," *The Guardian*, 15 March 2004.
69 Lauren Ploch, "Africa Command: U.S. Strategic Interests and the Role of the U.S. Military in Africa," Congressional Research Service Report to Congress, 21.
70 Donna Miles, "New Counterterrorism Initiative to Focus on Saharan Africa," *Armed Forces Press Service*, 16 May 2005, available at www.defense.gov/news/May2005/20050516_1126.html
71 Lauren Ploch, "Countering Terrorism in East Africa: The U.S. Response," Congressional Research Service Report 41473, 3 November 2010, 6–7.
72 For a detailed account of these events, see Ken Menkhaus, 2009, "Somalia: What Went Wrong?," *RUSI Journal*, 154:4, 6–12.

73 Frank Chothia, "Could Somali Famine Deal a Fatal Blow to al-Shabab?," *BBC News Africa*, 9 August 2011, available at www.bbc.co.uk/world-Africa 14373264
74 Ploch, "Countering Terrorism," 14.
75 "Fact Sheet: The President's Emergency Plan for AIDS Relief (PEPFAR)," Henry J. Kaiser Family Foundation, March 2013, available at www.kff.org/globalhealth/upload/8002–05.pdf
76 Frazer, 2010, "Reflections on U.S. Policy," 97.

4   The Establishment of AFRICOM

Africa's growing strategic importance and the increasing threats emanating from the region, especially since the August 1998 attacks on the U.S. embassies in Kenya and Tanzania, prompted a change of policy designed to focus more explicitly on security on the continent. President George Bush's February 2007 announcement that the U.S. would create a new U.S. Military Command for Africa (AFRICOM) clearly demonstrated a more systematic approach to security in Africa. Recognition that there was a lack of expertise in the Defense Department led to this reorganization of the U.S. Unified Command Plan.[1] Up until that point, responsibility for the continent had been divided among the European, Central, and Pacific Commands. AFRICOM unified responsibility for the continent in one combatant command and made Africa a more explicit part of the Unified Command Plan, the military's framework for geographic responsibility and military missions.[2] After a year of preparation in which the various military programs overseen by the three regional commands with previous responsibility were transferred to AFRICOM, the U.S. Military Command for Africa began formal operations on October 1, 2008.

As previously outlined, Africa's history of lagging development, political instability, insecurity, violent upheavals, and military coups makes for a complex security environment. Africa's sources of violence and insecurity are varied, and its security challenges are diverse. Violence is connected with Islamic extremism, issues related to poor governance, corruption, or the struggle for scarce resources among groups mobilized around divisions within society or some combination of those factors. A lack of military professionalism, combined with the armed forces operational incompetence, accounts for the difficulty in defeating insurgents or armed gangs and militia that are motivated primarily by the profit to be made from Africa's rich natural resources. Given the complicated sociopolitical environment, AFRICOM faces formidable challenges, made more acute by the circumstances surrounding the creation of the command.

Combatant Commands (COCOMs) are established by the president with the advice of the Joint Chiefs of Staff. They have a broad purview and are commanded by a four-star general and have an extensive and continuing mission. COCOMs integrate air, land, sea, and amphibious forces in support of U.S.

national security objectives. The geographic commands have access to units from the army, navy, air force, and marines. Commanders are responsible for carrying out assigned missions, joint training, logistics, and military operations. Funding for the commands comes from annual requests for operations and maintenance, while the support for the forces assigned to each command comes from their respective budgets. Operations carried out are funded separately and come primarily from the Overseas Contingency Operations account.[3]

As a joint effort with the State Department and USAID, AFRICOM represented a departure from the structure of existing military commands. The intention was to adopt an interagency approach that included representatives of other U.S. government stakeholders with interests in Africa. As the first AFRICOM commander, General William Ward, stated in testimony before the House Armed Services Committee in 2007, "We would like to realize a complementary mix of Department of Defense civilian and military staff and representatives from across the interagency departments of our government. Our intention is to move beyond the traditional concept of liaison officers and instead have our interagency partners serve alongside their DOD counterparts, working hand in hand every day on the matters most important to making a difference in Africa. As interagency representatives bring to bear the subject matter expertise of their parent organizations, USAFRICOM will complement, not compete with, the activities of other U.S. governmental organizations."[4] Ward went on to say, "I firmly believe security should be defined broadly and must be approached holistically. We will work to support on-going U.S. government efforts while finding additional ways to improve security related programs with the support of the Department of Defense. These can be military-to-military activities and exercises, or enhancing efforts led by another agency like USAID, State, Treasury, Commerce, or Justice."[5]

This approach signaled recognition of the multiple dimensions of security and sought to bring a range of expertise to the effort to enhance African security and establish a U.S.-African security partnership.

The structure of AFRICOM reflects the goal of developing a whole-of-government approach to African security with an emphasis on interagency cooperation. In addition to the four-star general who commands AFRICOM, there are two deputy commanders, a Deputy Commander for Military Operations (DCMO) and a Deputy to the Commander for Civil-Military Engagement (DCME), who is a senior State Department official. The DCME is a position unique to AFRICOM and has responsibility for helping to coordinate interagency cooperation and acts as a liaison with foreign governments and NGOs. USAID also contributes a senior development advisor for development-related issues.[6] The AFRICOM staff also includes some thirty representatives from more than ten federal agencies, including the Department of Homeland Security, the Department of Justice, Department of State, the Treasury Department, the Interior Department, and the Agriculture Department. Non-DOD representation is among the broadest of any combatant command, with representatives of other agencies embedded with DOD staff.[7]

The command was designed to address a broader security agenda than one focused on strictly military activities. According to a Defense Department official, AFRICOM's purpose is not to wage war but to establish the conditions for a more effective use of humanitarian and development assistance as well as to help Africans defeat terrorism.[8] The command's website describes its mission: "U.S. Africa Command protects and defends the national security interests of the United States by strengthening the defense capabilities of African states and regional organizations and, when directed, conducts military operations, in order to deter and defeat transnational threats and to provide a security environment conducive to good governance and development."[9]

Despite its lofty intentions, this ambitious effort to address a broader security agenda got off to a rocky start. AFRICOM's rollout was characterized by uncertainty about the scope of AFRICOM's mission; poor communications, particularly about where the command would be located; and mixed messages resulting in skepticism regarding its purpose. The result was a public relations disaster that overshadowed the launch of this new initiative.

Although planning for AFRICOM began in 2005 and was approved by President Bush in 2006,[10] information about the Bush administration's creation of AFRICOM was not well publicized. In his opening statement during hearings held by the House Foreign Affairs Subcommittee on Africa and Global Health in August 2007, the chairman of the subcommittee, Representative Donald Payne, expressed surprise at the news of AFRICOM's establishment. After expressing some concerns about the nature and scope of AFRICOM, Payne remarked, "My second concern is the way in which the initiative was announced and developed. I read about the administration's plans to establish a new command in the newspaper. I have had more calls from the press than I have had from the Department of Defense."[11] The limited consultation with Congress also raised additional questions. Expanding on his concerns, Chairman Payne said, "There has been no consultation with this committee about the establishment or structure of the command. The few briefings that we have had—which by the way are not consultations—have not been particularly informative." He also expressed concerns about what AFRICOM would do: "I do have some very serious concerns. One is about the administration's goals in setting up the command. On the one hand we have been told that the Department of Defense is not planning on taking on new tasks in Africa, that this is merely an organizational exercise. On the other hand we are told that the State Department and the USAID are being brought into the command so that they can inform the Department of Defense as it structures its programs. This implies that the programs and perhaps even the tasks that DOD carries out will be significantly different in some respects."[12]

The rollout was flawed in other ways as well. In their study of AFRICOM's establishment, Forest and Crispin found that the assumptions regarding AFRICOM's acceptance by other U.S. stakeholders were too optimistic, the planning process for AFRICOM was ad hoc and quicker than what might be expected for such an ambitious initiative, the transition team did not have adequate direction from the Office of the Secretary of Defense, and AFRICOM's establishment did not sufficiently take into account the challenges of establishing relationships among government agencies, NGOs, and foreign actors.[13]

The most visible dimension of the controversy surrounding the creation of AFRICOM was the location of AFRICOM's headquarters. Initial plans for the new command suggested that AFRICOM headquarters would be located on the continent. The original plan for U.S. operations involved a forward-basing approach in which supplies would be prepositioned at designated places. Initial DOD plans also included subregional offices to be established around the continent, with the command headquarters to be situated somewhere on the continent. DOD was forced to scale back its plans in the face of criticism from African countries and other U.S. stakeholders. One State Department official described the discussions between State and Defense about the headquarters location as contentious.[14]

Most of Africa reacted unfavorably to the prospect of a permanent U.S. military headquarters on the continent. African opposition to locating AFRICOM on the continent made it unlikely that the command would end up headquartered in Africa. With the exception of Liberia, no African state indicated a willingness to accept a U.S. headquarters, and many were outspoken in their opposition to a permanent U.S. presence in the region. The adverse African reaction was summed up by Dr. Wafula Okumu, head of the African Security Analysis Program at the Institute for Security Studies in South Africa, in testimony before the House Subcommittee on Africa and Global Health. He cited a range of statements in the African press questioning U.S. motives for establishing AFRICOM and recalled how U.S. policy had supported unpopular regimes during the Cold War. He went on to cite a lengthy list of reasons why Africans were opposed, including the view that AFRICOM would clash with African positions on defense and security, particularly those that discourage the hosting of foreign troops; concerns about the role of the military in development; a preference for dealing with diplomats rather than soldiers; skepticism regarding U.S. intentions in light of the U.S. invasion of Afghanistan and Iraq; past U.S. military involvement in Africa that amounted to a history of neglect and selective engagement; fears that AFRICOM would repeat the mission creep that accompanied the U.S. intervention in Somalia; lack of consultation with African governments on the establishment of AFRICOM; and mixed messages from U.S. officials regarding Africa's role in U.S. strategy.[15]

Adding to the skepticism regarding AFRICOM's purpose, the establishment of an African headquarters for AFRICOM would have been an exception to the basing of all but one of the other regional commands. Of the six regional U.S. military commands, only European Command and AFRICOM are headquartered outside the U.S. All other regional commands are located in the U.S., including those for areas that have traditionally had greater strategic importance than Africa. This may have contributed to the perception that AFRICOM was a plot to gain a foothold on the continent. The decision was eventually made to put AFRICOM's headquarters in Stuttgart, Germany, an understandable fallback position, since Stuttgart is the location of the U.S. European Command, from which most of the functions for AFRICOM were transferred. In 2012 testimony before Congress, General Carter Ham, then commander of AFRICOM, indicated that the headquarters decision was to be reviewed; there was again speculation about a move, but this time that speculation also involved a possible move back to the U.S. Nevertheless, AFRICOM remains headquartered at Kelley Barracks in Stuttgart, Germany.

Negative reactions to the decision to establish AFRICOM varied across the African continent. Many observers no doubt recalled U.S. policy during the Cold War, creating a wariness about U.S. motives and intentions. Some countries feared that association with the U.S., especially in counterterrorism efforts, would invite terrorist attacks and undermine regimes. Others feared that the establishment of AFRICOM, coming on the heels of the U.S. invasions of Afghanistan and Iraq, was a precursor to regime change on the continent. Still others, particularly South African officials, were concerned about AFRICOM's impact on their regional influence.[16] South Africa's negative reaction was also tied to lingering suspicion growing out of U.S. opposition to the ANC during the liberation struggle against apartheid, skepticism that U.S. concerns about African security were genuine, and Pretoria's opposition to the American invasions of Afghanistan and Iraq. In his response to Forest and Crispin's article, "AFRICOM: Troubled Infancy, Promising Future," South African security analyst Laurie Nathan ascribes the adverse reaction to AFRICOM to a deep-seated anti-imperialism in Africa. He asserts that anti-imperialism was the result of the history and realities of African politics and American foreign policy. It stemmed from U.S. hostility to national liberation movements and collaboration with dictatorial regimes, American support for the Israeli occupation of Palestinian territory, the U.S. stance on the International Criminal Court, American unilateralism, American aggression, and U.S. neglect of international law. He concludes that even a more effective rollout of AFRICOM would not have changed those views.[17]

A communications campaign was designed to ease skepticism about AFRICOM's purpose. The campaign emphasized the development of partnerships with African countries to provide training for peacekeeping, disaster relief, and counterterrorism. However, seemingly conflicting messages by American officials about resource access and strategic competition with China tended to undermine this effort.[18] Ultimately, the Defense Department's decision to place the headquarters outside the continent moderated opposition to AFRICOM among African countries.[19]

Nevertheless, the rollout of the plan for AFRICOM was a public relations blunder, and the failure to adequately consult with African countries on a policy that was certain to have an impact on their security interests was reminiscent of the 1996 controversy that surrounded the effort to establish the African Crisis Response Force. Given the history of U.S. security policy toward Africa and African sensitivity to any action that might be interpreted as neocolonial, opposition to a permanent base on the continent could certainly have been anticipated. Moreover, the U.S. invasion of Afghanistan and Iraq, combined with U.S. support for Ethiopia's 2006 incursion into Somalia, also made African states wary of the American plan for a new military command for Africa.

Africans were not the only actors wary about AFRICOM. There were also questions about the new command among other U.S. stakeholders given the proposed whole-of-government, interagency approach, particularly the collaboration among the Defense Department, the State Department, and other government agencies. One of the unique features of AFRICOM is that there are two deputies to the AFRICOM commander, the Deputy Commander for Military Operations (DCMO) and the Deputy Commander for Civil Military Engagement (DCME), who is a State Department official. As described by then Deputy Assistant Secretary of Defense Theresa Whelan, AFRICOM was to be an innovative command in several ways. Unlike a traditional Unified Command, AFRICOM focused on building African regional security and crisis response capacity. AFRICOM was also touted as a means to promote greater security ties between the United States and Africa, provide new opportunities to enhance bi-lateral military relationships, and strengthen the capacities of Africa's regional and subregional organizations. It was also supposed to include a significant and carefully selected number of representatives from other U.S. agencies within its staff, including officers from the Department of State and the U.S. Agency for International Development (USAID). Finally, Whelan noted that "USAFRICOM's focus is on war-prevention rather than war-fighting, the inner-workings of the command have been organized to best position it for theater security cooperation activities with a goal of preventing problems from becoming crises and preventing crises from becoming catastrophes."[20] As innovative as the idea behind the Command might have been, it still required implementation. Any interagency effort toward Africa was bound to raise concerns about how this new arrangement was going to address the goals of integrating defense, diplomacy, and development in practice. Among the obstacles has been the practice of staffing AFRICOM with representatives of other U.S. agencies. Despite its intuitive sense, interagency cooperation is an elusive goal, especially when resource allocations heavily favor one actor. Reductions in funding for the State Department and USAID limited the availability of personnel with the expertise to staff the positions set aside for agency partners. AFRICOM's plan was to embed experts from other agencies in the command, working together to coordinate U.S. security policy. By June 2010, the reported number of non-DOD agency personnel embedded in AFRICOM was well below anticipated levels. According to John H. Pendleton, the Director of Defense Capabilities and Management, the Department of State had five representatives, USAID had two, the Department of Homeland Security had six, the Office of the Director of National Intelligence had four, the Department of Justice had three, the Department of Transportation and the Department of Energy each had one, and the National Security Agency had four. The total of twenty-seven non-DOD personnel amounted to only 2% of the command's headquarters staff, and in FY2009 only 25% of the interagency staff authorized for AFRICOM was actually assigned. In contrast, 98% of the military's authorized positions were filled and 48% of the authorized DOD civilian positions were assigned.[21] Disproportionate staffing levels only added credibility to the argument that U.S. Africa policy was becoming increasingly militarized.

While the interagency approach adopted by AFRICOM signaled a more holistic view of security, it remains to be seen whether the DOD and other U.S. stakeholders can cooperate effectively to achieve this goal. Early indications were that the relationship between State and Defense got off to a rocky start, although cooperation has improved. The initial AFRICOM plan that envisioned a headquarters in Africa with regional offices spread out across the continent was unacceptable to the State Department, which had concerns over how the AFRICOM commander and DOS would exercise authority. DOS officials were uncomfortable with the regional DOD offices because they worried that these offices would not be operating under the ambassador's chief of mission authority.[22] Other concerns included staffing shortages at other federal agencies that reduced the availability of personnel to staff AFRICOM positions; AFRICOM's paucity of knowledge about how to coordinate with embassy staff; and the limited cultural training for AFRICOM staffers. Interagency partners were also critical of AFRICOM's inclusiveness. Some interagency officials said AFRICOM did not always involve other federal agencies in the formative stages of planning and did not fully utilize the expertise of embedded interagency personnel. Sometimes AFRICOM staff consulted with interagency personnel, but often staff had to insert themselves into meetings to influence decision making. According to a USAID official, the interagency staff asks the military staff how it can help, but that is the opposite of what should happen, since AFRICOM claims it is in a supporting role to USAID in development activities. From the DOS perspective, it had sufficient input into planning processes, but planning and decision making at the command's service components are separate from the process at AFRICOM headquarters, making coordination difficult. Even though AFRICOM works with State and USAID to incorporate their perspectives into the theater campaign plan, the timelines for planning and funding are different for AFRICOM, State, and USAID, making alignment difficult. A 2010 Government Accountability Office (GAO) report also found that AFRICOM had not developed the ability to conduct long-term assessments of its activities, making it difficult to make informed future planning decisions and to respond to its critics. Nevertheless, many U.S. embassies and federal partners believed that AFRICOM had the potential to make a positive contribution in Africa but that until it more fully integrated interagency partners in its activities it ran the risk of conducting activities that might run counter to U.S. foreign policy interests or lead to unintended consequences.[23]

AFRICOM's Roles and Missions

In conjunction with its subordinate commands, U.S. Army Africa (USARAF), U.S. Naval Forces Africa (NAVAF), U.S. Air Forces Africa (AFAFRICA), U.S. Marine Corps Forces Africa (MARFORAF), Combined Joint Task Force-Horn of Africa (CJTF-HOA), and U.S. Special Operations Command Africa (SOCAFRICA), AFRICOM has a full complement of military assets. When AFRICOM became operational in 2008, it took on responsibilities related to several existing security assistance programs that emphasize training, particularly for counterterrorism, and military professionalism and some programs that also have development-related components. These programs include the International Military Education Training (IMET) program, a Department of State(DOS)–funded program managed by AFRICOM that provides military education and training; the Africa Contingency Operations Training and Assistance program (ACOTA), a DOS-led program that is part of the Global Peace Operations Initiative to train peacekeeping forces; and the Foreign Military Financing (FMF) program, a joint DOD/DOS program to provide assistance to partner nations to acquire U.S. military equipment and training. Through its naval and marine components, AFRICOM also has responsibility for the African Partnership Station (APS) and the African Maritime Law Enforcement Partnership (AMLEP). These programs are meant to increase interoperability between the U.S. and its African partners and address the growing problems of piracy, drug trafficking, illegal fishing, and disruptions to maritime commerce in the region. The APS is designed to enhance African partner nations' maritime security within their inland waterways, territorial waters, and exclusive economic zones. AMLEP focuses on improving capacity to protect the coastal state marine environment through more effective and cooperative law enforcement.[24]

Combined Joint Task Force-Horn of Africa (CJTF-HOA), with some four thousand U.S. and allied military personnel as well as civilian personnel and U.S. contractors based at Camp Lemonnier in Djibouti, builds security cooperation and infrastructure and also has civil affairs teams that work with partners to improve civil-military relations with local communities. Operation Enduring Freedom-Trans-Sahara (OEF-TS) provides military support to the Trans-Sahara Counter-Terrorism Partnership, a DOS-led program focused on preventing the spread of extremism and terrorism. The State Partnership Program connects national guards from several U.S. states with African countries to provide training and build relationships. The Partnership for Integrated Logistics Operations and Tactics (PILOT) and the Africa Deployment Assistance Partnership Team (ADAPT) both provide logistics assistance and interoperability, particularly related to peacekeeping deployments. The Partner Military HIV/AIDS Program works to reduce the incidence of HIV/AIDS in African militaries, while the Pandemic Response Program, a joint AFRICOM-USAID program, is geared toward helping African militaries build the capacity to respond to outbreaks of contagious disease. Civil Military Assistance and Health programs also support USAID efforts; activities include constructing schools and health clinics, digging wells, seeking clothing and food donations, promoting stability, improving disaster response, and providing assistance to countries seriously affected by HIV/AIDS. AFRICOM also coordinates humanitarian aid efforts with USAID and the State Department.[25]

AFRICOM coordinates a number of joint training exercises with African militaries. Africa Endeavor is a communications and interoperability exercise to increase command, control, and communications capacity. Flintlock is an exercise directed by the Chairman of the Joint Chiefs of Staff, sponsored by AFRICOM, and conducted by Joint Special Operations Force Trans-Sahara; since its inception in 2005, it has been held annually and focuses on interoperability, combat skills, and counterterrorism. There are also four regional maritime capacity building and antipiracy exercises—Cutlass Express, Obangame Express, Phoenix Express, and Saharan Express—and four multidimensional exercises—Atlas Accord, Eastern Accord, Southern Accord and Western Accord—that provide training for deployment of humanitarian aid, peacekeeping, and disaster relief operations.[26]

AFRICOM's Challenges

Although foreign assistance is primarily the responsibility of the State Department, the Defense Department has historically had a role, particularly in three areas:

> responding to humanitarian and natural disasters; building foreign military capability through equipping and training foreign military forces for border and internal defense, counterterrorism, drug enforcement, and post-conflict state-building; and contributing to the legitimacy of foreign governments by strengthening law enforcement, and engaging in small-scale economic, health, political, and social projects.[27] Post-conflict state building became a focus as a result of the impact of DOD Directive 3000.05, Directive on Military Support for Stability, Transition, and Reconstruction Operations, issued in 2005. While now emphasizing this mission, at the same time DOD indicated doubt about the ability of civilian agencies in these efforts and said the Defense Department needed to develop its own capabilities. In a speech to the Association of the U.S. Army in 2007, then-Secretary of Defense Gates stated that until there was more funding for civilian agencies, Army personnel could be expected to be tasked with rebuilding public services, reconstructing infrastructure, and promoting good governance. He went on to say that these non-traditional capabilities had moved into the mainstream of military responsibility and were going to stay there.[28] Critics argued that the decline in resources for diplomacy and development relative to defense broadened the Defense Department's role in carrying out American foreign policy and was increasingly leading to the military taking on political and economic roles. Those concerns only intensified after the Directive 3000.05 was reissued in 2009. Stability operations were defined as "encompassing various military missions, tasks, and activities conducted outside the United States in coordination with other instruments of national power to maintain or reestablish a safe and secure environment, provide essential governmental services, emergency infrastructure reconstruction, and humanitarian relief."[29] Prior to this, the military regarded nation-building activities as inappropriate,

maintaining that they directed attention away from combat readiness. But Secretary Gates put these activities firmly on the agenda saying in his speech to the Association of the U.S. Army that "until our government decides to plus up our civilian agencies like USAID, Army soldiers can expect to be tasked with reviving public services, rebuilding infrastructure, and promoting good governance. All these so-called 'non-traditional' capabilities have moved into the mainstream of military thinking, planning and strategy, where they must stay."[30]

Since the Vietnam era, the military has developed a strong aversion to nation building, dismissing "military operations other than war," referred to as MOOTW ("mootwah") as unworthy, burdensome, outside the responsibilities of the military, and possibly detrimental to operational readiness.[31] Gates's emphasis on these new roles for the U.S. military stressed the military's role in both conflict prevention and state building. Although Directive 3000.05 sought to put stability operations on the same level as combat operations, it assigned the lead role in security, stability, transition, and reconstruction (SSTR) operations to the State Department and gave DOD a supporting role.[32] Despite Gates's 2010 article in *Foreign Affairs* acknowledging that capacity building was becoming a key mission for U.S. forces, his call for more funding for diplomacy and development highlighted the importance of coordination with the State Department in drafting and implementing U.S. foreign assistance.[33] Nevertheless, his statement failed to convince those worried about the militarization of U.S. policy, and it did not have a significant impact on funding for civilian agencies. This led to concerns that the State Department lead in foreign policy would be eclipsed by DOD dominance. A lead role for Defense was seen as potentially undermining the statutory basis for the conduct of U.S. foreign policy. It would give greater power and influence to the Defense Department's institutional culture, a "can-do" culture that is often more oriented toward accomplishing missions rather than attuned to the intricacies of indigenous culture, nuances of bilateral and multilateral relations, and the long-term objectives of foreign policy. For instance, the military's tendency to identify a problem and act quickly to address it can lead to community tensions and unsustainable projects. DOD's Humanitarian and Civic Assistance (HAC) and Overseas Humanitarian Disaster and Civic Assistance (OHDCA) programs are narrower in scope and have different time frames from DOS and USAID's longer-term development assistance programs. Because of the short duration and narrow goals of DOD programs and because planners have little familiarity with local custom and culture, DOD's humanitarian and disaster assistance and civic affairs efforts are not as effective as they could be. Moreover, inadequate follow-up and assessment of DOD programs prevent a thorough evaluation of the effectiveness DOD's programs.[34] The widespread history of coups in Africa led some officials to question whether an influential role for the U.S. military in development-related activities might not undermine U.S. efforts to promote democracy and clear civilian control of government.[35]

Because AFRICOM was supposed to help prevent conflicts and have a role in state building and civil affairs projects, there was a fear that military personnel would be in the forefront of U.S. Africa policy. Although the creation of a new combatant command was billed as a reorganization of responsibility to deal with the growing strategic importance of Africa, it also reflected growing military advantage and influence. The 1986 Goldwater-Nichols Act gave the combatant commanders (then called "commanders-in-chief") significant weight. They are responsible to the Secretary of Defense, have troops from all services at their disposal, have large staffs, and travel extensively. The creation of AFRICOM meant that AFRICOM's commander was in the lead of a new and expanding mission. Whether the combatant commanders are as powerful as some suggest or as constrained as others argue,[36] the new command was seen as a further evidence of DOD's dominance and the growing gap between Defense and its interagency partners. That balance had already been tilted heavily in favor of Defense by years of budget cuts to the State Department and USAID. The military's advantage was evident in other ways as well. Combatant commanders have multiple ways to engage with the region, including the State Department's International Military Education and Training (IMET) program, which is supposed to provide the opportunity to increase defense cooperation, augment partner state capabilities, and encourage military professionalism and respect for human rights, and Flintlock, a Joint Combined Exchange Training (JCET) exercise that provides training by special operations forces for counterterrorism and narcotics interdiction. Defense officials also engage with African militaries through the State Department's Foreign Military Financing (FMF) program, which provides funding for the purchase of military equipment.

As the U.S. has become more deeply involved in Africa, the U.S. experience in Iraq and Afghanistan has influenced U.S. military doctrine. The re-emergence of counterinsurgency (COIN) doctrine, influenced by American experience with postconflict stabilization and reconstruction efforts, offered a model for dealing with Africa's security, political, and economic challenges. Relying on his own experiences in Bosnia and Iraq and influenced by, among other sources, John A. Nagl's *Learning to Eat Soup with a Knife: Counterinsurgency Lessons from Malaya and Vietnam*, General David Petraeus revised the *U.S. Army Field Manual*, re-emphasizing counterinsurgency. Petraeus's experience in Bosnia convinced him that the military should not only fight the enemy but also deal with the underlying social, economic, and political bases of conflict.[37] Nagl, whose own experiences in Iraq informed his views, observed that "the fight to create a secure, democratic Iraq that does not provide a safe haven for terrorists is not primarily a military task. Counterinsurgency requires the integration of all elements of national power—diplomacy, information operations, intelligence, finance, the military—to achieve the predominately political objectives of establishing a stable national government that can secure itself against internal and external threats."[38] Although Nagl was focused on the lessons for fighting wars, the influence of counterinsurgency doctrine on

AFRICOM's mission is clear. In his introduction to the *Counterinsurgency Field Manual*, Nagl noted that counterinsurgency incorporates stability operations, which were previously considered a separate category of activity usually associated with multinational peacekeeping operations. The manual further directs U.S. forces to make securing the civilian rather than destroying the enemy the top priority and recognizes that COIN success relies on noncombat activities such as providing necessities, including electricity, jobs, and a functioning judicial system, and on expanded efforts along a rights continuum to provide not just physical security but also economic, social, civil, and political rights and a more holistic form of human security, while acknowledging that this is a complicated task. That task requires that civilians be engaged alongside combat forces integrating military and nonmilitary actors and tasks.[39] The idea of integrating civilian and military expertise meshed with both Defense Secretary Robert Gates's and Secretary of State Hillary Rodham Clinton's emphasis on defense, diplomacy, and development and in effect provided a blueprint for AFRICOM's operations.

The importance of human security to AFRICOM's role and mission was reinforced by the academic specialists invited to the U.S. military's first academic symposium, in June 2008, which brought together African specialists and AFRICOM personnel under the auspices of the African Center for Strategic Studies (ACSS). Throughout the symposium the discussion strongly emphasized the importance of human security.[40] The academic symposium has met repeatedly since that initial gathering to provide AFRICOM personnel with greater expertise on the politics and culture of the continent. The ACSS, associated with the National Defense University, is one of the DOD's five regional centers of excellence and focuses on research, training, and building collaborative relationships with African partners. ACSS provides a wide range of academic programs focusing on military professionalism and defense management, such as the Senior Leaders Seminar and the Next Generation of Security Sector Leaders Course, as well as courses on managing security resources, counterterrorism, transnational threats, and security sector reform.[41] Human security is also a component of the curriculum for ACSS training programs involving African security personnel.

The debate about "new wars"[42] or fourth-generation warfare[43] also poses a challenge to AFRICOM's operations. The causes of conflict in Africa are varied as the participants in these wars. Elements of new wars and fourth-generation warfare, which emphasize the importance of history, culture, and politics in explaining the causes of war, are evident in African conflict and instability. New wars blur the distinctions between inter-and intrastate warfare, organized criminal activity, and large-scale human rights abuses perpetrated by states and opposition forces. Africa's wars feature many of these characteristics. Called "low-intensity warfare" in the past, these wars involve a variety of transnational actors and connect the local and global levels of warfare. These wars occur in situations where state resources and security capabilities are limited and criminal activity and corruption are common. Africa's wars have involved national armed forces fighting against actors ranging from insurgent forces, to groups tied to the global Islamist insurgency, to criminal gangs.[44] The transnational dimensions of these conflicts do not easily lend themselves to a state-centered approach that focuses primarily on building armed forces' capacity, since regional and international actors often play a role in the trafficking in arms and resources that perpetuate these wars.

Not only do external actors and transnational links complicate AFRICOM's effort to create security partnerships, but conditions on the ground in conflict situations are often shifting. Opposition forces have displayed a tendency to splinter; this happened in the DRC, where there have been an estimated forty militias involved in the fighting, and in Darfur, where the Sudan Peoples Liberation Movement splintered, although not to the extent of the dizzying array of armed groups in the DRC. In the Sahel, Mokhtar Belmokhtar's Those Who Sign in Blood Battalion (al-Muwaqi-un Bil-Dima), which claimed responsibility for the 2013 gas-plant attack in Algeria, was a splinter group of al Qaeda. The group merged with MUJAO in 2013, reaffiliated with AQIM in 2015 and now operates as al Murabitoun. Al Qaeda offshoots Ansar al Dine and the Movement for Unity and Jihad in West Africa (MUJAO) eventually marginalized the Tuareg rebels who initiated the slide toward Mali's 2012 coup. In Nigeria, Ansaru split off from Boko Haram, compounding the threat. The splintering of militias creates a highly complex and volatile security environment in which it is difficult to keep track of the players. The circumstances are further complicated when splinter groups turn against one another.

America's partners have a weak record against their adversaries. During the crisis in northern Mali, not only did elements of the armed forces retreat when confronted by the rebels, but also some commanders of elite units trained by the U.S. defected to the rebels. There were also reports of Malian troops engaging in human rights abuses.[45] The officer who led the coup in Mali was also American trained. Developments such as these call into question the capabilities of the armed forces and the effectiveness of training.

Although Africa's wars are difficult to categorize, have various origins and a variety of actors, and raise questions of African forces' capability, the security environment is dominated by a primary focus on counterterrorism. Since even before the 1998 U.S. embassy bombings in Kenya and Tanzania, the threat of radical Islam has been increasing across the continent. The origins of this threat date to the early 1990s in Algeria, when the Armed Islamic Group emerged in opposition after the military suspended elections, which the Islamic Salvation Front was poised to win. In 2007, the Salafist Group for Preaching and Combat, an offshoot of the Armed Islamic Group, became al Qaeda in the Islamic Maghreb. In 2012, the U.S. claimed that there were connections linking al Qaeda and jihadists in the Sahel, al Shabaab in Somalia, and Boko Haram in Nigeria.[46] Al Qaeda has transformed from a specific threat to a more diffuse franchise operation in which each regional affiliate represents an increase in the threat to the U.S. and its African security partners. While the threat of terrorism in Africa has become more international as regional terrorist organizations have allied themselves with al Qaeda and, more recently, the Islamic State, it is local conditions that largely drive disillusionment and extremism. For instance, Boko Haram is at least in part the product of the poverty and disillusionment in Nigeria's north rather than aspirations to attack the U.S. Boko Haram's goals are the establishment of Islamic law and the replacement of what it regards as a corrupt government in which the Muslim north has been marginalized. In early 2015, Boko Haram announced its allegiance to the Islamic State, proclaiming itself the Islamic State West Africa Province. However, its breakaway faction, Ansaru, is more closely associated with AQIM, which has a broader international jihadist orientation. The two groups differ not only in their allegiances but also in their tactics. The split developed over a dispute about the targeting of Muslims, but there are indications that there are wider differences.[47] Although these organizations currently lack the capacity to strike the U.S. directly, that does not rule out the coalescence of a direct threat against the U.S. and its interests. The increase in terrorist incidents in Africa helps reinforce the view of radical Islam as a global insurgency for which the antidote is a retooled counterinsurgency doctrine combined with enhanced capacity for African armed forces. The al Qaeda– inspired jihadist movement is regarded as a global insurgency that requires an approach that includes paramilitary, political, economic, psychological, and civic actions along with a military effort.[48] Traditional counterinsurgency involved the application of military force as well as programs designed to "win hearts and minds." That entails not only protecting the civilians from the insurgents but also creating infrastructure and other civil affairs programs that improve living conditions and enhance the legitimacy of the government. In that sense, counterinsurgency has much in common with the goals of development.

The connection between security and development was evident in so-called Phase Zero or conflict-prevention operations, which involve a strategy of engagement focused on factors that contribute to terrorism. Phase Zero activities involve shaping operations to promote stability and peace by building partner capacity. Phase Zero became an integral part of theater security cooperation (TSC) activities before AFRICOM was even created. AFRICOM was given responsibility for Operation Enduring Freedom-Trans-Sahara, which was the first Joint Staff–directed TSC effort and the military component of the Trans-Sahara Counterterrorism Initiative. Operation Flintlock, now an annual exercise conducted by the Joint Special Operations Task Force Trans-Sahara, was the first OEF-Trans-Sahara exercise. It involved small-unit tactical training in marksmanship, land navigation, and basic infantry skills as well as in airborne operations and special operations aviation units. The goal was to improve interdiction of illicit weapons and human trafficking and to deny terrorists space to operate.[49] Phase Zero operations also share some features with counterinsurgency in the sense that the tasks associated with preventing conflict such as infrastructure and civil affairs projects are also part of an effective counterinsurgency. The focus of these operations is also similar to many of the challenges facing countries with low levels of development. All are characterized by the lack of the institutional capacity to provide security, justice, economic prosperity, and good governance, a task that is even more difficult in the aftermath of conflict, which adds the dimension of reconstruction and reconciliation. The convergence of these requirements and the military's growing role, combined with inadequate funding for diplomacy and development, has raised the U.S. military's visibility and led critics to fear that the military would be in the lead in U.S. policy toward Africa. Yet, despite its enormous advantage in resources, the Pentagon continues to face complex challenges in reaching AFRICOM's ambitious conflict prevention and counterinsurgency goals.

DOD's growing influence in foreign policy has not only encouraged the perception that U.S. Africa policy has become increasingly militarized but has also raised questions about the level of strategic coordination between Defense and State and whether there are the means to assure that DOD programs are sustainable.[50] Skeptics further questioned whether DOD state-building activities have sufficient strategic planning, apply economic-development best practices, have civilian input, integrate military and civilian efforts, and exercise sufficient oversight.[51] That skepticism increased with a 2010 GAO report that was critical of the CJTF-HOA. The report found that CJTF-HOA conducted activities without ensuring that they were having a positive effect on African partner countries over the long term, that the task force was not setting specific and measurable outcomes, and that there was no follow-up to its operations. The report also noted instances where CJTF-HOA personnel did not always understand embassy procedures for engaging African partners, creating strains among interagency partners. Some deficiencies in skills were attributed to limited training and the short duration of tours.[52]

Although under the 1961 Foreign Assistance Act the State Department has oversight of military assistance programs, in the aftermath of the September 11 attacks and the U.S. invasions of Afghanistan and Iraq DOD sought to develop greater capacity to provide training to American partners in those conflicts as well as to enhance the counterterrorism capabilities of foreign militaries. Concerned that its personnel lacked the country and regional expertise necessary to conduct training operations but equally concerned that the State Department lacked the necessary capacity to oversee training for counterterrorism, DOD pushed for greater authority to train foreign militaries. Section 1206, an amendment to the 2006 National Defense Authorization Act, allowed the Defense Department to use funds for training and equipping foreign militaries. The authority granted under the 2006 National Defense Authorization Act was extended through FY 2017. Although the selection of countries eligible for this assistance is made through an interagency process that involves both the Defense and State Departments, the controversy surrounding this authority illustrates tensions among interagency partners that surfaced with the establishment of AFRICOM. Some have suggested that the 1206 authority overlaps with the Foreign Military Financing (FMF) program run by the State Department, which also provides funds for training and equipment, although the DOD maintains that the two programs focus on different objectives. Critics say that the training and equipping of foreign military forces could be carried out by State through the FMF program, particularly if funding for the State Department were to be increased. Section 1206 funding for Africa has increased substantially over the past few years and has been used primarily for counterterrorism training, with funds also going to countries that participate in the AU's AMISOM mission. In fiscal year 2014, Niger was the second biggest recipient, at almost $37 million, while Kenya received $29 million. Funding for Africa increased from $44 million in 2012 to $100.7 million in 2013. That figure jumped further to $109.3 in 2014.[53] A Rand study found that AFRI-COM'S Building Partner Capacity (BPC) programs were ranked moderately high in efficiency and moderately low in effectiveness. Other DOS and DOD programs, including training and equipment provided under DOS's FMF, DOD's Section 1203 assistance to Yemen and East Africa, DOD's OEF-TS, DOD's Preact and Traditional Commander's Activities, and SOF JCET exercises, all ranked higher.[54]

In addition to the interagency challenges between State and Defense, other issues such as the role of private contractors and the relationship between the military and humanitarian NGOs have emerged in the debate surrounding AFRICOM. In his testimony before Congress in 2008, Mark Malan, Peacebuilding Program Officer with Refugees International, expressed concern not only about the policy framework for AFRICOM and the depth and balance of expertise in the command but also about the use of private contractors to train African peacekeepers and the State Department's ability to monitor the effectiveness of that training.[55] The use of contractors was also seen as a problem in the earlier stages of the ACOTA program, when some countries objected to working with military contractors rather than U.S. military personnel.[56] Some observers criticize the use of private contractors, citing a lack of accountability and the difficulty of monitoring their activities. The use of contractors undermines the U.S. emphasis on governance and military professionalism and contrasts with regional and subregional organizations' efforts to encourage transparent and accountable state security forces.[57]

Operational Record

Since its inception, in addition to its extensive training programs, AFRICOM has also participated in some high-profile operations on the continent. In March 2011, Operation Odyssey Dawn was launched to enforce the no-fly zone over Libya authorized by United Nations Security Council Resolution 1973. Designed to prevent Libya's Muammar Qaddafi from taking reprisals against regime opponents and to enforce an arms embargo authorized by the earlier Security Council resolution 1970, adopted in February 2011, the U.S. initially led an allied operation to enforce the no-fly zone. AFRICOM's commander, General Carter Ham, was in charge of the operation. Before turning operational command over to NATO on March 27, AFRICOM coordinated the initial U.S. operations among U.S. forces and oversaw the establishment and expansion of the no-fly zone and began operations to degrade Qaddafi's ground forces.[58]

Already engaged in fighting piracy off the Horn, the U.S. was drawn back to Somalia, albeit in a more limited way than before, by the weakness of the Transitional Federal Government (TFG), established in 2004, and by al Shabaab's growing control of much of southern Somalia. This situation, combined with the increasing level of piracy, made it imperative to try to establish effective central authority. Establishing a legitimate Somali government was made more difficult by Ethiopia's intervention against the Islamic Courts Union between 2006 and 2009. With America's consent, Ethiopia's 2006 intervention in support of the TFG led to the ouster of al Shabaab from many of its strongholds. But after Ethiopia's 2009 withdrawal, al Shabaab regained territory, and in 2011 Kenya, increasingly concerned about the prospect of radicalization, intervened against the Somali Islamists. Up to that point, Uganda and Burundi had provided the bulk of the African Union Mission in Somalia (AMISOM) authorized by the AU and endorsed by the UN in 2007. AMISOM troops also came to include armed forces from Djibouti, Sierra Leone, and Nigeria. The Kenyans formally linked up with AMISOM in 2012. U.S. contractors, backed by U.S. military personnel, have been involved in the training of AMISOM troops, the majority of which are Ugandan. The contractors are hired by the State Department and consist of U.S. Army or Marine veterans, many of whom have served in Iraq and Afghanistan. Between 2007 and 2013, the U.S. spent approximately $550 million to train, equip, and support AMISOM.[59]

In January 2007, in conjunction with an operation to root out extremist training camps in the Ras Kamboni region of Somalia, the U.S. conducted its first known operation in Somalia since the September 11 attacks. A series of air attacks was directed against extremist strongholds in the region. When AFRICOM became operational, in 2008, it assumed responsibility for continuing the fight against al Shabaab. Among the first operations after AFRICOM took over responsibility for the continent was a helicopter raid by American special forces in September 2009 that killed Saleh Ali Saleh Nabhan, wanted for his role in the 2002 Mombasa attacks.[60] In June 2011, the first lethal U.S. drone strikes in Somalia were reported. Since then, there have been at least eight drone strikes in Somalia.[61] At the end of October 2013, an American drone strike killed two al Shabaab members, one alleged to be the group's top explosives expert.[62] In the wake of the Westgate Mall attack in Nairobi in September 2013, U.S. special forces carried out a raid on the Somali coastal town of Baraawe to apprehend a Kenyan-born militant called Ikrima who, although not thought to be directly involved in the Nairobi attack, was linked to operatives associated with the 1998 embassy bombings and the 2002 attacks in Kenya. In that October 2013 raid, a SEAL team faced substantial resistance and withdrew without capturing its target. The operation came after a debate within the Obama administration about whether the use U.S. troops for direct action in Somalia was advisable.[63] While the Somalia operation did not achieve its objective, on the same day in Tripoli, Libya U.S. special forces apprehended Abu Anas al-Libi, accused of involvement in the 1998 embassy bombings in Kenya and Tanzania.[64] In 2014, U.S. special forces launched an operation in

Libya that apprehended Ahmed Abu Khattala, a suspect in the attack on the U.S. consulate in Benghazi, Libya. Khattala was taken to a U.S. naval vessel and interrogated on the way back to the U.S., where he faced charges.[65]

U.S. personnel began assisting in the fight against the Lord's Resistance Army (LRA) under the George W. Bush administration when team of counterterrorism advisers were sent to train Ugandan troops and the administration provided several million dollars in aid.[66] In 2009, AFRICOM helped to plan an attack against the LRA in the DRC, but the attack not only did not meet its objective of defeating the LRA but helped disperse the LRA across the region, resulting in further attacks against civilians. U.S. officials conceded the attack was unsuccessful but suggested that the Ugandan and Congolese troops that carried out the mission did not take their advice.[67] Following up on the Lord's Resistance Army Disarmament and Northern Uganda Recovery Act of 2009, signed into law in May 2010, in October 2011 President Barack Obama announced the deployment of a small contingent of one hundred U.S. special forces military advisers to assist the armed forces of Uganda, South Sudan, the DRC, and the Central African Republic in their joint effort, authorized by the AU, to defeat the LRA. U.S. objectives included protection of civilians; the capture of LRA leader Joseph Kony and senior leaders of the group; the encouragement of defections from the ranks of LRA fighters; disarmament, demobilization, and reintegration of LRA fighters; and provision of humanitarian assistance to those affected by the LRA.[68] A notorious militia that created havoc in Uganda for more than twenty years, the LRA was noted for brutality and particularly for abducting children to serve in the ranks as fighters, porters, and sex slaves. Reduced to a small, scattered, ragtag militia, the LRA has been marauding across the vast border regions of those four countries. U.S. personnel are not directly engaging the LRA; rather, the deployment was intended to provide training and logistical help for regional forces. Although cooperation was suspended after the coup in the CAR in 2013, the Obama administration resumed aid and increased the number of troops involved in 2014, when it sent several CV-22 Osprey aircraft and 150 Air Force Special Operations troops to augment the troops already deployed to help defeat the LRA. An Enough Project report claimed that the U.S. advisers were making progress against the LRA, with attacks dropping 53% and killings by the LRA dropping 67% from 2011 to 2012. Meanwhile, defections from the LRA's ranks rose.[69]

The 2012 coup in Mali occurred despite Mali's participation in America's ambitious counterterrorism and military training program in the Sahel. The U.S. considered Mali an exemplary partner, but when the fighting started, three of the four commanders of the units fighting in the north defected to the rebels, bringing their troops and weapons with them. The leaders of the units that defected had received U.S. training but were ethnic Tuareg, the very people who had been fighting against the government in Bamako.[70] The coup that resulted from the government's inept response to the rebel challenge was led by a U.S.-trained captain, Amadou Sanogo. Senior officers who might have prevented the coup remained on the sidelines. Prevented by law from assisting Mali in the aftermath of the coup, the U.S. provided support to the joint French and regional intervention that included troops from Niger, Senegal, Burkina Faso, Chad, and Nigeria. U.S. aid included airlift, refueling, and logistics.[71] The *Washington Post* reported that the U.S. also sent a small contingent of U.S. personnel to Mali to provide logistical support during the French-African operation against the extremists.[72] Once an analysis of the legality of providing further assistance was completed, the U.S. agreed to provide expanded aid to the French intervention, including refueling planes to help the French conduct airstrikes against the rebels. The analysis concluded that since the French were acting at the request of the Malian government and had notified the U.N. of that request, U.S. aid was legal.[73] With the swearing in of a democratically elected government in September 2013, the U.S. resumed some aid but continued to evaluate the resumption of military aid. The renewed aid was supposed to prioritize security-sector reform, military professionalism, the reassertion of civilian authority, accountability, and the rule of law.[74]

AFRICOM has also overseen the development of a network of intelligence-gathering facilities across the continent. U.S. surveillance activities have originated in Burkina Faso, Mauritania, Uganda, Ethiopia, Djibouti, Kenya, and the Seychelles. They consist mostly of flights originating at secluded hangars located at military or civilian bases. The operations are overseen by special operations forces but also rely on contractors as well as support from African troops. These operations use both small planes and unarmed drones to track terrorists. A key hub for these surveillance activities in the Sahel, code-named Creek Sand, has been in Ouagadougou, Burkina Faso, near the Sahel region where groups associated with al Qaeda have been active.[75] In 2015, *Foreign Policy* reported that the U.S. special forces troops from the Joint Special Operations Command were operating drones out of Somalia, a charge the U.S. government has not confirmed, but AFRICOM spokesman Chuck Pritchard acknowledged that there was a small SOF contingent in AFRICOM's area of responsibility. Aside from asserting that no troops were in combat roles, he would not say what operations U.S. forces were engaged in, citing security risks. The CIA is also reported to be training personnel in Somalia, U.S. forces are assisting AMISOM, and contractors are training Somali commandos. Contractors from Bancroft International who are training the Somali troops are paid through reimbursements to Uganda, which initially pays the cost of the contract.[76]

The theater strategy and subordinate regional campaign plans guide AFRICOM's operations and focus on five functional areas: combating violent extremist organizations, strengthening maritime security and countering illicit trafficking, strengthening defense capabilities, maintaining strategic posture, and preparing for and responding to crises. AFRICOM has compiled an extensive list of exercises and training missions since beginning operations. In FY 2013, AFRICOM engaged in fifty-five operations, ten exercises, and 481 security cooperation activities. Among those were U.S. support for the

AU Regional Task Force assigned to pursue the LRA; the U.S. assisted in thirty-three operations to disrupt LRA activities.[77] In 2012, U.S. Air Force Africa (AFAFRICA), in conjunction with its European counterpart (USAFE), launched African Partnership Flight, which promotes regional cooperation and strengthens African partner capabilities to provide airlift support to UN and AU peacekeeping operations.[78]

AFRICOM was also in the lead on the U.S. military response to the Ebola outbreak in late 2014. Operation United Assistance deployed some three thousand military personnel to the U.S. effort to combat the epidemic. Military personnel provided logistics and training and built labs and treatment units. The military spent about $400 million to combat the epidemic before most American troops returned home in early 2015 after the disease had peaked. Although the military response ended, the U.S. continued to support efforts to contain the disease.[79]

In an effort to improve familiarity with the region, AFRICOM is the first combatant command to be supported by the Army's Regionally Aligned Forces (RAF), a program that designates units that will engage in long-term relationships with the combatant commands. These forces will receive linguistic and cultural training linking them to the command's area of responsibility. This will better equip soldiers to anticipate conflicts before they escalate and better position U.S. forces for success when they engage. Activities include influencing local populations, establishing relationships with local leaders, and strengthening military to military cooperation.[80]

AFRICOM's engagement with African countries consists of a wide and growing array of operations and training. The establishment of AFRICOM indicates increased attention to a region long regarded as peripheral to U.S. interests. Clearly Africa's connection to international terrorism is a major component of U.S. military strategy on the continent, but Africa's strategic importance includes a broader range of strategic interests.

Notes

1 Personal interview, U.S. State Department personnel, April 2014.
2 Gregg Garbesi, 2004, "U.S. Unified Command Plan," in Derek S. Reveron, ed., *America's Viceroys: The Military and U.S. Foreign Policy* (New York: Palgrave Macmillan), 17.
3 Andrew Feickert, 2013, "The Unified Command Plan and Combatant Commands: Background and Issues for Congress," Congressional Research Service Report 2013-FTD-0010, 2, 11–12.
4 Statement of William Ward, Commander, United States Africa Command, before the U.S. House of Representatives Committee on Armed Services, 14 November 2007, SUDOC # Y4.AR5/2A:2007–2008/100.
5 Ward, Statement, 14 November 2007.
6 Robert G. Berschinski, "AFRICOM's Dilemma: The Global War on Terrorism, Capacity Building, Humanitarianism, and the Future of U.S. Security Policy in Africa," Strategic Studies Institute, 6-7, available at www.strategicstudiesinstitute. army.mil

7 United States Africa Command, "About the Command-Interagency," available at www.africom.mil/about-the-command/interagency

8 Jim Fisher-Thompson, "New African Command to Have Unique Structure, Mission," USINFO, 22 June 2007, available at http://uninfo.state.gov/xarchives/display.html?p=washfile-english&y=2007&m=june&x=

9 See website for United States Africa Command, available at www.africom.mil

10 Jeff Schogol, "Africa Command Approved by Bush, DOD Officials Confirm," *Stars and Stripes*, 30 December 2006.

11 Statement of Representative Donald Payne, U.S. House of Representatives Committee on Foreign Affairs, Subcommittee on Africa and Global Health, 2 August 2007.

12 Payne, Statement, 2 August 2007.

13 James J. F. Forest & Rebecca Crispin, 2009, "AFRICOM: Troubled Infancy, Promising Future," *Contemporary Security Policy*, 30:1, 11.

14 See U.S. Government Accountability Office Report to the Subcommittee on National Security and Foreign Affairs, Committee on Oversight and Government Reform, "Defense Management: Actions Needed to Address Stakeholder Concerns, Improve Interagency Collaboration, and Determine Full Costs Associated with the U.S. Africa Command," GAO-09-181, February 2009.

15 Statement of Dr. Wafula Okumu, Head, African Security Analysis Program, Institute for Security Studies, before the U.S. House of Representatives, Committee on Foreign Affairs, Subcommittee on Africa and Global Health, 2 August 2007.

16 Stephen F. Burgess, 2009, "In the National Interest? Authoritarian Decision-making and the Problematic Creation of US African Command," *Contemporary Security Policy*, 30:1, 94.

17 Laurie Nathan, 2009, "AFRICOM: A Threat to Africa's Security," *Contemporary Security Policy,* 30:1, 58.

18 Burgess, "In the National Interest?," 91.

19 Burgess, "In the National Interest?," 93.

20 Statement of Theresa Whelan, Deputy Assistant Secretary for African Affairs, Department of Defense, before the U.S. House of Representatives, Committee on Oversight and Government Reform, Subcommittee on National Security and Foreign Affairs, 110th Congress, Second session, 16 July 2008, SUDOC y4.g47/7: 110–204.

21 Statement of John H. Pendleton, Director, Defense Capabilities and Management, Government Accounting Office, before the U.S. House of Representatives, Committee on Oversight and Government Reform, Subcommittee on National Security and Foreign Affairs, 111th Congress Second Session, 28 July 2010, 11.

22 "Defense Headquarters: DOD Needs to Reassess Options for Permanent Location of U.S. Africa Command," Government Accounting Office Report to Senate Foreign Relations Committee, GAO-13-646, September 2013, 6.

23 "Defense Management," Government Accountability Office Report 10-794, 4–43.

24 See Statement of General Carter Ham, Commander, United States Africa Command, before the U.S. Senate Armed Services Committee, 7 March 2013, available at www.africom.mil; "African Maritime Law Enforcement Partnership" and "African Partnership Station," all available at www.africom.mil.

25 Fuller descriptions of these programs can be found on the AFRICOM website, available at www.africom.mil.

26 Summaries of these programs can be found on the AFRICOM website, available at www.africom.mil.

27 Nina M. Serafino, Christine Dale, Richard F. Grimmett, Rhoda Margesson, John Rollins, Tiaji Salaam-Blyther, Curt Tarnoff, my F. Woolf, Liana Sun Wyler, & Steve Bowman, 2008, "The Department of Defense Role in Foreign Assistance:

Background, Major Issues, and Options for Congress," Congressional Research Service Report RL34639, 9 December 2008, 1.

28 Serafino, et. al., "Department of Defense Role," 4.
29 "Stability Operations," Department of Defense Instruction No. 3000.05, 16 September 2009, 1.
30 Serafino, et. al. "Department of Defense Role," 4, 16.
31 For a fuller discussion of this issue, see Fred Kaplan, 2013, *The Insurgents: David Petraeus and the Plot to Change the American Way of War* (New York: Simon and Schuster).
32 Jessica Piombo, 2015, "Evolving Civilian and Military Missions," in Jessica Piombo, ed., *The U.S. Military in Africa: Enhancing Security and Development?* (Boulder: FirstForum Press), 46.
33 Robert M. Gates, "Helping Others Defend Themselves: The Future of U.S. Security Assistance," *Foreign Affairs*, 89:3 (May/June 2010).
34 For a full discussion of these issues see Government Accountability Office Report to Congressional Committees, "Humanitarian and Development Assistance," GAO Report 12–359, February 2012.
35 Nina Serafino et al., 2011, "Building Civilian Interagency Capacity for Missions Abroad: Key Proposals and Issues for Congress," Congressional Research Service Report 7–5700, 22 December 2011, 19.
36 See, for instance, Dana Priest, 2004, The Mission: Waging War and Keeping Peace with America's Military (New York: W. W. Norton, 2004); Christopher J. Fettweis, 2004, "Militarizing Diplomacy: Warrior-Diplomats and the Foreign Policy Process," in Derek S. Reveron, ed., *America's Viceroys: The Military and U.S. Foreign Policy* (New York: Palgrave Macmillan), 47–70; and Stephen D. Wrage, 2004, "U.S. Combatant Commander: The Man in the Middle," in Derek Reveron, ed., *America's Viceroys: The Military U.S. Foreign Policy* (New York: Palgrave Macmillan), 185–202.
37 Kaplan, *The Insurgents*, 67.
38 John A Nagl, 2002. *Learning to Eat Soup with a Knife: Counterinsurgency Lessons from Malaysia and Vietnam* (Chicago: University of Chicago Press), xvi.
39 Sarah Sewell, 2007, "Introduction: A Radical Field Manual," *U.S. Army/Marine Corps Counterinsurgency Field Manual* (Chicago: University of Chicago Press), xxv–xxx.
40 The author was a participant in the 2008 symposium.
41 See the ACSS website at http://africacenter.org/programs/
42 See Mary Kaldor, 2006, *New and Old Wars*, 2nd edition (Cambridge: Polity Press).
43 See Thomas X. Hammes, 2005, "War Evolves into the Fourth Generation," *Contemporary Security Policy*, 26:2, 189–221.
44 Paul Jackson, 2007, "Are Africa's Wars Part of a Fourth Generation of Warfare?," *Contemporary Security Policy*, 28:2, 269–271.
45 Lydia Polgreen, "Mali Army, Riding U.S. Hopes, Is No Match for Militants," *New York Times*, 24 January 2013.
46 See Zachary Laub & Jonathan Masters, "Backgrounder: Al Qaeda in the Islamic Maghreb," Council on Foreign Relations, 8 January 2014.
47 See Thomas Joscelyn, "Jihadist Divisions Grow in Nigeria," *The Long War Journal*, 23 February 2015.
48 Sewell, "Introduction," xlii.
49 Charles F. Wald, "The Phase Zero Campaign," *Joint Forces Quarterly*, 43, October 2006.
50 Serafino, et. al. "Department of Defense Role," 2.
51 Serafino, et. al. "Department of Defense Role," 16.

52 Government Accountability Office Report to the House of Representatives, Committee on Oversight and Government Reform, Subcommittee on National Security and Foreign Affairs, "Defense Management: DOD Needs to Determine the Future of Its Horn of Africa Task Force," GAO Report 10–504, April 2010.

53 Nina M. Serafino, "Security Assistance Reform: 'Section 1206' Background and Issues for Congress," Congressional Research Service Report RS22855, December 8, 2014, 7.

54 Serafino, "Security Assistance Reform," 5, 7, 17–18. This report contains a concise summary of the debate surrounding this program and the funding for 1206 authority.

55 Statement of Mark Malan, Peacebuilding Program Officer, Refugees International, before the U.S. House of Representatives Committee on Oversight and Government Reform, Subcommittee on National Security and Foreign Affairs, 23 July 2008.

56 A. Sarjoh Bah & Kwesi Aning, 2008, "U.S. Peace Operations Policy in Africa: From ACRI to AFRICOM," *International Peacekeeping*, 15:1, 121.

57 Boubacar N'Diaye & Sndy Africa, 2009, "AFRICOM and the Interests of Africans: Beyond Perceptions and Strategic Communication," *Contemporary Security Review*, 30:1, 65.

58 For a more detailed summary and analysis of this operation see Jeremiah Gertler et al., "Operation Odyssey Dawn (Libya): Background and Issues for Congress," Congressional Research Service Report R41725, 30 March 2011; Jonathan Stevenson, "Snapshot: AFRICOM's Libya Experience," *Foreign Affairs*, available at www.foreignaffairs.com/print/67779; Eric Schmitt, "Libya Crisis Thrusts U.S. Africa Command into Leadership Role," *New York Times*, 22 March 2011.

59 Craig Whitlock, "U.S. Trains African Soldiers for Somalia Mission," *Washington Post*, 13 May 2013.

60 Karen De Young, "Special Forces Raid in Somalia Killed Terrorist with al Qaeda Links, U.S. Says," *Washington Post*, 15 September 2009.

61 For a full accounting of U.S. military operations in Somalia, see "Somalia: U.S. Covert Actions," Bureau of Investigative Journalism, available at www.thebureauinvestigates.com/2012/02/22/get-the-data-somalias-hidden-war/

62 David Smith, "U.S. Drone Strike in Somalia Kills Top al Shabaab Explosives Expert," *The Guardian*, 29 October 2013.

63 Nicholas Kulish, Eric Sachmitt, & Mark Mazzetti, "Target of U.S. Raid in Somalia Is Called Top Shabaab Planner of Attacks Abroad," *New York Times*, 6 October 2013.

64 Kevin Rawlinson, "U.S. Special Forces Raids Target Islamist Militants in Libya and Somalia," *The Guardian*, 6 October 2013.

65 Karen DeYoung, Adam Goldman, & Julie Tate, "U.S. Captures Benghazi Suspect in Secret Raid," *Washington Post*, 17 June 2014.

66 Thom Shanker & Rick Gladstone, "Armed U.S. Advisers to Help Fight African Renegade Group," *New York Times*, 14 October 2011, available at www.nytimes.com/2011/10/15/worls www.nytimes.com/2011/10/15/world/africa/barack-obama-sending-100-armed-advisers-to-africa-to-help-fight-lords-resistance-army.html

67 Jeffrey Gettleman & Eric Schmitt, "U.S. Aided a Failed Plan to Rout Ugandan Rebels," *New York Times*, 6 February 2009.

68 Testimony of Deputy Assistant Secretary of State for African Affairs Don Yamamoto before the U.S. House of Representatives, Committee on Foreign Affairs, 25 October 2011, available at www.state.gov/p/af/rls/rm/2011/176160.htm

69 Kasper Agger, "Completing the Mission: U.S. Special Forces Are Essential for Ending the LRA," The Enough Project, October 2013.

70 Adam Nossiter, Eric Schmitt, & Mark Mazzeti, "French Strikes in Mali Supplant Caution of U.S.," *New York Times*, 13 January 2013.

71 Statement of General Carter Ham, Commander, United States Africa Command, before the Senate Armed Services Committee, 7 March 2013, available at www.africom.mil

72 Craig Whitlock, "Pentagon Deploys Small Number of Troops to War-Torn Mali," *Washington Post,* 30 April 2013.

73 Ernesto Londono, "U.S. Expands Aid to French Mission in Mali," *Washington Post,* 26 January 2013.

74 "U.S. Resumes Aid to Mali after New President Takes Office," Reuters, 6 September 2013.

75 Craig Whitlock, "U.S. Expands Secret Intelligence Operations in Africa," *Washington Post,* 13 June 2012.

76 Ty McCormack, "Exclusive: U.S. Operates Drones from Secret Bases in Somalia," *Foreign Policy,* online edition, 2 July 2015.

77 Statement of General David M. Rodriguez, Commander AFRICOM, before the Senate Armed Services Committee Posture Hearing, 6 March 2014.

78 Statement of General David Rodriguez before the Subcommittee on Defense of the House Appropriations Committee, 25 April 2013.

79 Dion Nissanbaum & Julian E. Barnes, "U.S. Military to End African Ebola Role," *Wall Street Journal,* 10 February 2015.

80 See Rosa Brooks, 2014, "Portrait of the Army as a Work in Progress," *Foreign Policy,* May/June 2014, 44.

5 Africa's Strategic Environment and the U.S. Global Posture

Since the September 11 attacks, a major American security priority in Africa has been countering the spread of extremism in the continent's weak states and ungoverned territories. Although the establishment of AFRICOM and its role in training African armed forces also focuses on capacity building for humanitarian and peacekeeping missions, training is also geared heavily toward counterterrorism. Beyond its importance to counterterrorism, Africa has strategic significance in other areas, including the continent's vast energy and mineral resources, its growing trade potential, its geographical position astride major sea lanes, its influence in international forums where African countries make up the single largest voting bloc, and its role in the transnational trafficking in drugs, arms, people, and other contraband, activities that often fund extremism. These elements of Africa's strategic significance, some of which overlap with the terrorist threat, exemplify the broader dimensions of security interests and threats.

African Security Engagement with Europe, China, India, Russia, and Brazil

The U.S. is not the only power increasing its engagement with Africa. Violent conflicts, humanitarian crises fueled by arms trafficking and famine, and state fragility in the post–Cold War era provided the backdrop for EU-African security cooperation. Going back to the 2000 Cairo Joint Declaration and Action Plan, there was a recognition of the connection between security and development. Europe's security engagement with Africa takes place primarily under the auspices of the Joint Africa-European Union Strategy (JAES), adopted at the Lisbon Summit in 2007. Prior to that, the former colonial powers maintained varying levels of bilateral security relations. France in particular maintained forces in former colonial possessions under the terms of defense and military cooperation agreements.

First among the JAES eight cooperative areas is peace and security. The document provides the roadmap for EU-Africa security relations and reflects a more holistic approach to security on the continent, coinciding with the formation of the AU and the establishment of the African security architecture, which also involves a comprehensive peace and security regime.[1] The EU's African

Peace Facility, established in 2004, is the main source of funding to support the AU and African regional economic communities' peace and security efforts, including capacity building for peace support operations (PSOs), and funds for the African Peace and Security Architecture (APSA), comprising the Peace and Security Council, the Continental Early Warning System, the African Standby Force, Panel of the Wise, and the Peace Fund, as well as support for the Early Response Mechanism (ESM).[2]

Information on Sino-African military cooperation is not detailed and does not often go beyond announcements of exchange visits, personnel participating, and statements about good military ties.[3] China's security cooperation with Africa, though modest in comparison with its other forms of engagement on the continent, is significant nevertheless. China's military links are primarily directed toward ensuring access to raw materials and expanding markets. Military ties are used primarily to strengthen political relations. Cooperation varies from state to state, but Chinese security assistance has included financial assistance for military infrastructure, de-mining efforts, and training for African armed forces.[4] China provides at least some military aid or training to all African countries with which it has diplomatic relations. In a January 2006 policy document, China pledged to promote high-level military exchanges, provide military-related technical exchanges, and improve overall cooperation. The document also maintained that China would help train African militaries and support defense and military improvements to enhance African security.[5]

Arms sales have also become a growing component of China's Africa policy. Between 2000 and 2004, China's conventional arms transfers to Africa were only $1.4 billion, just 5% of the U.S. transfers of $25.9 billion.[6] The African market became more important to China between 2006 and 2010, when Africa became the destination for 11% of Chinese arms exports.[7] China's arms transfers raised questions regarding Beijing's compliance with UN arms embargoes. There were allegations that China had failed to give a complete accounting to a UN panel and had used its Security Council clout to prevent disclosure of unfavorable information about the origin of weapons in conflict zones.[8]

Small arms fuel much of the conflict in Africa, and of particular concern is China's growing role as a source of small arms and light weapons (SALW). Because of the murky world of arms transfers, tracking these weapons is difficult. By some estimates, China has become one of the biggest suppliers of SALW to Africa, partly as a result of the relatively inexpensive weapons and ammunition it sells. China's SALWs have ended up in the hands of nonstate actors such as rebel factions in the DRC, which have used them to commit human rights abuses. China's policy of noninterference in other nations' internal affairs means that it is willing to supply weapons to states that may use them against government opponents.[9] China's willingness to do business with authoritarian regimes was evident in the high-profile case of a shipment of Chinese weapons bound for Zimbabwe in 2008 that was turned away from the port of Durban in South Africa. The available data shows that China exports a wide range of military equipment to several African countries.[10]

Not only does China export arms to Africa, but a troubling 2014 report by Amnesty International and the Omega Foundation titled *China's Trade in Tools of Torture and Repression* asserts that some 130 Chinese companies, many state-owned, supply devices such as electric shock batons, spiked batons, and a variety of restraint devices to countries around the world. Although some products marketed by Chinese companies have legitimate law enforcement uses, several products are associated with human rights abuses and torture. The report found that twenty-nine Chinese companies advertised products that were inherently cruel and that some of their customers were countries in which human rights violations were common. One company, China Xinxing Import/Export Corporation, which advertised thumb cuffs, restraint chairs, electric shock stun guns, and batons, stated in 2012 that it had links with forty African countries and that its trade with the continent was worth in excess of $100 million.[11]

Ironically, in contrast to its record of arms transfers and sales of torture devices, China is by far the largest contributor of peacekeeping troops among the UN Security Council's permanent members. As of the end of July 2014, China had 2,196 peacekeepers deployed around the world, compared to 116 from the U.S., 287 from the U.K., 942 from France, and 107 from Russia.[12] In September 2014, China announced that it would send seven hundred troops to join the UN peacekeeping mission in South Sudan, the first time China has sent an entire battalion of troops to a UN peacekeeping operation. In 2013, China sent a smaller number of troops to the UN mission in Mali. According to China's Foreign Ministry, China now has some 1,800 peacekeepers deployed in Africa.[13] Moreover, China's share of the peacekeeping budget was set to increase from 3% to 6% by 2015, making it the sixth-largest contributor to UN peacekeeping. With that increase, it is likely that China will gain even greater influence in peacekeeping decision making.[14] China also dispatched naval vessels to the coast of the Horn, where they cooperate with the international antipiracy effort and have played an important role in reducing attacks while gaining operational experience and international good will.[15]

China's participation in UN peacekeeping and maritime security offers several benefits. Participation affords China's armed forces useful experience and access to intelligence on a region that is of growing importance; it also extends China's naval capability and provides cover to deflect criticism of China's policy of obtaining oil from Sudan and supplying the country with arms.[16]

In addition to its participation in UN peacekeeping missions in Africa, India has also been engaged in training programs on the continent. India has developed security relationships with several African countries, especially along the Indian Ocean coast, where it is concerned about piracy, security of trade routes, and Chinese naval expansion into the region. India has also participated in the international antipiracy efforts off Somalia. India has signed defense agreements with Kenya, Madagascar, and Mozambique and has joint training programs with Kenya, Mozambique, South Africa, and Tanzania. Madagascar, Mauritius, and the Seychelles also cooperate with India on maritime surveillance and intelligence, while South Africa and India have conducted joint naval exercises.[17] India has also deployed military training teams to Botswana, Zambia, Lesotho, the Seychelles, Nigeria, and Tanzania. In addition, a number of African military officers have received training in India. Advocates of stronger military ties argue that such links would expand India's influence in Africa as well as address common security concerns, including Indian Ocean maritime security and nonconventional threats such as drugs and small-arms trafficking.[18] To that end, India has stepped up its engagement at both domestic training facilities and on the ground in Ethiopia and Namibia. Indian defense personnel are also conducting training missions in other African countries that are not involved in internal conflicts.[19]

As one of the world's largest arms suppliers, Russia has also provided arms to the continent and according to the Stockholm International Peace Research Institute (SIPRI). Between 2006 and 2010, Russia provided arms to Sudan, Chad, Niger, Senegal, and Uganda. Moreover, SIPRI noted that Russia's role as an arms supplier was expected to grow.[20] Much of this activity takes place outside official channels, and there are reports that some weapons ended up fueling the conflict in the DRC. Between 2000 and 2007, Russia sold MiG-29 fighters to Sudan and Algeria, which received $7.5 billion in Russian arms as part of an energy deal.[21] Russian security involvement in Africa also involves participation in UN peacekeeping missions. As of 2010, Russia was reported to be participating in all UN peacekeeping missions in Africa and also trained African personnel for peacekeeping.[22] By 2015, small numbers of Russian military personnel were participating in six of the nine U.N. peacekeeping operations in Africa, including the DRC, Western Sahara, Cote d'Ivoire, South Sudan, Sudan, and Liberia.[23]

Brazil's growing trade ties with Africa, combined with its own coastal and Exclusive Economic Zone (EEZ) maritime security concerns, account for Brazil's growing security interests in Africa. Brazil's national defense strategy focuses on the South Atlantic, through which some 95% of its trade flows. Brazil also has significant energy reserves offshore and in its EEZ.[24] Security relations with the African countries along the South Atlantic coast are a key interest, especially in light of the recent increase in piracy in the Gulf of Guinea. While Brazil does not yet have either extensive military ties to Africa or major representation in UN peacekeeping operations in Africa, Brazilian defense doctrine gives the South Atlantic a high priority. As a result, Brazil has sought to strengthen maritime cooperation with its African counterparts. This includes training programs, transfers of military vessels and equipment, and capacity building. Brazil also sees Africa as a market for its military hardware.[25]

Resources, Trade, and Investment

Africa's vast natural resource wealth is a prime example of a blessing and a curse. Indeed, it was the promise of the continent's riches that provided the incentive for the colonial-era scramble for Africa among the European powers. In the independence era, revenues from resource extraction have often been described as the resource curse. Its resource trade is key to Africa's future prosperity, but growth also depends on diversification of Africa's economies and fuller participation in global markets. A new scramble for Africa's resources is now under way, with China, India, Brazil, Russia, Turkey, and other emerging markets joining the former colonial powers and the U.S. in the effort to ensure access to Africa's energy and mineral wealth.[26] African markets also offer greater opportunity for investment and trade, for which security is essential.

While its mineral resources are the most plentiful in the world, Africa is still underexplored. The continent is estimated to have about 30% of the world's total mineral reserves, and several African countries depend heavily on mineral production, although Africa accounts for only about 8% of global mineral production. Of the fifty-four countries in Africa, twenty-four rely on a relatively few minerals to generate more than 75% of export earnings.[27] In 2005, Africa ranked first in both production and reserves of platinum, gold, chrome, vanadium, cobalt, and diamonds. It ranked second in the world in the production of manganese, and its reserves of that mineral were the largest in the world.[28]

Africa's minerals have been a critical component of China's industrialization. Between 1995 and 2005, China's contribution to world industrial production doubled to 12%. From 2000 to 2007, China more than doubled its share of global demand for aluminum, copper, and zinc; tripled demand for lead; and quadrupled demand for nickel. During that period, China's share of iron ore imports also tripled, from 16% to 48%, accounting for 32% of total crude steel demand. Although China has been a main driver of Africa's economic growth, many other countries at similar stages of development, such as Brazil, Russia, Turkey, and several Southeast Asian countries, are interested in imports of Africa's minerals.[29] Although China's economic growth has slowed and is likely to have an impact on demand, Africa's resources figure prominently in what Michael Klare calls the "Race for What's Left."[30]

In the past several years, Africa's energy reserves have attracted even more attention than its mineral wealth. According to the U.S. Energy Information Agency, sixteen of Africa's fifty-four countries are oil producers, and the continent's proven oil reserves grew by almost 120%, up from 57 billion barrels in 1980 to 124 billion barrels in 2012. There are also an estimated 100 billion barrels offshore.[31] In 2012, sub-Saharan Africa produced nearly 6 million barrels per day, amounting to about 7% of total world production. Oil production in the region grew by an annual average of 3% between 2003 and 2013.[32] New producers include Ghana, which began producing from its Jubilee offshore field in late 2010. East Africa also has great potential. Uganda, which could have the largest onshore deposits,[33] is due to begin oil production by 2017–18, and oil was discovered in northern Kenya in 2010. Onshore deposits require construction of pipelines to get the oil to the market. Construction of those pipelines not only would increase African oil production but would be an estimated $16 billion project that could benefit Kenya, Ethiopia, South Sudan, and Uganda. Discussions between these countries on a joint pipeline have stalled due to regional differences and lack of agreement on a route for the pipeline. The Western oil companies Total and Tullow as well as the China National Offshore Oil Corporation (CNOOC) are interested in the project.[34] While depressed demand for oil may postpone oil export plans, demand, especially from industrializing states, is likely to rebound in the future.

Africa is also a growing source of natural gas production. Estimates of natural gas reserves grew 140% between 1980 and 2012, increasing from 210 to 509 trillion cubic feet. In 2012, twenty-four African countries were known to have gas reserves. Nigeria, Algeria, and Egypt are three of the world's top gas producers, with Nigeria the region's top exporter. Nigeria, with 82% of the proven gas reserves in sub-Saharan Africa, was already the world's fourth-largest liquid natural gas exporter in 2012, accounting for about 8% of total world exports. Overall, gas production in sub-Saharan Africa grew by an annual average of 10% in the ten years between 2003 and 2013. In 2011, sub-Saharan Africa produced more than 1.6 trillion cubic feet of natural gas, about 1% of total world production.[35] Gas strikes off East Africa have led to predictions that the region could become the world's third-largest exporter of natural gas in the long term. Tanzania is now producing natural gas, as is Namibia.[36] As more exploration takes place and new producers come online, Africa's share of world production will increase further, especially as natural gas becomes an environmentally conscious alternative to oil and coal.

China has become a major influence on the continent through its trade and investment, and China's rapid economic growth has fueled demand for oil and minerals to sustain its massive industrialization. Africa has become an important source of China's imports of energy and raw materials. China accounts for more than 13% of world demand for oil and petroleum products, second only to the U.S.[37] Angola was the second leading oil exporter to China, accounting for 15% of China's crude oil imports in 2012. Overall, China was the largest importer of crude oil from Africa in 2012,[38] and Africa's oil exports to China are expected to increase further as it overtakes the U.S. as the largest net importer of oil by 2020.[39]

China has relied on a dual strategy in its effort to secure oil supplies. It uses its export-import bank to finance development projects in oil-producing countries and gets part of the loan repaid in oil. China's Eximbank extended a $2 billion loan to Angola in 2004. After five years, Angola was to set aside some fifteen thousand barrels of oil per day, with the amount to increase to forty thousand barrels per day until the loan was repaid. The Chinese paid market price for the oil; the proceeds go into an escrow account from which the loan payments are paid, while the Angolan government gets the remainder. The loan was to fund infrastructure projects, for which Chinese companies secured the contracts.[40]

By using its considerable currency reserves and its state-run export-import bank to extend loans, China gets access to Angolan oil and the good will of the Angolan government. Angola gets infrastructure development and an alternative to financing such projects through Western financial institutions, which require greater transparency and accountability. Angola is notorious for its lack of transparency in accounting for its oil revenues, and China's policy of noninterference in the internal affairs of its business partners reduces the pressure to hold the Angolan government more accountable.

Chinese investment in oil production in Sudan also came under scrutiny because of China's willingness to do business with a government that has engaged in widespread human rights abuses, especially in Darfur. Although China eventually agreed to authorize a UN peacekeeping mission to Darfur, as far as the Chinese are concerned the principle of sovereignty precludes any further interference in Sudan. China refuses to pass judgment on the actions of countries with which it does business, nor does it require any standards of conduct.[41] Sudan's president, Omar al-Bashir, attended China's 2015 military celebration commemorating the seventieth anniversary of China's World War II defeat of Japan. Not only did China not detain Bashir on the ICC warrant for his arrest, but Bashir secured Chinese investment contracts during his visit.[42]

Although China does not have the security that comes with equity oil, that is, oil that the Chinese government actually owns, deals such as the loan advanced to Angola or the production-sharing agreement negotiated with Sudan lock in a reliable supply. Moreover, African partners see China as an attractive alternative to doing business with Western multinationals. The Chinese alternative not only helps prop up authoritarian regimes but gives African countries greater leverage in negotiations with foreign governments to develop their resources.[43]

Africa's economic growth and expanding middle class have opened greater global trade opportunities. Aside from energy, China's interests include opening African markets to Chinese exports and cultivating African countries' support in regional and international organizations.[44] China's trade with sub-Saharan Africa has been expanding rapidly, growing from $10 billion in 2000 to about $50 billion by 2007.[45] China surpassed the U.S. as Africa's largest trading partner in 2009, and China's trade with Africa rose sharply to $200 billion in 2013. That figure included a 44% jump in Chinese foreign investment. In contrast, U.S. trade in goods was $85 billion in 2013, while trade in services amounted to another $11billion.[46] If China maintains its growth rate at 7%, it will continue to rely on Africa for resources. China's continued growth and demand for resources could help Africa to maintain its recent average growth rate of about 5% and also help Africa take advantage of the demographic dividend of its young population.

Approximately 40% of Africa's total exports to Asia are to China, while some 30% of Asia's total exports to Africa are from China.[47] China's imports are concentrated in oil and minerals, but it also fishes off Africa's coasts, grows crops in Zimbabwe and Madagascar for shipment back to China, and recently began importing cotton from Mozambique. Its exports to Africa account for a smaller proportion of its $200 billion in trade than its imports, but China is increasingly taking advantage of Africa's markets for consumer goods. China also sells African governments jet fighters, military equipment and ammunition, uniforms, communications technology, agricultural equipment, road machinery, and turbines and generators. It has also shipped patrol boats capable of carrying helicopters to Nigeria to help protect offshore oil installations.[48]

Almost all African countries have been the beneficiaries of China's infra-structure construction, which includes the building or refurbishing of dams, hydroelectric plants, roads, hospitals, stadiums, railways, and port facilities. The top beneficiaries of China's assistance and concessionary loans between 2000 and 2011 were Ghana ($11.4 billion), Nigeria ($8.4 billion), Sudan and Ethiopia ($5.4 billion), Mauritania ($4.6 billion), Angola ($4.2 billion), Equa-torial Guinea and Zimbabwe ($3.8 billion), and South Africa ($2.3 billion).[49]

While most African countries welcome China's trade and investment as an alternative to seeking partnerships in the West[50] and like China's emphasis on sovereignty and noninterference, there are African critics of Chinese involve-ment on the continent. After the death in 2006 of forty-nine workers in factory in Zambia that made explosives for a Chinese copper mine, a Zambian presi-dential candidate, Michael Sata, was critical of labor practices, especially in Chinese-run mines, charging that workers were mistreated and poorly paid.[51] He continued these criticisms in his successful 2011 campaign.[52] In a speech in Tanzania in March 2013, Chinese president Xi Jinping tried to allay African concerns about Chinese competition in African markets and the impact on jobs and industrialization. He acknowledged difficulties in Sino-African economic cooperation and pledged to take steps to ensure that Africa benefited from the relationship. He announced that China would follow through on the promise of $20 billion in loans for infrastructure, farming, and business, as well as funding for training programs and scholarships.[53]

Critics also question trade patterns in which African raw materials are used to produce Chinese goods that are then exported to Africa, undermining Afri-can efforts to industrialize and costing jobs. China also wins the bulk of the construction contracts that are awarded by African countries and paid for by Chinese loans. There has also been widespread criticism of China for bringing its own workers to complete infrastructure projects while providing poor pay and hard working conditions for the African workers Chinese firms do employ. Small-scale Chinese merchants have also flooded into Africa in recent years, competing with indigenous traders. There are estimates that up to 1 million Chinese now live in Africa and pursue business opportunities there.[54]

China is not the only emerging market player on the African continent. India is the world's fifth-largest energy consumer and is expected to double its energy consumption by 2030, overtaking Japan and Russia to move into third place behind the U.S. and China. The quest for energy security is one of the major factors driving Indian investment in Africa.[55] Although India's recent economic growth has slowed, coming in at 4.6% in the first quarter of 2014, about the same rate as the previous quarter, analysts expect the economy to grow on the heels of the election of Narendra Modi, who is seen as an economic reformer, as prime minister.[56] India faces a potential energy crisis in the future as it tries to sustain its economic growth. Its own oil reserves are very small, and it too has turned to Africa to supply its growing energy needs. India has invested in oil exploitation in a number of African countries, including Nigeria, Sudan, and Côte d'Ivoire, and Indian oil companies have also expressed interest in Mauritius, Burkina Faso, Equatorial Guinea, Ghana, Guinea-Bissau, and Senegal. India is also interested in Africa's mineral resources, investing in Zambian copper, Liberian iron ore, and Senegalese phosphorous. Africa's agricultural resources are also seen as a way to provide for India's food security. Indian firms have already invested in Uganda and have plans to invest in Kenya as well.[57]

India's bilateral trade with Africa grew at 31.8% annually from 2005 to 2011. Bilateral trade increased from $5.3 billion in 2001 to $63 billion in 2011, outstripping Indian trade with the U.S. in 2011, which stood at $56 billion. Africa-India trade value was projected to reach $176 billion by 2015, with African exports to India projected at $121.5 billion and African imports at $54.5 billion if the annual growth rates between 2001 and 2011 continue. India is the fastest-growing market for African exports, with growth of more than 41.8% per year between 2005 and 2011, higher than the 28% growth in African exports to China. Nevertheless, China's total trade value with Africa of $166 billion in 2011 still substantially exceeded India's, which was $63 for that year.[58] There has also been strong growth in Indian private investment, with large investments in telecommunications, information technology, energy, and the automobile sector. Indian multinational firms also encourage the integration of local workers.[59] Indian commercial ties with Africa are concentrated in the telecommunications, pharmaceuticals, and manufacturing sectors, but the highest priority is the energy sector. India has had impressive economic growth rates and that is expected to continue, making it likely that India will expand its ties to Africa.[60]

Although Russia was deeply engaged in Africa during the Cold War, the collapse of the Soviet Union and the end of the East-West ideological struggle led to Russia's withdrawal from extensive contact with the continent. In an effort to regain its position as a major power under President Vladimir Putin, Russia has re-engaged with Africa. Although possessing some of the world's largest energy reserves and not dependent on Africa for its energy, Russia has sought to gain leverage in energy markets through deals, particularly with African natural gas producers, as part of its effort to enhance its political and economic power. It has also sought to deal with its shortage of critical minerals such as aluminum, chrome, manganese, mercury, and titanium and to hedge against depletion of its own reserves of copper, nickel, tin, and zinc.[61]

Brazil also has interests in African resources and markets. Although Brazil achieved energy self-sufficiency in 2006, its state oil company has operations in Angola, Benin, Gabon, Nigeria, Namibia, Senegal, and Tanzania. A leader in the production of biofuels, it has also started cooperative programs to produce biofuels with Angola and Mozambique, and those programs could expand to other African countries.[62] According to the Brazilian Ministry of Development, Industry, and Foreign Trade, oil and other resources accounted for almost 90% of imports from Africa, mainly connected to large-scale Brazilian companies specializing largely in resources. Nevertheless, although Brazil's involvement with Africa trails that of other emerging markets, Brazil competes with China for energy exploration rights on the continent.[63]

Brazil's trade with Africa increased from $4 billion in 2000 to $20 billion in 2010. Brazil's top ten trading partners in Africa are Nigeria, South Africa, Angola, Ghana, DRC, Senegal, Côte d'Ivoire, Cape Verde, Benin, and Mauritania. During his tenure in office, former Brazilian president Luis Inacio da Silva visited Africa twelve times, often accompanied by representatives from the private sector. By 2010, Brazil's exports to Africa amounted to 4.54% of total exports. Brazilian foreign direct investment reached $32 billion in 2010, with Angola, Nigeria, and South Africa accounting for 40% of that investment. Unlike Chinese companies, Brazilian companies tend to hire local workers.[64] Despite a focus on resources, Brazilian businesses see their biggest potential as the export of machinery, technical equipment, and consumer goods. Some 42% of Brazil's exports to Africa consist of manufactured goods. Brazil's foreign policy toward Africa also emphasizes poverty and hunger reduction. Benefiting from its own experience in confronting those problems, along with its similar geography and climate, Brazil may be able to adapt its agricultural expertise more easily to conditions in Africa. Its emphasis on social development and health also coincides with Africa's development needs.[65]

In contrast to increases elsewhere, U.S. trade in goods with Africa has steadily declined since 2011. Trade went down from $125 billion in 2011 to $99 billion in 2012, dropping further to $85 billion in 2013, $72 billion in 2014, and just over $48.2 billion in 2015.[66] A major reason for the decline is a drop in oil and gas imports. U.S. oil consumption began a 9% decline in 2008, decreasing from 20.7 million to 18.9 million barrels per day in 2013. During that time, oil and gas imports from countries covered under the Africa Growth and Opportunity Act (AGOA) declined by 66%, from $60 billion to $20 billion. By contrast, nonoil exports dropped only 6% during that same period.[67] Boosting American trade with Africa is complicated by poor infrastructure on the continent and bureaucratic delays as well as by opposition by U.S. agricultural and textile interests to expanding the list of products covered by AGOA. In addition, the U.S. sought to strengthen the criteria for access to certain AGOA benefits by tying access to issues such as workers' rights.[68]

With its declining trade, the U.S. faces the prospect of losing leverage with which to push for political and economic reform in Africa. According to a survey done in Nigeria, South Africa, Ghana, and Kenya, Africans think that U.S. trade prospects with the continent are hurt by American demands for good governance and democratic reform. In contrast, a survey conducted by the *Wall Street Journal* found that the majority of its readers surveyed did not think that these requirements harmed business prospects.[69] China offers an attractive alternative to the U.S. since Chinese trade and investments emphasize business relationships and are not tied to governance, democratic reform, or a good human rights record, which are required to qualify for AGOA. China's emphasis on sovereignty and noninterference in internal affairs also means

that there is little likelihood that China will be critical of its trade and investment partners' human rights records. On the other hand, China has come in for
criticism for its willingness to do business with some of the continent's worst
human rights abusers.

Political and Diplomatic Support

There is clearly a clash of diplomatic engagement models between the U.S.
and China. The U.S. and its Western allies have been exerting pressure, albeit
selectively, on African countries to adopt democratic governance, while China
utilizes its non-Western status, the success of its development model, and
its strong support for sovereignty to rally support in international forums. Its
strong support for sovereignty and noninterference and its appeal to postcolonial sentiment in African countries are key components of China's effort to
build a strategic partnership with Africa, which, because of its voting strength
in international forums, is an important part of China's effort to complete its
"peaceful rise" as a global power and counter the hegemony of the West. With
a combination of economic reform and political control, the Chinese development model has lifted hundreds of million out of poverty, provided political
stability, and increased China's international influence.[70] This model is especially attractive to authoritarian African regimes.

Among China's strategic goals is the cultivation of African support for
Beijing in the UN and other international organizations. China seeks to bolster support for its policies and to expand its role as a spokesman for the
developing world at the UN and in other international forums. China's self-
identification as a developing country and its emphasis on sovereignty also
help account for its effort to work through international and regional organizations. China appeals to African countries not only by portraying itself as a
champion of the developing world but also through its skepticism about the
promotion of human rights, especially at the expense of sovereignty. African
countries make up the largest single voting bloc at the UN, and African support has been important in blocking greater UN interaction with Taiwan and in
deflecting criticism of China's human rights record.[71] China's firm insistence
on the inviolability of sovereignty also supplies cover for its relations with
allies like Sudan.

Like China, India also portrays itself as a spokesman for the developing
world, and its support for multilateralism and reductions in global inequality,
as well as for a larger role for the developing world in multilateral institutions,
resonates in Africa. India has demonstrated a commitment to the reform of
the international order, particularly with regard to the issue of global inequality. This resonates with African countries, which boosts India's relations with
Africa and helps in its implicit competition with China for influence.[72] India
has also participated in several UN peacekeeping deployments in Africa and
has made no secret of its desire to gain a seat on the UN Security Council,
from which it would be better positioned in its rivalry with China over global

influence. Relations with Africa are an important component of India's efforts to enhance its influence in international affairs. To that end, India has increased its diplomatic activity in Africa and in 2008 organized its own variation of China's Forum on China-Africa Cooperation (FOCAC) to focus attention on its efforts to strengthen ties with Africa. In 2003, India also joined with Brazil and South Africa to form the India, Brazil, South Africa Dialogue (IBSA), designed to highlight South-South cooperation and to challenge the West on global governance issues.[73] At the 2014 meeting of the heads of state of Brazil, Russia, India, China, and South Africa, the BRICS announced the establishment of the New Development Bank, which they hope will eventually become an alternative to the IMF and the World Bank. India will serve as the president of the Bank for the first six years of operation.[74]

Russia also seeks to bolster international support for its policy positions and to counter American and Chinese influence both globally and on the African continent. Russia needs African support for its initiatives in international forums not only to achieve its policy aims but also to strengthen its claim to major power status. Like China and India, Russia emphasizes its links to the continent, especially its support for decolonization and liberation movements in several African countries. If need be, Russia can exercise its Security Council veto to demonstrate its support of sovereignty and its rejection of international intervention, positions that resonate in Africa. Russia's opposition to Western dominance in international affairs and its rhetoric regarding multilateralism are also appealing to Africa. The Russians are also bolstering their soft-power approach through revival of Soviet-era approaches emphasizing cultural exchanges and educational opportunities.[75]

Other emerging regional powers such as Iran, Turkey, and Vietnam have increased their engagement with Africa. Most of Iran's interest has been tied to trade and investment. Iran's 2010 trade with Africa totaled $3.9 billion in exports, while it imported $268 million worth of African goods. Iran has sought to engage a number of African countries, but it has especially sought to build ties to northeastern African countries as well as Indian Ocean coastal countries. Despite Iran's efforts to expand ties, illustrated by the 2010 Iran-Africa summit in Teheran, Iran has had some missteps. In 2010, Nigerian authorities intercepted an arms shipment bound for rebels in Gambia and Senegal, and broke diplomatic relations with Iran over the affair. Turkey has also increased its contacts with the continent. Trade between Africa and Turkey accounts for about 8% of Turkey's exports and 3% of its imports, and Turkish companies have provided some $1 billion in foreign investment. Turkey has also undertaken some modest development projects. Following the Chinese model, Turkey held its first Turkey-Africa cooperation summit in 2008. Turkey also hosted a conference on Somalia in 2011 and opened an embassy in Mogadishu in 2012. Vietnam held its first Vietnam-Africa International Forum in 2003, with a follow-up in 2010. Vietnam's trade with Africa is small, only $1.5 billion in 2010, most of it Vietnamese exports to Africa. Vietnam's investment is concentrated in the energy sector.[76]

Sea Lanes, Piracy, and Transnational Criminal Activity

Africa's strategic importance is also tied to its geographic location astride important sea lanes and to the growing threat of lawlessness in some areas off the continent. The Indian Ocean sea lanes are among the most strategically important in the world. According to the *Journal of the Indian Ocean Region*, more than 80% of the world's seaborne trade in oil travels through chokepoints such as the Straits of Hormuz, the Malacca Straits, and the Bab al-Mandab, all of which provide access to the Indian Ocean. More than half of the world's armed conflicts are in the Indian Ocean region, and the region is the site of other evolving strategic developments, including competition between India and China, the spread of Islamic radicalism, and the management of ocean resources such as fisheries.[77]

While piracy has dropped in the Gulf of Aden and off the Horn, the strategic importance of the Indian Ocean sea lanes to global trade and maritime traffic remains. Oil shipments through the region to the U.S. and the rest of the West as well as to India, China, and the rest of Asia are the major concern. Some 75% of East Asian oil and gas imports traverse the Indian Ocean, and disruption would have serious consequences for the global economy.[78] The growing commercial trade among Africa, India, and China also traverses these sea lanes.

An additional strategic nautical challenge will be to avoid tensions as China develops its blue-water naval capability. As Chinese naval-power projection capability grows, there is the possibility of tension or confrontation between the U.S. and China. Moreover, cooperation between India and the U.S. to off-set China's growing maritime influence in the Indian Ocean cannot be ruled out. Given its location, along with its existing naval capability, India has a significant stake in the maritime security of the region. China's development of relations and port facilities around the Indian Ocean littoral, stretching to Africa, highlights its expanding maritime strategy. Concerns about Chinese naval projection ensure that India will also play a role in the future security of the Indian Ocean.[79] The Chinese proposal of a "maritime silk road" in the Indian Ocean is seen by some Indian strategists as a ploy to justify a larger Chinese presence in the region.[80]

In addition to its importance to maritime security, eastern Africa is also the site of substantial drug and human trafficking. Among the findings of a 2013 UN Office on Drugs and Crime report were that conflict and poverty in East Africa produce a large and vulnerable stream of smuggled migrants who are exploited during their journey. It was estimated that more than 100,000 people paid smugglers to transport them across the Red Sea and the Gulf of Aden to Yemen in 2012. Heroin is also trafficked to and through the region. While the region has been a transshipment point for heroin since at least the 1980s, recent seizures have indicated an increased flow. It is believed that the local market absorbs about 2.5 tons, but the total volume trafficked is estimated at 22 tons, indicating substantial transhipment. East Africa is also a major source for illegal ivory, which is decimating elephant populations. In 2011, ivory worth an estimated $30 million, two-thirds of which was bound for Asia, passed through the region.[81]

The surge in piracy off the coast of Somalia between 2005 and its peak in 2011 led to the formation of an international naval patrol off the Horn of Africa. The effectiveness of these international patrols, combined with the use of armed guards on cargo vessels and the strengthening of Somalia's fledgling government, have had a significant impact. Incidents of piracy have plummeted, with only 15 reported in 2013, down from 75 in 2012 and a drastic reduction from the 237 reported in 2011. However, as piracy off the coast of Somalia declined, there was a surge in attacks in the Gulf of Guinea, home to almost 70% of Africa's oil production. The oil giants Nigeria and Angola produce some 2 million barrels per day, and Congo-Brazzaville, Gabon, Equatorial Guinea, and Cameroon produce several hundred thousand additional barrels. Oil has recently been discovered in Ghana, Sierra Leone, and Sao Tome and Principe. In 2010, Ghana began production from its offshore Jubilee oil field with production of 120,000 barrels per day, set to double within three years. In 2012, the region shipped 1.5 million barrels to the U.S. and 1 million barrels to Europe every day, as well as 850,000 barrels to China and 330,000 barrels to India.[82] Piracy in the Gulf of Guinea has risen, accounting for 19% of pirate attacks in 2013. Overall, Nigerian pirates accounted for thirty-one of the fifty-one attacks in the Gulf of Guinea region.[83] Piracy in West Africa differs from that off the Horn. Somali pirates were primarily interested in ransoms paid to release the ships and their crews. The primary focus of pirates in the Gulf of Guinea is the theft of oil shipments; since the condition of the crew is less important, these attacks are more prone to violence.

Nigeria has been at the center of this surge in piracy, but maritime insecurity and criminal activity have also increased due to tensions in Nigeria's Niger Delta. Decades of oil extraction in the Niger Delta region have created a volatile mix of political opposition and criminal activity. Inequitable distribution of oil revenue and the fouling of the environment in the region have sharpened political opposition. Oil spills from aging pipelines, illegal refining, pipeline sabotage, and oil theft have decreased fish stocks and contaminated water and arable land. A UN Environmental Program study of Ogoniland found the problem ongoing and stated that the damage could take twenty-five to thirty years to repair.[84] High poverty rates in a region that produces much of Nigeria's wealth led to the formation of the insurgent group the Movement for the Emancipation of the Niger Delta (MEND), in 2005. MEND began a campaign against the government and the oil industry, including theft of oil from pipelines and tankers and kidnappings of oil workers. Opportunistic criminals also took part in these activities, and it was difficult to distinguish clearly between those who were motivated by political and economic reasons and those who were simply using the unrest as cover for purely criminal purposes. The Nigerian government tried to gain control of the situation in 2009, using a combination of military action coupled with an amnesty that included monthly stipends and a training program for insurgents. That did not stop the criminals, nor did it completely end the insurgent attacks, although, after the implementation of the stipend and training program, the attacks tapered off.[85]

West Africa's coastal defense capabilities are limited, although the region faces major maritime challenges. There is little patrol and interception capability among the region's navies and coast guards, making the region a prime location for piracy, arms, drugs, human trafficking, and toxic waste disposal.[86] New offshore oil fields in the region increase the likelihood that, barring effective deterrence, pirates will attack tankers and perhaps ships carrying other valuable resources bound for the global market. At the same time, contention over maritime boundaries and the resources at stake in such a potentially rich and relatively underexplored region could create tensions between coastal states.[87]

Criminal activity in West Africa also presents a regional and international security challenge. The combination of weak maritime security, the region's uninhabited islands, and the existence of established criminal gangs linked to corrupt government officials all facilitate criminal activity, especially the drug trade. The Gulf of Guinea region has become a major transshipment point for the drug trade. Drugs have been seized in Guinea-Bissau, Cape Verde, Gambia, Ghana, Mauritania, and Senegal. In fact, Guinea-Bissau has earned the reputation as a narco state because of the deep involvement of state officials in the drug trade.[88] A 2012 military coup brought the role of the armed forces in the drug trade more into the open. In 2013, the U.S. Justice Department alleged that government officials, including the army chief of staff, Antonio Indjai, were involved in drug and arms trafficking. These developments also pointed to the connections between the South Atlantic drug trade and extremist and criminal networks stretching across West Africa and the Sahel. In 2009, the wreckage of a jet believed to have been carrying five to ten tons of cocaine was found in northern Mali. Evidence suggests that drug trafficking helps finance AQIM's activities. Algerian intelligence estimates that drug trafficking and kidnapping contributed more than $100 million to AQIM between 2003 and 2010.[89] There are also indications that the drug trade reaches into Guinea, Senegal, and Ghana.[90] Smuggling routes are seldom restricted to one illicit cargo; trafficking routes may also be used to smuggle weapons, other contraband, and humans. The lawlessness and corruption that accompany smuggling weaken military, police, and border and customs officials and influence their motivation, with broader consequences for the legitimacy and transparency of state governments.[91] The problem is not confined to coastal areas in West Africa. Inland; political unrest has been mixed with banditry, terrorism, and the trade in drugs, arms, persons, and cigarettes.[92] The illicit trade routes through the Sahel and the Sahara not only provide a conduit for illegal trade and contribute to the coffers of terrorists but also line the pockets of local officials and encourage further corruption. The focus on the threat from AQIM and related groups has overshadowed the growth of criminal activity in the region and its links to state officials and political leaders and the international networks that prop up corrupt regimes. The crisis in northern

Mali demonstrates the complex interaction of corrupt government officials, militants, and criminal elements.[93]

Looming on the horizon, the effects of climate change are likely to have an impact on the strategic calculus and the security environment in the future. An erratic climate will affect food security and contribute to health and human security concerns in the future. In 2003–2004, heavy rain in the Sahel dramatically increased the locust population and contributed to famine in Niger in 2005–2006. Flooding in Ghana in 2007 increased the incidence of waterborne disease and destroyed crops. Unscrupulous politicians and warlords have already been known to manipulate the competition for scarce resources for their own purposes, and the further deterioration of the environment can only aggravate that tendency.[94] Climate change has already contributed to conflict in Darfur, where tensions between herders and farmers over increasingly scarce arable land developed characteristics of identity politics and ethnic conflict. The 2014 *U.S. Quadrennial Defense Review* specifically mentioned the growing security threat associated with climate change. Specifically, the QDR noted that "Climate change may exacerbate water scarcity and lead to sharp increases in food costs. The pressures caused by climate change will influence resource competition while placing additional burdens on economies, societies, and governance institutions around the world. These effects are threat multipliers that will aggravate stressors abroad such as poverty, environmental degradation, political instability, and social tensions—conditions that can enable terrorist activity and other forms of violence."[95] A *New York Times* report states that the authors of the QDR concluded that desertification of the Sahel in Mali killed crops and devastated farmland, contributing to the jihadist threat in 2012.[96]

The impact of climate change will be compounded by Africa's projected population surge. Projections of Africa's population now forecast a doubling from 1.2 to 2.4 billion between 2015 and 2050 and climbing to 4.2 billion by 2100. Moreover, more than half of the projected growth in global population between 2015 and 2050 is expected to take place in Africa. By then, close to 41% of the world's births, 40% of those under age five, and 37% of those under age eighteen will be African.[97] While such a large youth bulge is potentially good for Africa's demographic transition and economic prospects, it also means that a thriving economy will be essential to avoid disillusionment, frustration, radicalization, and instability. Such a large population increase is unquestionably going to put even greater pressure on the environment.

U.S. Security Strategy: Global Challenges and Constraints

While Africa represents a range of security challenges, U.S. interests and influence are global. Yet, confidence in its international leadership has declined at a time when U.S. foreign policy is a topic of considerable debate around the world as well as at home. The reverberations from the September 11 attacks continue to shape U.S. security policy. Despite the withdrawal of U.S. combat troops from Iraq and the scaling down of U.S. involvement in Afghanistan, these experiences are likely to have a long-term impact on U.S. willingness to intervene overseas. Boko Haram's allegiance to the Islamic State (IS) and the continued threat posed by groups associated with al Qaeda in the Islamic Maghreb are sure to reinforce the U.S. focus on counterterrorism, especially in the aftermath of the terrorist attacks on hotels in Mali in November 2015 and Burkina Faso in January 2016. Africa will continue to be a focus, albeit a secondary one, because of its strategic importance to counterterrorism efforts, which overshadow other dimensions of strategic value.

Even before the ISIS challenge, the U.S. had a full national security agenda. The Defense Department's 2012 report "Sustaining U.S. Global Leadership: Priorities for 21st Century Defense" noted that the global security environment presented an increasingly complex set of challenges and opportunities that would require the application of the full spectrum of American power. The report went on to outline the broad parameters of the American security agenda and the primary missions of the U.S. armed forces. These included engaging in counterterrorism and irregular warfare, deterring and defeating aggression, projecting American power despite the challenges posted by limited access, countering the spread of weapons of mass destruction, operating effectively in cyberspace and space, maintaining an effective nuclear deterrent, defending the homeland, providing a stabilizing presence abroad, conducting stability and counterinsurgency operations, and carrying out humanitarian, disaster relief, and other operations.[98]

Although the U.S. still has the world's most powerful military, with a full spectrum of capabilities, such a broad security agenda under any circumstances would be both complicated and expensive. As Bruce Jentleson noted, in a world where there is decreasing agreement on the nature of threats, military power may not translate into other forms of power and influence. An effective security strategy must take into account the costs of maintaining U.S. hegemony, the impact of security reassessments by American allies and the extent to which those reassessments coincide with U.S. interests, the threats associated with intrastate war, and a broadening security agenda that now includes environmental and health issues.[99] It must also contend with the particular challenges Africa represents, such as institutional weakness and porous borders, uneven growth, and potential strategic competition with China and the increase in interaction between Africa and other emerging markets. These challenges come at a time when the U.S. is juggling the crises in the Middle East, Chinese assertiveness, and a resurgent Russia. Political partisanship and economic realities at home also constrain American action.

After the September 11 attacks, counterterrorism became the dominant concern of U.S. security policy, resulting in the strengthening of U.S. military and intelligence capabilities. The defense budget rose rapidly between 2001 and 2010, with new counterinsurgency initiatives, the formation of AFRICOM, and expansion of the American presence abroad contributing to this increase.[100] The U.S. invasions of Afghanistan and Iraq added even more to the cost of defense. Not only will these wars have cost the U.S. in excess of $2 trillion, but the estimated total, including medical care for wounded veterans and rebuilding of depleted capabilities, will come to between $4 and $6 trillion.[101] As the wars in Iraq and Afghanistan wound down, the prospect of refocusing U.S. defense and security accelerated. The financial crisis that began in 2008 weakened the U.S. economy and put further downward pressure on defense spending. Bitter political wrangling and political gridlock in Washington drove the defense budget even lower. With Congress unable to reach agreement on government spending, the 2011 Budget Control Act called for deep cuts, of which half were to come from defense programs. The 2013 Bipartisan Budget Act provided some immediate relief from automatic cuts of $50 billion annually under sequestration, while the Bipartisan Budget Act of 2015 provided some further relief from sequestration, increasing defense spending by $33 billion in 2016 and $23 billion in 2017.[102]

The 2014 Quadrennial Defense Review (QDR) focused on rebalancing defense in an era of fiscal restraint. Building on DOD's 2012 "Sustaining U.S. Global Leadership," which provided the strategic guidance, the DOD strategy outlined in the QDR rests on three pillars:

> 1) deterring and defeating attacks on the U.S. and supporting civil authorities in the event of attacks or natural disasters; 2) preserving regional stability, deterring adversaries, supporting allies and partners, and cooperating with others to meet common security challenges; projecting American power to defeat aggression, disrupting and destroying terrorist networks; and 3) providing humanitarian assistance and disaster relief. The QDR listed priorities that included a re-balancing to the Asia-Pacific, maintaining a strong commitment to security and stability in Europe and the Middle East, sustaining a global effort to counter violent extremists and terrorist threats with an emphasis on the Middle East and Africa, continuing to protect and prioritize key investments in technology while the armed forces shrink, and building innovative partnerships and strengthening key alliances and partnerships.[103]

The Project for a United and Strong America, a report authored by a collection of foreign policy and national security experts, offered recommendations for meeting those challenges. The report suggested a light U.S. military footprint around the world, with flexible forces able to operate with partners at the national and regional levels. If military operations are necessary, the U.S. should act with its allies and partners as well as regional organizations. To that end, it recommended that the U.S. expand the capabilities of allies and partners by providing equipment and training and that it engage in joint exercises and capacity building. Foreign aid should include humanitarian assistance, disaster relief, security assistance, and training aimed at preventing human rights abuses and providing for democracy development.[104] While these priorities reflect the elements of U.S. Africa policy, it remains to be seen how effectively they can be implemented.

U.S. experience in Iraq and Afghanistan, combined with a counterterrorism focus and budgetary constraints, have had an important impact on military doctrine. The invasions of Afghanistan and Iraq and the long military campaigns that followed initially revived interest in counterinsurgency and nation building. Even though nation-building has been undermined by the U.S. experience in Iraq and Afghanistan, counterinsurgency, stability operations, and nation building have influenced the roles and capabilities of the armed forces and shifted the emphasis of American training and security assistance to Africa. In October 2014, the U.S. Army announced that it was scrapping its AirLand battle operating concept in favor of a new strategy called Unified Land Operations. Instead of focusing on one big battle, Army Chief of Staff Ray Odierno described the new Army operating concept as the ability to do multiple small-scale things simultaneously. He emphasized flexibility, adaptability, and the development of new capabilities to understand economic, political, and cultural environments and to operate around the world. The new plan also envisions a joint force of U.S. Army, Navy, Marines, and Air Force personnel working with other agencies such as the State Department and capable of operating in terrain ranging from large cities to ungoverned space. Much of this new operating concept was the result of the Army's experience of war since 2001.[105]

The Army's new approach also involves developing regionally aligned forces (RAF), units that receive language and cultural training and that will support specific combatant commands. RAFs are supposed to provide a better understanding of a region that will permit troops to anticipate conflicts before they escalate, build relations with local leaders, and facilitate military-to-military cooperation. This effort is also an outgrowth of the U.S. experience in Iraq and Afghanistan, which demonstrated that military might alone did not ensure success against insurgents. The first of the RAFs, the First Infantry Division's Second Armored Brigade Combat Team, based at Fort Riley, Kansas, was designated to AFRICOM. Regional deployments began in early 2013 with a small training mission in Niger for peacekeeping troops bound for Mali.[106] Between March and mid-September 2013, the AFRICOM RAF conducted approximately seventy-nine missions in more than thirty countries.[107]

The Obama administration had hoped that the withdrawal of troops from Iraq and Afghanistan would allow the U.S. to move from the war footing it has been on since 2001. While some had hoped that the end of the wars would free up personnel for operations in other parts of the world, such as Africa, the continent will remain a secondary priority and deployments are likely to be limited, as indicated by the reliance on prepositioning instead of permanent facilities. Regarding Africa, the 2012 strategic guidance document says only that the U.S. will "seek to be the security partner of choice, pursuing new partnerships with a growing number of nations, including those in Africa and Latin America."[108] It goes on to say that the U.S. will, whenever possible, develop innovative, low-cost, and small-footprint operations that rely on exercises with countries in the region, troop rotations, and advisory capabilities. Toward the end of the list of priorities the report mentions conducting stability and counterinsurgency operations in limited circumstances where military cooperation is insufficient. U.S. forces will continue to refine the lessons learned, the expertise gained, and the specialized capabilities developed in stability and counterinsurgency in Afghanistan and Iraq. The document states unequivocally that the U.S. will not size its forces for large-scale, prolonged stability operations. The U.S. will also conduct humanitarian and disaster relief operations, using its capability in air and sea lift, medical care and evacuation, and communications in support of lead relief agencies.[109]

Nevertheless, counterterrorism still leads the list of U.S. priorities, while Africa's fragile states, low levels of development, maritime capabilities, natural-resource wealth, and diplomatic support accentuate other security challenges. U.S. policy faces the task of channeling assistance to both improve military capability and target the underlying causes of conflict and instability on the continent. That type of assistance is costly, and as the debate over AFRICOM demonstrates, it is also controversial. Such a multidimensional policy will undoubtedly be affected by a backlash against American involvement overseas, divisions over strategy and tactics, continuing budgetary constraints at home, and disagreements on the appropriate use of American power. While the U.S. has a worldwide security agenda, of which Africa should certainly be an important component, the availability of budgetary resources with which to pursue the broad agenda Africa represents remains uncertain. Effective security cooperation with Africa is dependent on identifying the sources of insecurity, reconciling U.S. and African security challenges, rationalizing these challenges to the resources available, and negotiating the array of constraints on U.S. policy toward Africa.

Notes

1 Toni Haastrup, 2013, "Africa-EU Partnership on Peace and Security," in Jack Mangala, ed., *Africa and the European Union: A Strategic Partnership* (New York: Palgrave Macmillan), 48–50.
2 "Africa-EU Continental Cooperation," European Commission, available at https://ec.europa.eu/europeaid/regions/africa-eu-continental cooperation.html
3 David H. Shinn, 2009, "Africa: The United States and China Court the Continent," *Journal of International Affairs*, 62:2, 42.
4 "China's Growing Role in African Peace and Security," Saferworld, January 2011, iii, available at www.saferworld.org.uk/resources/view-resource/500-chinas-growing-role-in-african-peace-and-security
5 David H. Shinn, 2008, "Military and Security Relations: China, Africa, and the Rest of the World," in Robert I. Rotberg, ed., *China into Africa: Trade Aid and Influence* (Washington, DC: The Brookings Institution/World Peace Foundation,), 162.
6 Shinn, "Military and Security Relations," 176.
7 Pieter D. Wezeman, Siemon T. Wezeman, & Lucie Beraud-Sudreau, 2011, "Arms Flows to Sub-Saharan Africa," SIPRI Policy Paper No. 30, Stockholm International Peace Research Institute, December 2011, 11.
8 Colum Lynch, "China's Arms Exports Flooding Sub-Saharan Africa," *Washington Post*, 25 August 2012.

9 Mark Bromley, Mathieu Duchatel, & Paul Holtom, "China's Exports of Small Arms and Light Weapons," SIPRI Policy Paper No. 38, Stockholm International Peace Research Institute, October 2013, 42.
10 "China's Growing Role in African Peace and Security," iv, 46.
11 "Africa: China's Booming Torture Trade Revealed," Press Release, Amnesty International, AllAfrica.com, 23 September 2014. For the full report see www.amnesty.org/en/library/asset/ASA17/042/2014/en/7dcccd64–15c2–423a-93dd-2841687f6655/asa170422014en.pdf
12 "UN Peacekeeping Statistics," available at www.un.org/en/peacekeeping/resources/statistics/
13 "South Sudan: China to Send Troops for U.N. Mission," *New York Times*, 26 September 2014, A8.
14 Colleen Wong, 2023, "China Embraces Peacekeeping Mission," *The Diplomat*, 9 August 2013.
15 For a full discussion of China's antipiracy role see Andrew S. Erickson & Austin M. Strange, 2013, "No Substitute for Experience: Chinese Antipiracy Operations in the Gulf of Aden," U.S. Naval War College China Maritime Study No. 10, available at atwww.usnwc.edu/Research—-Gaming/China-Maritime-Studies-Institute/Publications.aspx
16 Shinn, "Military and Security Relations,"183.
17 David Shinn, "Emerging Powers Expand Ties with Africa," *International Policy Digest*, 17 September 2012.
18 Arvind Dutta, 2008, "Indo-African Defense Cooperation: Need for Enhanced Trust," *Journal of Defense Studies*, 2:2, 174–177.
19 Dipanjan Roy Chaudhury, "Global Strategic Move: India Increases Defense Training in Asia, Africa, and Latin America," *The Economic Times* (India), 5 September 2014.
20 Wezeman et al., "Arms Flows," 12.
21 David Shinn, "Emerging Powers Expand Ties with Africa," *International Policy Digest*, 17 September 2012.
22 Vladimir Schubin, 2010, "Russia and Africa: Coming Back?," *Russian Analytical Digest*, 83, 24 September 2010, 6, quoted in Keir Giles, "Russian Interests in Sub-Saharan Africa," Strategic Studies Institute, U.S. Army War College, July 2013, 13.
23 "Current Peacekeeping Operations Facts and Figures," United Nations Peacekeeping Operations, available at www.un.org/en/peacekeeping/operations/current.shtml
24 See Adriana Erthal Abdenur & Danilo Marcondes de Souza Neto, "Brazil's Growing Relevance to Peace and Security in Africa," Norwegian Peacebuilding Resource Center Report, March 2014.
25 Abdenur & de Souza Neto, "Brazil's Growing Relevance," 5–7.
26 See, for example, Padraig Carmody, 2011, *The New Scramble for Africa* (Malden, MA: Polity Press).
27 "Mining Industry Prospects in Africa," African Development Bank Group, 26 December 2012, available at www.afdb.org/en/blogs/afdb-championing-inclusive-growth-across-africa/post/mining-industry-prospects-in-africa-10177/
28 "Africa's Non-Renewable Natural Resources," African Development Report 2007, 63, available at www.afdb.org
29 "Minerals and Africa's Development: The International Study Group Report on Africa's Minerals Regimes," Economic Commission for Africa, 2011, 21, 25.
30 Michael T. Klare, 2012, *The Race for What's Left: The Global Scramble for the World's Last Resources* (New York: Picador).
31 "Oil and Gas in Africa: Africa's Reserves, Potential and Prospects," KPMG Full Sector Report, 2013, available at www.KPMG.com/Africa

32 "Oil and Natural Gas in Sub-Saharan Africa," U.S. Energy Information Administration, 8/1/2013, 4–5, available at www.eia.gov/pressroom/presentations/howard_08012013.pdf
33 "Oil and Natural Gas in Sub-Saharan Africa," 6.
34 "Pipeline Poker," *The Economist*, 25 May 2013.
35 "Oil and Natural Gas in Sub-Saharan Africa," 18.
36 "Oil and Natural Gas in Sub-Saharan Africa," 17.
37 Robert I. Rotberg, 2008, "China's Quest for Resources, Opportunities, and Influence in Africa," in Robert I. Rotberg, ed., *China into Africa: Trade Aid and Influence* (Washington, DC: The Brookings Institution/World Peace Foundation), 3.
38 "Oil and Natural Gas in Sub-Saharan Africa," 10.
39 "Oil and Natural Gas in Sub-Saharan Africa," 5.
40 Henry Lee & Dan Shalmon, 2008, "Searching for Oil: China's Oil Strategies in Africa," in Robert I. Rotberg, ed., *China into Africa: Trade Aid and Influence* (Washington, DC: The Brookings Institution/World Peace Foundation), 119.
41 Lee & Shalmon, "Searching for Oil," 112.
42 Mohammed Amin, "Sudan's President Bashir Bags Goodies on China Trip," *The East African*, 4 September 2015.
43 Lee & Shalmon, "Searching for Oil," 132–133.
44 Shinn, "Africa: The United States and China Court the Continent," 39.
45 Rotberg, " China's Quest for Resources," 3.
46 Robert Rotberg, "China's Trade with Africa at Record High," *Christian Science Monitor*, 19 March 2014.
47 Rotberg, "China's Quest for Resources," 4.
48 Rotberg, "China's Trade with Africa at Record High."
49 Rotberg, "China's Trade with Africa at Record High,"
50 Shinn, "Africa: The United States and China Court the Continent," 47.
51 Padraig Carmody, 2011, *The New Scramble for Africa* (Cambridge, UK: Polity Press), 86.
52 Jeffrey Gettleman, "Opposition Leader Is Handed Reins in Zambia," *New York Times*, 23 September 2011; for a more in-depth discussion of this criticism, see also Howard W. French, 2014, *China's Second Continent: How a Million Migrants Are Building a New Empire in Africa* (New York: Alfred A. Knopf).
53 Chris Buckley, "China's New leader Tries to Calm African Fears of His Country's Economic Power," *New York Times,* 26 March 2013, A6.
54 For a detailed discussion of Chinese migration and business practices in Africa, see French, *China's Second Continent*.
55 "Minerals and Africa's Development," 40.
56 "India's Economic Growth Disappoints," BBC Business News, 30 May 2014, available at www.bbc.com/news/business-27638906
57 J. Peter Pham, 2010, "India's New Engagement of Africa," in Jack Mangala, ed., *Africa and the New World Era* (New York: Palgrave Macmillan), 118–119.
58 "India-Africa: South-South Trade and Investment for Development," World Trade Organization/Confederation of Indian Industry, 2013, 15–18, 64.
59 "India-Africa: South-South Trade," Introduction, 18.
60 Ian Taylor, 2012, "India's Rise in Africa," *International Affairs*, 88:4, 780.
61 J. Peter Pham, 2010, "Back to Africa: Russia's New African Engagement," in Jack Mangala, ed., *Africa and the New World Era* (New York: Palgrave Macmillan), 76.
62 "Bridging the Atlantic Brazil and Sub-Saharan Africa: South-South Partnering for Growth," World Bank Working Paper 68970, 2012, 69,72, available at http://documents.worldbank.org/curated/en/2012/01/16279478/bridging-atlantic-brazil-sub-saharan-africa-south-south-partnering-growth

63 Christina Stolte, 2012, "Brazil in Africa: Just Another BRICS Country Seeking Resources?," Chatham House Africa Program and Americas Program Briefing Paper 1, 4, 8.
64 "Bridging the Atlantic," 40, 90, 95–96.
65 Stolte, "Brazil in Africa," 8, 11.
66 "Trade in Goods with Africa," United States Census Bureau, available at www.census.gov/foreign-trade/balance/c0013.htm/#204
67 Yun Sun, "American and Chinese Trade with Africa: Rhetoric vs. Reality," *The Hill*, 5 August 2014, available at http://thehill.com/blogs/pundits-blog/international/214270-american-and-chinese-trade-with-africa-rhetoric-vs-reality
68 William Mauldin, "U.S., Africa Aim to Boost Trade," *Wall Street Journal*, 4 August 2014.
69 "Africans See U.S. Trade Policy Hindering American Firms," *Wall Street Journal*, 11 August 2014, available at http://blogs.wsj.com/frontiers/2014/08/11/africans-see-us-trade-policy-limiting-opportunities-for-american-firms/
70 Chin-Hao Huang, 2008, "China's Renewed Partnership with Africa; Implications for the United States," in Robert I. Rotberg, ed., *China into Africa: Trade Aid and Influence* (Washington, DC: The Brookings Institution/World Peace Foundation), 296–298.
71 "China's Growing Role in African Peace and Security," *Saferworld*, January 2011, 9, available at www.saferworld.org.uk
72 Taylor, "India's Rise in Africa," 783.
73 Taylor, "India's Rise in Africa," 783–785.
74 See Raj M. Desai & James Raymond Vreeland, "What the New Bank of BRICS Is All About," *Washington Post*, 17 July 2014, available at www.washingtonpost.com/blogs/monkey-cage/wp/2014/07/17/what-the-new-bank-of-brics-is-all-about/
75 See Keir Giles, "Russian Interests in Sub-Saharan Africa," Strategic Studies Institute, U.S. Army War College, July 2013, 12–13 and J. Peter Pham, 2010, "Back to Africa: Russia's New African Engagement," in Jack Mangala, ed., *Africa and the New World Era: From Humanitarianism to a Strategic View* (New York: Palgrave Macmillan), 75–77.
76 Shinn, "Emerging Powers."
77 Sergei DeSilva-Ranasinghe, "Why the Indian Ocean Matters," *The Diplomat*, 2 March 2011.
78 Michael J. Green & Andrew Shearer, 2012, "Defining U.S. Indian Ocean Strategy," *Washington Quarterly*, 35:2, 117.
79 For a detailed strategic analysis of the Indian Ocean region see Anthony Cordesman & Abdullah Toucan, *The Indian Ocean Region: A Strategic Net Assessment*, Center for Strategic and International Studies, April 1, 2014.
80 Jonathan Eyal, "Commonality, Competition between China and India," *Straits Times*, 25 September 2014.
81 "Transnational Organized Crime in Eastern Africa: A Threat Assessment," UN Office on Drugs and Crime, September 2013.
82 Freedom C. Onuoha, 2012, "Oil Piracy in the Gulf of Guinea," *Conflict Trends*, 4, 29.
83 "Somali Pirate Clampdown Caused Drop in Global Piracy IMB Reveals," International Chamber of Commerce Commercial Crime Services, 15 January 2014.
84 "Nigeria," *Analysis*, U.S. Energy Information Administration, 30 December 2013, available at www.eia.gov/country/cab.cfm?fips=NI
85 "The Gulf of Guinea: The New Danger Zone," International Crisis Group Africa Report 195, 12 December 2012, 9–10.
86 Abdel-Fatau Musah, "West Africa: Governance and Security in a Changing Region," Africa Program Working Paper Series, International Institute of Peace, February 2009, 2.

87 Kamal-Deen Ali & Martin Tsamenyi, 2013, "Fault Lines in Maritime Security," *African Security Review*, 103.

88 Musah, "West Africa," 2.

89 Max Hoffman & Conor Lane, "Guinea-Bissau and the South Atlantic Cocaine Trade," Center for American Progress, 22 August 2013, 2–4, available at http://www.americanprogress.org/issues/security/report/2013/08/22/72557/guinea-bissau-and-the-south-atlantic-cocaine-trade

90 See Davin O'Ragan, "The Evolving Drug Trade in Guinea-Bissau and West Africa," International Relations and Security Network, Swiss Federal Institute of Technology Zurich, available at www.isn.ethz.ch/Digital-Library/Articles/Detail/?lng=en&id=182200

91 Kwesi Aning & John Pokoo, 2014, "Understanding the Nature and Threats of Drug Trafficking to National and Regional Security in West Africa," *Stability: International Journal of Security and Development*, 3:1, 1–2.

92 Musah, "West Africa," 3.

93 Wolfram Lacher, "Organized Crime and Conflict in the Sahel-Sahara Region," *The Carnegie Papers*, Carnegie Endowment, September 2012, 3, 11–17.

94 Musah, "West Africa," 3–4.

95 "Quadrennial Defense Review 2014," U.S. Department of Defense, 8, available at www.defense.gov/pubs/2014_Quadrennial_Defense_Review.pdf

96 Coral Davenport, "Climate Change Deemed Growing Threat by Military Researchers," *New York Times*, 13 May 2014.

97 "Generation 2030 Africa, Executive Summary," UNICEF Division of Data, Research, and Policy, 7.

98 "Sustaining U.S. Global Leadership: Priorities for 21st Century Defense," Department of Defense, January 2012, 1, 4.

99 Bruce W. Jentleson, 2014, "Strategic Recalibration: Framework for a 21st Century National Security Strategy," *Washington Quarterly*, 37:1, 118–120.

100 Melvyn P. Leffler, 2011, "9/11 in Retrospect: George W. Bush's Grand Strategy, Reconsidered," *Foreign Affairs*, 90:5, 35.

101 Ernesto Londono, "Study: Iraq, Afghan War Costs to Top $4 Trillion," *Washington Post*, 28 March 2013.

102 Harry Stein, 2015, "Congress Passed a Budget Deal. Now What?" Center for American Progress, November 2, 2015, available at www.americanprogress.org/issues/budget/news/2015/11/02/124733/congress-passed-a-budget-deal-now-what

103 "Quadrennial Defense Review 2014, Executive Summary," U.S. Department of Defense, iv–v, available at www.defense.gov/pubs/2014_Quadrennial_Defense_Review.pdf

104 "Setting Priorities for American Leadership: New National Security Strategy for the United States," Project for a United and Strong America, March 2013, 9–11.

105 Michelle Tan, "Army Unveils New Plan to 'Win in a Complex World'" *Army Times*, 13 October 2014.

106 Rosa Brooks, 2014, "Portrait of the Army as a Work in Progress," *Foreign Policy*, May/June 2014, 44–45.

107 Kimberly Field, James Learmont, & Jason Charland, 2013, "Regionally Aligned Forces: Business Not as Usual," *Parameters*, 43.3 (Autumn).

108 "Sustaining U.S. Global Leadership: Priorities for 21st Century Defense," 2–3, available at www.defense.gov/news/defense_strategic_guidance.pdf

109 "Sustaining U.S. Global Leadership," 6.

Conclusion
A New Approach to Security in Africa?

Africa's increasing strategic importance highlights the many security challenges on the continent. In many ways, Africa is the world's last best place, with its abundance of natural resources and its growing market driven by urbanization, population growth, and the recent record of economic success. But in several states, weak institutions, low levels of development, conflict, instability, and extremism continue to threaten the security crucial to further improving the living conditions of the population. Africa's complicated security environment involves the nature of the state and patterns of politics and intersects with shifting conceptions of security and the exigencies of complex conflicts with regional and international dimensions. U.S.-African security cooperation is at the nexus of a debate over both the security-development challenge and the response to extremism. Growing U.S. security cooperation on the continent, especially the creation of AFRICOM, has generated considerable discussion of U.S. policy. U.S.-African security cooperation is a complicated policy, doctrine, practice, perspective, and political puzzle.

Africa's Patterns of Politics and Security

Political patterns have a significant impact on African security. In 2014, only one of the forty-four African countries listed in the 2014 Economist Intelligence Unit's index of democracy was classified as a full democracy, while there were eight flawed democracies, fourteen hybrid regimes, and twenty-two authoritarian regimes. The region's democracy index average between 2006 and 2014 changed very little, with a slight drop between 2013 and 2014. Africa's average is the second lowest in the world, behind only the Middle East and North Africa.[1]

Several African states are not only undemocratic, they are fragile. According to the 2015 Fragile States Index, the top four and nineteen of the twenty-five most fragile states are African countries. Among the components that make up the rankings, Africa's low scores on the political and military indicators are indicative of the continent's security challenges. These categories of the index include measures of state legitimacy, provision of public services, human rights and rule of law, the security apparatus, and factionalization of elites.[2] These fragile states also have neither full control of their territory nor a monopoly on the legitimate use of force.[3] To compound problems, Africa's fragile states' boundaries rarely correspond to community boundaries with which citizens identify, leading to greater identification along ethnic than national lines.[4] In Africa's weak and fragile states, institutions and administration are inefficient and often corrupt, have little legitimacy, lack the resources to provide public goods for all its citizens, and are frequently fragmented along ethnic or communal lines. Africa's weak, fragile, and undemocratic states are regional and international security concerns and pose a particular challenge to U.S. security policy.

African armed forces are the critical interface in U.S. security partnerships. The armed forces are essential to security, but African militaries lack the capabilities to confront complex security threats, and all too often African armed forces themselves have been a major source of state and individual insecurity. Because the major challenges to African states are internal, the armed forces have become an important player in African politics. The combination of Africa's artificial borders and incomplete or ineffective nation building has encouraged ethnic and communal tensions that fuel conflict while patronage and neopatrimonial relations exacerbate tensions over the distribution of public goods. These tensions may prompt a challenge to the government and draw the armed forces into the fray. In that case, the primary objective in many states is regime preservation, and the armed forces are frequently configured for that purpose, not state security. Dysfunctional civil-military relations compound the problems. Africa's record of coups and countercoups, the use of the armed forces to suppress challenges to existing regimes, and a disturbing tendency toward human rights abuses undermine the effectiveness of the armed forces and complicate U.S. security cooperation.

Africa's politics have had an impact on the armed forces' professionalism and propensity to intervene in politics. The widespread existence of neopatrimonialism, which consists of personal networks embedded in formal government structures, has encouraged personal rule, patronage, institutional weakness, a politicized bureaucracy, and corruption.[5] These factors have had an impact on the armed forces. Neopatrimonialism's patronage networks may extend to the military, where they undermine capacity and cohesiveness. Patronage relationships may also encourage coups. Guinea's 2008 coup was in part the result of junior officers at the bottom of patronage networks seeking to alter the arrangements that favored senior officers under President Conte. In multiethnic societies, as one faction gains at the expense of others, coups can be an attractive way to rearrange power relationships. Coups also represent a route for the armed forces to access more resources.[6]

Despite a clear regional and international rejection of coups, political instability continues to prompt military intervention into politics. In yet another example that coups are still a feature of African politics, Burkina Faso was plunged into crisis during 2014–2015, when civil unrest ousted President Blaise Campaore, who had sought to extend his twenty-seven years in power.

The armed forces initially announced that they were assuming power, but pressure from ECOWAS and the AU soon forced the military to accept a civilian-led transitional government. However, in September 2015, with elections only a few weeks away, troops from Campaore's presidential guard, the RSP, carried out a brief coup. Regional and international condemnation was quick, with Burkina Faso suspended from the AU and threatened with sanctions. That rebuke, combined with the threat of a showdown between the RSP and regular army troops, forced the head of the presidential guard to step down and reinstate the transitional government. Not only does this demonstrate the military's political role; it also illustrates the potential for splits between units whose function is to protect the president and regular army troops. Demands that the RSP be integrated into the regular army played a role in the short-lived 2015 coup.[7] In the absence of democratic civil-military relations and military professionalism, political, corporate, and personal motives for intervention cannot be excluded. The potential for future coups will continue to be influenced by the state's political dynamics.

Africa's Conflicts

Africa has long been one of the most conflict-prone regions of the world. The Armed Conflict Location and Event Data (ACLED) Project database shows an increase in the number of organized armed-conflict events in Africa, which rose to 10,174 in 2014 from 8,379 in 2013. The majority of the violence spread in a band across Africa from the Sahel to the Horn and extended south to the CAR and the DRC.[8] Since 2013, political militias, defined as militant groups that use violence to alter the existing political system but do not seek to overthrow the government, have been the most active. In 2014, militias reached their highest levels of activity since ALCED began keeping records. Their targets are increasingly civilians, and they accounted for more than 8,800 civilian deaths in 2014, almost double the number for 2013. Militia attacks against government forces declined by about 8% from 2013. Governments are the second most active force in perpetrating political violence.[9] More than 34% of all conflict-related fatalities in 2014 involved civilians, and there were four thousand more civilian fatalities in that year than in 2013. Attacks by political militias that targeted civilians largely accounted for this increase.[10]

Africa's conflicts reflect the prevalence of intrastate conflict based on ethnic and communal tensions, patterns of African politics, transnational threats, and terrorism. Africa's conflicts also reflect the concepts of fourth-generation warfare characterized by political and social networks and the protracted duration of conflicts, and are the antithesis of the high-technology, short wars the DOD would prefer to fight.[11] The evolving nature of war requires viable strategies for fighting these new wars lest they continue to spread.[12]

Despite these new forms of warfare, spending on conventional military components continues. SIPRI reported that military spending in Africa grew by

8.3% in 2013, and two out of three African countries increased spending over the previous decade. As a whole, the continent increased military spending by 65% after fifteen years of stagnation. Purchases included tanks and fighter jets, and there was speculation that the purchases had been prompted by revenues from higher commodity prices, the desire for prestigious weapons systems, or were seen by corrupt officials as a way to skim profits off of the deals. State fragility creates concern not only about corruption but also that weapons could fall into the wrong hands as they did after the fall of Qaddafi in Libya.[13]

Obviously terrorism is a global challenge, and Africa has felt its effects. Using data from the Lawson Terrorism Information Center, Bangura and Tate listed some 550 terrorist incidents in Africa between 1998 and 2007, with 4,525 fatalities.[14] That averaged out to just over five hundred deaths per year attributable to terrorist activity. There was a sharp increase in terrorist attacks in sub-Saharan Africa beginning in about 2010, with close to 2,400 incidents by 2014 and a corresponding increase in fatalities. A majority of these attacks were carried out by the Islamic extremist groups Boko Haram and al Shabaab.[15] While critics have suggested that the increase is connected to an increased U.S. presence in the region,[16] it is also likely that Boko Haram became emboldened by its string of successes in capturing territory and that al Shabaab's loss of territory has caused it to shift its tactics in favor of terrorist attacks. Regional successes against Boko Haram now seem to have produced a similar dynamic toward more indiscriminate terrorist attacks. While deaths from terrorist attacks are a growing threat, as evidenced by the hotel attacks in Mali and Burkina Faso, the number of deaths from terrorist attacks is lower than the number caused by a wide variety of other security threats.

While the threat of terrorism has grown considerably, the continent's widespread poverty, disease, deprivation, environmental degradation, and lagging development clearly indicate that Africa faces challenges that affect more citizens than terrorism. Paul Collier asserts that poverty, economic stagnation, and dependence on the export of primary products correlate with conflict and insecurity.[17] Primary production made up 64.3% of Africa's exports in 2011.[18] He also suggests that the potential for conflict rises when there is a large population of young men, increasingly disillusioned due to poverty and low economic-growth rates, who make a ready pool of recruits for rebel movements and terrorist organizations.[19] With slightly less than half of Africa's population under the age of twenty in 2014, it is unlikely that the pool will dry up soon, particularly in the absence of a concerted effort to promote security and development.

Africa's conflicts have a well-documented tendency to spill across borders and create regional security threats. The regionalism of African conflicts also illustrates the role of networks that profit from conflict and highlights the connection between fighting at the local level and its connection to the global economy. From blood diamonds in Sierra Leone to coltan extraction in the DRC to the illegal timber trade in the CAR, the illicit exploitation of natural resources has helped to perpetuate conflicts across the continent. A 2015 report by Global Witness detailed the extent to which logging has contributed to the fighting in the CAR. Pointing specifically to Europe's contribution to prolonging the conflict, the report charged that European companies paid rebels in the CAR to continue logging illegally, that European markets were a prime destination for illegal timber, and that aid and timber contracts were not promoting development but fueling the fighting.[20]

Other forms of crime continue to contribute to insecurity. Networks extending from West Africa to the Horn and from North Africa to the Gulf of Guinea provide the conduit for human trafficking, drug, and weapons smuggling. Drug cartels and criminal syndicates use commercial airliners, fishing vessels, and container ships to move contraband such as drugs, people, small arms, crude oil, cigarettes, counterfeit medicines, and toxic waste through the region. The UN Office on Drugs and Crime estimates that terrorist financing, drugs, arms, human trafficking, and other criminal activity generate about $3.34 billion per year.[21]

Criminal activity is undermining the growth in fast-growing African economies, increasing vulnerabilities, and adding to insecurity and instability. Illicit markets are growing across the continent to meet the demand for arms, counterfeit goods, cigarettes, diamonds and other precious minerals, wildlife, stolen luxury vehicles, and other illegal goods. This illicit trade is feeding destabilization across West Africa, the Sahel, and the Maghreb.[22] Citing the testimony of James Clapper, Director of National Intelligence, before the Senate Select Committee on Intelligence, David M. Luna, the Director of Programs, Bureau of International Narcotics and Law Enforcement Affairs at the State Department, pointed to the emergence of extremists and rebels that African governments lack the capacity or the will to confront. The youth bulge in the region is likely to result in unfulfilled economic expectations, frustration, increase conflict over land and water, strengthen criminal networks, undermine political and economic stability, hamper development, and affect continent's ability to absorb foreign assistance to improve the stability and security that make it harder for terrorists to operate.[23]

Africa's conflicts are unlikely to subside until the local-global dimension of these conflicts is addressed. The trade in conflict resources helps to perpetuate the fighting in the CAR and the DRC, much as the conflict diamond trade did in Sierra Leone's civil war. The Kimberley Process, developed to certify diamonds as conflict free, and the Extractive Industries Transparency Initiative, which seeks to encourage openness about raw-materials production, are among the efforts to reduce the corruption and the conflict that too frequently accompany resource extraction. Provisions of the U.S. Dodd-Frank legislation are also intended to reduce the flow of conflict minerals. While these initiatives demonstrate acknowledgment of the problem, their impact has been uneven, and more needs to be done to break the links between illegal extraction and global resource markets.

U.S. Policy and AFRICOM

Given Africa's growing strategic importance and the wide range of security threats throughout the region, the consolidation of American military responsibility for Africa made sense. The creation of AFRICOM, in 2007, not only consolidated responsibility for the continent in one regional combatant command but also focused more broadly on Africa's security challenges. AFRICOM marked a departure for the U.S. armed forces and signified acknowledgment of the connection between security and development and the influence of a human security perspective. The creation of AFRICOM and the inclusion of the State Department and USAID along with other U.S. government stakeholders reflect the understanding that security is not exclusively a military responsibility and that a holistic approach that recognizes the connection between security and development and reflects a human security perspective is essential to security in Africa. After the September 11 attacks, the recognition that state weakness and low levels of development were contributing factors in the spread of terrorism led to the emphasis on a whole-of-government approach linking AFRICOM to the State Department, USAID, and other government stakeholders in an effort to address the root causes of terrorist activity and to provide better coordination of policy. Recognition of the link between security and development has increased the importance of the human security perspective and its relevance to U.S. security policy.

In June 2012, the Obama administration released "U.S. Strategy toward Sub-Saharan Africa." The document was an effort to address the criticism that the U.S. lacked a clear strategic vision for the continent. Recognizing Africa's strategic importance, it outlined the four pillars of U.S. strategy, including strengthening democratic institutions; spurring economic growth, trade and investment; advancing peace and security; and promoting opportunity and development. It also noted the importance of democratic institutions in mitigating conflict, countering transnational threats, and strengthening American partners.[24] Although short on details, it identified the primary American goals and provided at least an outline for policy. The U.S. security footprint in Africa remains focused on building capacity, and the modest funding levels for AFRICOM have remained relatively flat since its establishment. The U.S. military's budget for AFRICOM peaked at $273.7 million in 2010 and then declined to $261.6 million in 2014; the 2015 request was $244.5 million.[25] That amounts to slightly less than the cost of two of the military's newest, most advanced model F-35 fighter jets. Even if one were to be able to accurately total all the security assistance, intelligence, and contingency expenditures by the military services in support of their operations on the continent, the figure would still not exceed the $7.5 billion in humanitarian and development aid that went to Africa in 2015.[26]

According to AFRICOM commander General David Rodriguez in the 2015 AFRICOM Posture Statement, in Fiscal Year 2014 the command conducted 68 operations, 11 major joint exercises, and 595 security cooperation exercises.

In comparison, in 2013 AFRICOM conducted 55 operations, 10 major joint exercises, and 481 security cooperation activities. Requirements are expanding faster than resources are increasing.[27] Beyond that, in support of operational training, the Africa Center for Strategic Studies provides a wide range of training on security-sector governance and civil-military relations for African military personnel. As AFRICOM has ramped up its operations, observers have referred to America's "pivot" to Africa.[28] There is little question that American security engagement has accelerated. It has also become more accepted, even if modestly funded.

Despite the disastrous launch of AFRICOM, evidence indicates that opposition to AFRICOM among African states has diminished as engagement has expanded. By 2015, there were thirty-four U.S. Offices of Security Cooperation to coordinate DOD programs in partner countries across the continent. There are also "small U.S. advisory teams embedded in allied partner strategic, operational, and tactical headquarters to support programs and build confidence and trust."[29] Just prior to the U.S.-Africa summit in 2014, the Obama administration also proposed the Security Governance Initiative, an aid program to help combat extremism and provide a more secure environment for U.S. investment. In addition, the U.S. has access to eleven Cooperative Security Locations (CSLs) throughout the region. These so-called lily pads are designed to provide supply and staging facilities for U.S. troops. Particularly in the aftermath of the 2012 deaths of the U.S. ambassador to Libya, Christopher Stevens, and his security detail, the goal is to position these facilities so as to make hot spots across the region accessible within four hours.[30]

Despite the skepticism over the creation of AFRICOM, a 2013 Pew Foundation survey of selected African countries found very positive approval ratings for the U.S. in Ghana (83%), Senegal (81%), Kenya (81%), Uganda (73%), South Africa (72%), and Nigeria (69%).[31] Prior to Obama's 2015 trip to Africa, a Pew Center review of recent surveys found that the U.S. received more favorable ratings in Africa than in any other region of the world. Opinion surveys found that Obama was highly popular and that Africans embraced key elements of American soft power, and a majority thought American aid was having a positive impact.[32] These views position the U.S. to expand positive relations with Africa through important health initiatives such the anti-HIV program PEPFAR and the response to the Ebola crisis, as well as through American economic, governance, and humanitarian programs. The danger is that an increasing military presence and the focus on counterterrorism will reinforce perceptions of the militarization of U.S. policy and overshadow aid programs, despite the fact that the bulk of U.S. foreign assistance goes to those programs.[33]

To realize the benefits of positive views, the U.S. military footprint must remain small enough not to call into question U.S. motives and reinforce neocolonialist perceptions. Given the U.S. support for undemocratic regimes during the Cold War, it is important to avoid connections to authoritarian regimes and maintain a strong commitment to human rights. U.S. policy on these fronts has an uneven record. As Jessica Piombo pointed out, "Washington has a consistent record of backing governments that support U.S. strategic, economic, or military interests, regardless of the governments' domestic or regional behavior."[34] American policy continues to rely on certain regional powers. Major U.S. partners include Ethiopia, Kenya, Uganda, and Nigeria, all of which have questionable democratic and human rights credentials. Support for these countries is not necessarily axiomatic, however. Tensions between the U.S. and Nigeria regarding U.S. support for the fight against Boko Haram revolved around U.S. refusal to provide training and equipment to Nigerian troops found to have engaged in abuses. It is not just human rights abuses that are a concern. American trained troops in Mali defected to the extremist side, and the colonel who came to power in the coup was a recipient of U.S. training. The leader of Burkina Faso's brief 2014 coup had also received U.S. training.[35] The leader of Burkina Faso's 2015 coup was Campaore's former chief of staff, General Gilbert Diendere, who stepped down from the leadership of the RSP in 2014 and who had reportedly participated in counterterrorism exercises with U.S. troops.[36]

In recognition of the economic-development dimension of security, the Obama administration focused more intently on economic infrastructure with the 2013 Power Africa initiative, designed to expand Africa's electrical grid. Power Africa is supposed to increase U.S. investment in the power infrastructure to make Africa more attractive to U.S. investors, encourage industrialization, and diversify individual countries' economies. The summit of African leaders in Washington in 2014 and the president's trip to Africa in July 2015, during which he attended the Global Entrepreneurship Summit, were also designed to encourage more investment in Africa. Just before the president's departure for Africa, the Africa Growth and Opportunity Act, which allows African goods duty-free access to American markets, was reauthorized for an additional ten years. While these initiatives reinforced the impression that the U.S. was trying to challenge the Chinese, the fact is that U.S. investment is unlikely to challenge Chinese investments on the continent. African markets are not large enough to attract American investment, infrastructure is weak, and conflict and instability make investors wary. Obama's initiatives are broadly in alignment with the goals of promoting investment, boosting economic growth, and increasing emphasis on transparency and accountability. The initiatives also reflect the differing perspectives of the U.S. and Africa on the most important policy objectives. According to a report by the Center for Global Leadership, while the U.S. targets funding toward health and education, Africans emphasize jobs, the economy, and infrastructure as the top priorities.[37]

African Regional Security Architecture

There is also a growing African security architecture across the continent involving the AU and subregional organizations. Although African peacekeeping missions still require significant external funding and logistical help, if African countries' capability becomes more fully developed they will be in a more advantageous position to be an effective security partner and better able to take advantage of U.S. training and security assistance to meet their security challenges. As Paul Williams has noted, Africa has developed a complex set of overlapping security institutions at the subregional and regional levels. Although there may be coordination problems and differences in priorities, building institutions that emphasize democracy and the rule of law is a crucial part of changing security dynamics in the region.[38] Regional cooperation encourages contributions from the U.S. and the West to address Africa's conflicts while also building African military capacity and increasing African countries' ownership of their own security. African countries have realized that conflict and instability require a regional approach, and this has contributed to greater cooperation, while Western countries have recognized the importance of contributing to African efforts to deal with challenges posed by the region's ungoverned spaces.[39] The AU's Peace and Security Council authorizes regional peacekeeping missions and since its inception, in 2004, has authorized the deployment of more than sixty thousand peacekeeping troops across the continent. Deployments continue to rely on outside contributions as the AU member states contribute only 2.3% of the operating budget. The results of AU peacekeeping missions have been mixed. The missions in Liberia and Sierra Leone in the 1990s were considered successful, while more recent operations have been less successful in providing stability. Peacekeepers have also been criticized for failing to protect civilians and committing human rights abuses.[40]

As part of the African Peace and Security Architecture, the AU proposed the African Standby Force in 2003. A rapid-response force made up of troops organized into regional brigades, the creation of this force was delayed several times. Because of the delay in getting the ASF off the ground, the AU Assembly authorized the formation of the African Capacity for Immediate Response to Crises (ACIRC) to provide a rapid-response capability until the ASF became operational. Amani Africa II, a training exercise that finally inaugurated the ASF and also included the ACIRC, took place in October 2015. The exercise was meant to determine the readiness of the forces, but it remained uncertain if and how these two forces will be merged.[41]

Human security has clearly been securitized in Africa. African regional organizations have embraced a human security agenda, as evidenced in documents and policy statements. While these developments have shifted the focus toward this perspective, it is unclear how this concept can be operationalized, especially in the face of lagging capability and inadequate resources.

The U.S. is also cooperating with regional organizations. Since 2005, the U.S. has had a representative for peace and security at the AU and has supported both AU and UN peacekeeping operations on the continent, providing funding and training for African peacekeepers. Between 2009 and 2014, the U.S. provided more than $890 million in support of African peacekeeping and related institutions. At the 2014 African leaders summit, the administration announced the African Peacekeeping Rapid Response Partnership, a $110 million-per-year program over three to five years to build a rapid-peacekeeping-deployment capability. DOD also provides training on interoperability for complex operations and works to strengthen the ASF for its eventual deployment. The U.S. also supplies equipment for African peacekeeping forces in Somalia and the CAR.[42]

The Geostrategic Dimension

Although countering violent extremism is the primary focus of U.S. policy, there is clearly much more at stake in the push for greater African security. There is considerable debate over U.S. national security strategy in the post-Iraq and -Afghanistan era. Some speculate that China's "peaceful rise" will result in strategic competition between the U.S. and China. Africa has already been identified as an arena for this competition. Others point out that the U.S. does not necessarily see China as a strategic competitor in Africa. The Chinese are pursuing trade and investment opportunities and securing access to raw materials, just as others are trying to do. As President Obama acknowledged during his 2015 trip to Africa, their infrastructure construction not only is good for Africa but increases the attractiveness of investment for other countries. On the other hand, the Chinese are suspicious that U.S. security activities on the continent are an attempt to thwart their influence.[43] While China sees Africa's security in relation to access to oil and minerals and will continue to engage in military cooperation particularly with those states that supply it, Sino-African relations also demonstrate China's effort to increase its soft power.[44] China's soft-power resources include trade and investment, which have had a powerful impact on the continent's economic growth as well as providing an alternative development strategy that appeals to autocratic leaders. Although Chinese soft power falls short with respect to cultural influence, it is trying to play catch-up by creating cultural centers and offering Chinese-language instruction. While its authoritarian model may be attractive to Africa's autocrats, the West's emphasis on transparency and accountability resonates with African civil society organizations and human rights campaigners. Moreover, American cultural influences are much more attractive to Africans.

China's expanding power projection capabilities are also a reason to see Africa in geostrategic terms. Currently U.S. air and sea power, in conjunction with regional partnerships, play a major role in securing Persian Gulf oil exports and ensuring maritime security. The U.S. remains vitally important in the region and gives the Middle East and Asia high priority in its security strategy. The American role in the Indian Ocean will depend on whether the U.S. will continue to deploy its forces in an effort to maintain its influence or whether growing domestic energy production will result in a reduced U.S. presence. Some observers speculate that the American commitment will decrease because of a decline in U.S. energy imports, the pivot to Asia, and the impact of sequestration and budget cuts.[45] Forming the western littoral of the Indian Ocean, East Africa has a potentially important role in securing maritime commerce and U.S. power projection. Although, with the exception of

South Africa, countries along the coast have very limited coastal protection and seaward projection capability, they may provide important port and supply facilities for the U.S. Coastal states are sharing the same rapid population growth as the rest of the region and this creates economic and governance pressures and the need for education, job creation, and infrastructure development.[46] A 2013 draft of the U.S. National Security Strategy identified defense of critical waterways through which global oil supplies travel as an objective. According to the draft document, the U.S. must be prepared to defend strategic points that may not be essential to ensuring domestic oil supplies but that could have an impact on worldwide oil supplies if threatened.[47] Political stability and the development of sustained U.S. partnerships with African coastal states will be part of the American strategy to protect sea lanes in the Indian Ocean, around the tip of Africa, and in the Gulf of Guinea.

A Complicated Policy Arena

Africa represents a particular challenge to the U.S. security agenda. The U.S. is increasingly engaged in a multidimensional African regional security environment in which it provides support for preventing conflicts, improving stability, providing peacekeeping training, increasing human security, and confronting the extremist threat. So far, U.S. policy has had mixed success. More than 250,000 African troops have been trained for peacekeeping under the State Department's ACOTA program, a part of the Global Peace Operations Initiative. Those troops have been deployed to several hot spots on the continent and beyond. U.S. training has helped AMISOM make some progress against al Shabaab in Somalia. African troops have received training on a wide range of tasks, including logistics, medical care, disaster management, and gender mainstreaming in the armed forces. AFRICOM has also engaged in civil-military operations, including development-related activities and functions usually provided by local, regional, and national governments. These operations are part of the effort to shape the security environment and to build capacity.[48] These programs are indicative of a more positive policy direction.

Despite the U.S. emphasis on training programs, doubts about U.S. goals and methods persist.[49] Cooperation with partners whose commitment to democracy, human rights, and military professionalism is tenuous raises questions about the extent to which the U.S. is willing to overlook these deficiencies in pursuit of its larger security goals. Moreover, the expansion of intelligence gathering, drone reconnaissance, and special forces' covert operations on the continent are reminiscent of Cold War intrigue.

The persistence of coups in countries where the U.S. has trained troops is also troubling. Failure to instill the importance of a democratic pattern of civil-military relations raises doubts about the emphasis and effectiveness of training. It also demonstrates that the exigencies of national politics continue to trump reform efforts. It is difficult enough to establish a partnership with militaries that lack equipment and training, let alone with armed forces that are more motivated by political or corporate interests than they are by national security. Although professionalism is a component of U.S. training, the primary emphasis is on enhancing operational capacity, especially in the area of counterterrorism. The counterterrorism priority can produce serious dilemmas. The Leahy Amendment rightly prohibits assistance to states whose armed forces have poor human rights records. Citing this law, the U.S. restricted assistance to Nigeria, creating friction over assistance in the fight against Boko Haram. Nevertheless, the law can be undermined by workarounds. Defense Security Cooperation Agency documents showed that the U.S. was going to ship military equipment to Nigeria anyway. The State Department confirmed that the delivery was pending. However, the equipment is meant to go only to units that are approved recipients.[50] Prior to the dispute with Nigeria, the prohibition on aid to human rights violators drew criticism from some U.S. military commanders, including Admiral William McRaven, who headed the Special Operations Command at the time. These critics said that the law hurts the ability to train African forces to combat extremists. Although the critics said they supported the spirit of the law, they asserted that changes to the law to strengthen its enforcement complicated training.[51] Any effort to undermine the Leahy Amendment would only fuel further skepticism about U.S. intentions.

Mineral resources and geostrategic value remain key components of Africa's importance, but the importance of access to Africa's abundant energy supplies has been eclipsed for the time being by the rapid increase in U.S. domestic energy production and the sharp decline in oil prices amidst excess production worldwide. Demand for Africa's other commodities has also declined as economic growth in China has slipped. Nevertheless, as China increases its ability to project its growing naval power, Africa will become more important to the monitoring of Chinese movements, much as it was to the monitoring of the Soviets during the Cold War. As both the U.S. and China seek greater influence in Africa, their activities also create the perception of strategic competition on the continent, reminiscent of the Cold War. Even if the U.S. is content to let China play the economic role it has been taking on, there are still strategic concerns, and, as China's global power projection capabilities improve, the strategic importance of African coastal regions, especially those bordering the Indian Ocean, will encourage U.S. engagement with the region in order to thwart the expansion of Chinese maritime influence. It is unlikely that a U.S.–Chinese geostrategic power projection rivalry will skip the African continent.

Nevertheless, Africa remains a second-tier policy focus, and this position is unlikely to change, especially given the first-order challenges of growing Chinese military capability and assertiveness in the South China Sea, the civil war in Syria and U.S. bombing campaign against Islamic State forces, continuing fighting in Iraq and Afghanistan, and a resurgent Russia. As a second-tier interest, Africa is also unlikely to get sufficient attention in a highly polarized U.S. political climate immersed in more high-visibility security issues.

In many ways, U.S. security policy toward Africa is both an operational and a conceptual experiment. Since the aftermath of U.S. inaction in Rwanda, U.S.

policy has evolved from that first articulation of "African solutions for African problems," the Africa Crisis Response Force proposed back in 1996. As a result of involvement in Iraq and Afghanistan, U.S. policymakers have come to recognize the importance of stability operations and counterinsurgency. Because large scale operations such as those are unlikely in the future and because the flaws of American policy in Somalia remain fresh, the U.S. has sought ways to promote security partnerships to create more capable African armed forces, enhance U.S. ability to cooperate with those forces to contend with common security threats, and address human security concerns.

While the holistic approach to security is a progressive concept, especially given African political patterns and the characteristics of its conflict zones, it is a difficult policy to implement. Stability operations, Phase Zero, counterterrorism, humanitarian assistance, human security, and the promotion of political and economic development share some common elements, but fitting together the pieces of a multidimensional policy that bridges all those elements, particularly with constrained resources, is a significant challenge. It is especially difficult due to deficiencies in African armed forces' capabilities and U.S. funding levels that leave the civilian component of a holistic approach at huge disadvantage. While the U.S. armed forces are certainly more active across a spectrum of activities in Africa, the perception that the military has the lead stems at least in part from the dearth of civilian development specialists. Further complicating matters, the whole-of-government approach is also inevitably deeply bureaucratic, especially with the array of U.S. stakeholders involved in a broader conception of security.

Problems of policy coordination and implementation do not involve only government actors and African countries. Humanitarian NGOs also operate throughout conflict zones, caring for refugees or providing postconflict assistance. NGOs operate apart from governments, and their impartiality, essential in the conditions under which they work, can be undermined by cooperation with American armed forces. While the military has the logistical expertise and equipment for humanitarian operations, it may lack sufficient knowledge of the local population and culture.[52] Regionally aligned forces (RAFs) may help to counteract the military's unfamiliarity with local culture and conditions in Africa and develop long-term relationships that improve the military's ability to anticipate conflicts and prevent them from escalating. This includes building local relationships and military-to-military links.[53] These goals are in keeping with Phase Zero's emphasis on shaping the security environment. RAFs may also provide greater familiarity with the political patterns that help to account for the low levels of capacity of the armed forces and the ways in which the political circumstances contribute to conflict and instability.

Given the breadth of the policy challenges facing the U.S., it is not surprising that security cooperation with Africa has come under scrutiny. The wide purview of holistic security has suffered from a lack of coherent focus and effective coordination.[54] Improvement in interagency coordination continues to be an obstacle because of the "complexity among interagency organizational structures, cultures, time horizons, funding and staffing levels, operating procedures, and mandates"[55] that define DOS, USAID and DOD. Moreover, although some of the initial goals of the whole-of-government approach have been realized, many of the "developmental and interagency aspects have been scaled back."[56] While the AFRICOM website notes that there are some thirty representatives of other government agencies embedded at AFRICOM headquarters, this representation is well below what was initially anticipated.

There is a strong incentive to get policy right. Saving lives, refining techniques to prevent and resolve conflicts, protecting human rights, encouraging democratic reform, emphasizing military professionalism, promoting development, and fighting extremism are essential to both African and American security. Africa's strategic importance is sure to increase, provided its economy expands to keep pace with its rapid population growth and conflict and instability are reduced. At the same time, there is also a distinct possibility that climate change will sharpen Africa's conflicts, making an effective multidimensional policy response even more essential.

U.S. training reflects the recognition of the relevance of a human security approach. The emphasis on capability, peacekeeping, and humanitarian assistance not only addresses important current problems but may also help to steer the role and mission of African militaries in a new direction. In *The Ultimate Weapon Is No Weapon*, Shannon Beebe and Mary Kaldor advocated "a blending of police, military, and development experts to create an organization along the lines of a civilian protection and development corps," noting that nowhere is this concept more applicable than in Africa.[57] While still retaining the capability to protect the population, such engagement brigades would focus on human security and conflict prevention rather than on traditional war-fighting skills.[58] Along these lines, one provision of the 2008 DRC government's security-sector reform plan suggested the creation of a "development army" that would contribute to reconstruction in postconflict situations, including infrastructure construction as well as agricultural production to provide food for troops.[59] While such a nontraditional shift is not likely to occur any time soon, some of the training activities AFRICOM touts on its website help to steer military roles and missions in that direction. They also coincide with the African emphasis on human security and regional response.

U.S. policy is a patchwork that seeks to weave together the fight against extremism and a holistic, human security–oriented perspective that recognizes the other dimensions of African security. The effort to integrate these diverse policy strands clearly remains a work in progress. It remains to be seen whether U.S. security cooperation with Africa will lead to a more comprehensive, coordinated, and effective U.S. policy toward Africa that combines security and development. Given the circumstances, that is a tall order but fitting the pieces of such a policy together more effectively would best ensure both African and U.S. security interests.

Notes

1 "Democracy Index 2014," The Economist Intelligence Unit, 16–17, at www.eiu. com/public/topical_report.aspx?campaignid=Democracy0115
2 "Fragile States Index 2015," Fund for Peace, available at http://library.fundfor peace.org/fsi15-report
3 "What Does State Fragility Mean?," *Fragile States Index*, Fund for Peace, 2015.
4 Lothar Brock, Hans-Henrik Holm, Georg Sorensen, & Michael Stohl, 2012, *Fragile States* (Malden, MA: Polity Press), 16–17.
5 Pierre Englebert & Kevin C. Dunn, 2013, *Inside African Politics* (Boulder: Lynne Rienner Publishers), 130.
6 Englebert & Dunn, *Inside African Politics*, 153.
7 See "Burkina Faso Coup: Michael Kafando Reinstated as President," *BBC News Africa*, 23 September 2015.
8 "Rates of Violence in 2014," Armed Conflict Locator and Event Data Project, available at www.acleddata.com/rates-of-violence-in-2014/
9 "Agents of Violence in 2014," Armed Conflict Locator and Event Data Project, available at www.acleddata.com/agents-of-violence-in-2014/
10 "Violence against Civilians 2014," Armed Conflict Locator and Event Data Project, available at www.acleddata.com/violence-against-civilians-in-2014/
11 Thomas X. Hammes, 2005, "War Evolves into the Fourth Generation," *Contemporary Security Policy*, 26:2, 190.
12 Martin Van Creveld, 2005, "It Will Continue to Conquer and Spread," *Contemporary Security Policy*, 26:2, 232.
13 "Arms and the African," *The Economist*, 22 November 2014.
14 Abdul Karim Bangura & Billie D. Tate, 2010, "Africa's Responses to International Terrorism and the War against It," in Jack Mangala, ed., *New Security Threats and Crises in Africa Regional and International Perspectives* (New York: Palgrave Macmillan), 59–86.
15 "Sub-Saharan Africa," Global Terrorism Database, available atwww.start.umd. edu/gtd/search/Results.aspx?chart=overtime&casualties_type=&casualties_ max=&region=11
16 See, for instance, Nick Turse, "Tomgram: Nothing Succeeds Like Failure," TomDispatch, 10 September 2015, available at www.tomdispatch.com/
17 See Paul Collier, 2007, *The Bottom Billion: Why the Poorest Countries Are Failing and What Can Be Done about It* (Oxford: Oxford University Press), 18–35.
18 "World Merchandise Exports by Product Group and Region, 2011," *International Trade Statistics*, World Trade Organization, 62, available at www.wto.org/English/ res_e/statis_e/its2012_e/its12_merch_trade_product_e.pdf
19 Collier, *The Bottom Billion*, 20–21.
20 "Blood Timber: How Europe Played a Significant Role in Funding War in the Central African Republic," *Global Witness Report*, July 15, 2015.
21 Remarks by David M. Luna, Director of Anticrime Programs, Bureau of International Narcotics and Law Enforcement Affairs, Department of State, at AFSEC 14, West African Coastal Surveillance and Maritime Security Summit, Casablanca, Morocco, 25–27 February 2014, available at www.state.gov/j/inl/rls/rm/2014/222591.htm
22 Luna, Remarks.
23 Luna, Remarks, 14.
24 "U.S. Strategy toward Sub-Saharan Africa," The White House, June 2012, 2.
25 Gopal Ratnam, "Africa Military Moves by U.S. Reflect Iraq, Afghan Wars," *Bloomberg News*, 1 August 2014.
26 "Africa: Military vs Economic Aid," *Security Assistance Monitor*, available at http://securityassistance.org/africa

27 "United States Africa Command 2015 Posture Statement," available at www.africom.mil

28 See, for instance, Rosa Brooks, 2012, " The Pivot to Africa," Foreign Policy, available at www.foreignpolicy.com/articles/2012/08/16/the_pivot_to_africa; Hilary Matfess, 2013, "Are We Pivoting to Africa Rather Than Asia?," *The Atlantic*, available at www.theatlantic.com/international/ /print/2013/10/are-we-pivoting-to africa-rather-than asia

29 Statement of AFRICOM Commander General David Rodriguez before the House Appropriations Committee, Subcommittee on Defense, March 3, 2015, 12.

30 John Vandiver, "Staging Sites Enable AFRICOM to Reach Hot Spots 'within 4 Hours,' Leader Says," *Stars and Stripes*, 8 May 2015.

31 "Attitudes towards the United States," *America's Global Image Remains More Positive Than China's*, Pew Research Center, 18 July 2013, 8.

32 Richard Wike, "Five Charts on America's (Very Positive) Image in Africa," *Fact Tank: News in the Numbers*, Pew Foundation, 23 July 2015.

33 Jessica Piombo, 2012, "U.S. Africa Policy: Rhetoric versus Reality," *Current History*, 11:745 (May).

34 Piombo, "U.S. Africa Policy," 194.

35 Craig Whitlock, "Coup Leader in Burkina Faso Had Received U.S. Military Training," *Washington Post*, 3 November 2014.

36 Colby Goodman, "Post-coup Leader in Burkina Faso Helped Steer U.S. Military Exercises," *Security Assistance Monitor*, 18 September 2015.

37 Quoted in Jonathan Grieg, "News Analysis: Fixing Mismatch between US Aid Policy and Africa's Needs," *Business Day*, 17 December 2013, available at www.bdlive.co.za/africa/africannews/2013/12/17/news-analysis-fixing-mismatch-between-us-aid-policy-and-africas-needs

38 Paul D. Williams, 2007, "Thinking about Security in Africa," *International Affairs*, 83:6, 1037.

39 Greg Mills, 2012, "The Regionalization of African Security," *Current History*, 111:745 (May), 175–176.

40 Danielle Renwick, "Peace Operations in Africa," *Council on Foreign Relations Backgrounder*, 15 May 2015.

41 Peter Fabricius, "Standing By or Standing Up: Is the African Standby Force Nearly Ready for Action?," *ISS Today*, 23 July 2015, available at www.issafrica.org/iss-today/standing-by-or-standing-up-is-the-african-standby-force-nearly-ready-for-action

42 "Fact Sheet: U.S. Support for Peacekeeping in Africa," The White House, Office of the Press Secretary, 6 August 2014.

43 Larry Hanover & Lyle J. Morris, 2014, *Chinese Engagement in Africa: Drivers, Reactions, and Implications for U.S. Policy* (Santa Monica, CA: Rand Corporation), 102–104.

44 Shinn, "Military and Security Relations,"183.

45 Anthony Cordesman & Abdullah Toucan, *The Indian Ocean Region: A Strategic Net Assessment*, Center for Strategic and International Studies, April 1, 2014, vii.

46 Cordesman & Toukan, *The Indian Ocean Region*, viii.

47 "National Security Strategy 2013," Final Draft, 7–8, available at www.utexas.edu/lbj/sites/default/files/file/news/National%20Security%20Strategy%202013%20%28Final%20Draft%29.pdf

48 Maureen Farrell & Jessica Lee, 2015, "Civil-Military Operations in East Africa: Coordinated Approaches," in Jessica Piombo, ed., *The U.S. Military in Africa: Enhancing Security and Development?* (Boulder: FirstForum Press), 104.

49 See, for instance, Nick Turse, 2015, *Tomorrow's Battlefield: U.S. Proxy Wars and Secret Ops in Africa* (Chicago: Haymarket Books).

50 Michel Arseneault, "US Exporting Arms to Nigeria Despite 'Ban'" *RFI(English)*, 14 August 2015.

51 Eric Schmitt, "Military Says Law Barring U.S. Aid to Rights Violators Hurts Training Mission," *New York Times*, 20 June 2013.
52 Jessica Piombo, "Evolving Civilian and Military Missions," in Jessica Piombo, ed., *The U.S. Military in Africa: Enhancing Security and Development?* (Boulder: First-Forum Press), 55–57.
53 Rosa Brooks, 2014, "Portrait of the Army as a Work in Progress," *Foreign Policy*, May/June 2014, 44.
54 William M. Bellamy, "U.S. Security Engagement in Africa," *Africa Security Brief*, Africa Center for Strategic Studies, No. 1, June 2009; Nicolas Van De Walle, 2009, "U.S. Policy towards Africa: The Bush Legacy and the Obama Administration," *African Affairs*, 109:434, 1–21.
55 Jessica Piombo, 2015, "Pursuing Multidimensional Security," in Jessica Piombo, ed., *The U.S. Military in Africa: Enhancing Security and Development?* (Boulder: FirstForum Press), 226.
56 Piombo, "Pursuing Multidimensional Security," 216.
57 Shannon D. Beebe & Mary Kaldor, 2010, *The Ultimate Weapon Is No Weapon* (New York: Public Affairs), 178.
58 Beebe & Kaldor, *The Ultimate Weapon Is No Weapon*, 179.
59 Henri Boshoff, "Security Sector Reform in the Congo: The Status of Military Reform," *African Security Review*, 17:2, 64.

Bibliography

Achu Check, Nacasius and Thabani Mdlongwa. 2012. "The Hegleg Oil Conflict: An Exercise of Sovereignty or an Act of Aggression?" *Policy Brief* 78. August. Pretoria, South Africa: Africa Institute of South Africa.

Africa Leadership Forum. 1991. *The Kampala Document. Towards a Conference on Security, Stability, Development and Cooperation in Africa.* Accessed October 17, 2015. www.africaleadership.org/rc/the%20kampala%20document.pdf

Africa Research Bulletin. 2002. "Bin Laden's $20m African Blood Diamond Deals." Vol. 39, no. 11 (November): 15093.

Africa Research Bulletin. 2002. "Somali SAMS?" Vol. 39, no. 12 (December): 15134.

African Development Bank Group. 2007. "Africa's Non-Renewable Natural Resources." *African Development Report*: 55–95. Accessed October 21, 2015. www.afdb.org/fileadmin/uploads/afdb/Documents/Publications/(D)%20AfricanBank%202007%20Ch3.pdf

African Development Bank Group. 2012. "Mining Industry Prospects in Africa." December 26. Accessed October 21, 2015. www.afdb.org/en/blogs/afdb-championing-inclusive-growth-across-africa/post/mining-industry-prospects-in-africa-10177

Agger, Kasper. 2013. "Completing the Mission: U.S. Special Forces Are Essential for Ending the LRA." *Enough Project.* October. Washington, DC: Center for American Progress. Accessed October 20, 2015. www.enoughproject.org/files/Completing-The-Mission-US-Special-Forces-Essential-to-Ending-LRA.pdf

Ahmed, Abdel Ghaffar M. 2008. "Multiple Complexity and Prospects for Reconciliation and Unity: Sudan Conundrum." In: *The Roots of African Conflicts. The Causes and Costs*, edited by Alfred Nhema and Paul Tiyambe Zeleza, 71–87. Oxford, UK: James Currey.

Ake, Claude. 1996. *Democracy and Development in Africa.* Washington, DC: The Brookings Institution.

Al Jazeera. 2012. "Congo's M23 Rebels Threaten to Take Goma." July 11. Accessed October 25, 2015. www.aljazeera.com/news/africa/2012/07/2012711172138525791.html

Al Jazeera. 2013. "UN: Over 1,000 Killed in Boko Haram Attacks." December 16. Accessed October 12, 2015. www.aljazeera.com/news/africa/2013/12/un-1224-killed-boko-haram-attacks-20131216175810115265.html

Al Jazeera. 2014. "Nigeria Seals State Border with Cameroon." February 23. Accessed October 16, 2015. www.aljazeera.com/news/africa/2014/02/nigeria-seals-state-border-with-cameroon-2014223154723696322.html

Al Jazeera. 2015. "DR Congo Launches Offensive against FDLR Rebels." February 26. Accessed October 25, 2015. www.aljazeera.com/news/2015/02/dr-congo-offensive-fdlr-rebels-150226021624157.html

Al Jazeera. 2015. "Rebel Leader Gives Ultimatum to South Sudan President." July 8. Accessed October 25, 2015. www.aljazeera.com/news/2015/07/rebel-leader-ultimatum-south-sudan-president-150708124822677.html

Alexander, Paul. 2013. "Fallout From Somalia Still Haunts U.S. Policy 20 Years Later." *Stars and Stripes*. October 3. Accessed October 25, 2015. www.stripes.com/news/fallout-from-somalia-still-haunts-us-policy-20-years-later-1.244957

Ali, Kamal-Deen and Martin Tsamenyi. 2013. "Fault Lines in Maritime Security." *African Security Review* 22, no. 3: 95–110.

Allison, Simon. 2014. "Burkina Faso: Is the Cure More Dangerous Than the Disease?" *The Daily Maverick*. November 04. Accessed October 15, 2015. www.dailymaverick.co.za/article/2014-11-04-burkina-faso-is-the-cure-more-dangerous-than-the-disease

Amin, Mohammed. 2015. "Sudan President Bashir Bags Goodies on China Trip." *The East African*. September 4. Accessed October 25, 2015. www.theeastafrican.co.ke/news/Sudan-President-Bashir-bags-goodies-on-China-trip/-/2558/2858434/-/rtrbtj/-/index.html

Amnesty International. 2014. *Africa: China's Booming Torture Trade Revealed*. September 23. London, UK: Amnesty International Ltd.

Amnesty International. 2015. *Stars on Their Shoulders, Blood on Their Hands. War Crimes Committed by the Nigerian Military. AFR44/1657/2015*. June. London, UK: Amnesty International Ltd.

Aning, Kwesi and John Pokoo. 2014. "Understanding the Nature and Threats of Drug Trafficking to National and Regional Security in West Africa." *Stability: International Journal of Security and Development* 3, no. 1: 1–13.

Armed Conflict Location & Event Data Project. 2015. "Agents of Violence in 2014." Accessed October 22, 2015. www.acleddata.com/agents-of-violence-in-2014/

Armed Conflict Location & Event Data Project. 2015. "Rates of Violence in 2014." Accessed October 22, 2015. www.acleddata.com/rates-of-violence-in-2014/

Armed Conflict Location & Event Data Project. 2015. "Violence against Civilians in 2014." Accessed October 22, 2015. www.acleddata.com/violence-against-civilians-in-2014/

Arseneault, Michel. 2015. "U.S. Exporting Arms to Nigeria despite 'Ban'." *Radio France Internationale*. August 14. Accessed October 25, 2015. www.english.rfi.fr/africa/20150814-us-exporting-arms-nigeria-despite-ban

Associated Press. 2002. "About 1,000 More Americans Headed to Hunt for al-Qaeda in and around Horn of Africa." November 8.

Associated Press. 2002. "Pentagon Creating New Military Command in Djibouti to Monitor Terrorists in the Horn of Africa." November 4.

Ayoob, Mohammed. 1995. *The Third World Security Predicament: State Making, Regional Conflict, and the International System*. Boulder, CO: Lynne Rienner Publishers.

Ayoob, Mohammed. 1997. "Defining Security: A Subaltern Realist Perspective." In: *Critical Security Studies: Concepts and Cases*, edited by Keith Krause and Michael C. Williams, 121–148. Minneapolis, MN: University of Minnesota Press.

Bangura, Abdul Karim and Billie D. Tate. 2010. "Africa's Responses to International Terrorism and the War against It." In: *New Security Threats and Crises in Africa: Regional and International Perspectives*, edited by Jack Mangala, 59–85. New York, NY: Palgrave Macmillan.

BBC News. 2003. "UN Warns of Somalia Terror Link." November 4. Accessed October 18, 2015. http://news.bbc.co.uk/2/hi/africa/3241021.stm

BBC News. 2012. "DR Congo's M23 Rebels Attacked by UN Forces." July 25. Accessed October 17, 2015. www.bbc.co.uk/news/world-africa-18983159

BBC News. 2012. "Nigeria Gunmen Storm Oil Ship-Two Dead, Four Kidnapped." August 4. Accessed October 18, 2015. www.bbc.com/news/world-africa-19127704

BBC News. 2012. "Nigeria's Precarious Oil Amnesty." August 1. Accessed October 18, 2015. www.bbc.com/news/world-africa-19067711

BBC News. 2014. "India's Economic Growth Disappoints." May 30. Accessed October 22, 2015. www.bbc.com/news/business-27638906

BBC News. 2014. "Nigeria Violence: Cameroon Boosts anti-Boko Haram Border Forces." May 27. Accessed October 16, 2015. www.bbc.com/news/world-africa-27593163

BBC News. 2015. "Burkina Faso Coup: Michael Kafando Reinstated as President." September 23. Accessed October 25, 2015. www.bbc.com/news/world-africa-34334430

BBC News. 2015. "Guinea Profile Timeline." October 14. Accessed October 18, 2015. www.bbc.co.uk/news/world-africa-13443183

Beebe, Shannon D. and Mary Kaldor. 2010. *The Ultimate Weapon Is No Weapon: Human Security and the New Rules of War and Peace*. New York, NY: Public Affairs.

Bellamy, William M. 2009. "U.S. Security Engagement in Africa." *Africa Security Brief* 1. June. Washington, DC: Africa Center for Strategic Studies.

Ben Barka, Habiba and Mthuli Ncube. 2012. "Political Fragility in Africa: Are Military Coups d'Etat a Never-Ending Phenomena?" *African Development Economic Briefs*. October 19. Accessed October 15, 2015. www.afdb.org/en/documents/document/economic-brief-political-fragility-in-africa-are-military-coups-detat-a-never-ending-phenomenon-29430/

Berdal, Mats. 2003. "How 'New' Are 'New Wars'? Global Economic Change and the Study of Civil War." *Global Governance* 9: 477–502.

Berman, Eric G. 2004. "Recent Developments in U.S. Peacekeeping Policy and Assistance to Africa." *African Security Review* 13, no. 2: 133–136.

Berschinski, Robert G. 2014. *AFRICOM's Dilemma: The Global War on Terrorism, Capacity Building, Humanitarianism, and the Future of U.S. Security Policy in Africa*. Carlisle, PA: Strategic Studies Institute.

Blunt, Elizabeth. 2004. "U.S. Targets Sahara Militant Threat." *BBC News*. January 14. Accessed October 18, 2015. http://news.bbc.co.uk/2/hi/africa/3397001.stm

Booth, Ken and Peter Vale. 1997. "Critical Security Studies and Regional Insecurity: The Case of Southern Africa." In: *Critical Security Studies: Concepts and Cases*, edited by Keith Krause and Michael C. Williams, 329–358. Minneapolis, MN: University of Minnesota Press.

Boshoff, Henri. 2008. "Security Sector Reform in the Democratic Republic of Congo: The Status of Military Reform." *African Security Review* 17, no. 2: 60–65.

Brock, Lothar, Hans-Henrik Holm, Georg Sorenson, and Michael Stohl. 2012. *Fragile States*. Malden, MA: Polity Press.

Bromley, Mark, Mathieu Duchâtel, and Paul Holtom. 2013. "China's Exports of Small Arms and Light Weapons." *SIPRI Policy Paper* 38. October. Stockholm, Sweden: Stockholm International Peace Research Institute.

Brooks, Rosa. 2012. "The Pivot to Africa." *Foreign Policy*. August 16.

Brooks, Rosa. 2014. "Portrait of the Army as a Work in Progress." *Foreign Policy*. May/June.

Brown, Oli and Alec Crawford. 2009. *Climate Change and Security in Africa*. Winnipeg, Canada: International Institute for Sustainable Development.

Buckley, Chris. 2013. "China's Leader Tries to Calm African Fears of His Country's Economic Power." *New York Times*. March 25. Accessed October 25, 2015. www.nytimes.com/2013/03/26/world/asia/chinese-leader-xi-jinping-offers-africa-assurance-and-aid.html?_r=0

Bugnacki, John. 2015. "Critical Issues Facing Africa: Terrorism, War, and Political Violence." *American Security Project*. January 17. Accessed October 17, 2015. www.americansecurityproject.org/critical-issues-facing-africa-terrorism-war-and-political-violence/

Burgess, Stephen F. 2009. "In the National Interest? Authoritarian Decision-making and the Problematic Creation of US African Command." *Contemporary Security Policy* 30, no. 1: 79–99.

Buzan, Barry. 1983. *People, States, and Fear*. Chapel Hill, NC: The University of North Carolina Press.

Buzan, Barry and Lene Hansen. 2009. *The Evolution of International Security Studies*. Cambridge, UK: Cambridge University Press.

Buzan, Barry and Ole Waever. 2003. *Regions and Powers: The Structure of International Security*. Cambridge, UK: Cambridge University Press.

Campbell, John and Asch Harwood. 2013. "Why a Terrifying Religious Conflict Is Raging in Nigeria." *The Atlantic*. July 10.

Carmody, Pádraig. 2011. *The New Scramble for Africa*. Malden, MA: Polity Press.

Center for International Policy. 2015. "Africa." *Security Assistance Monitor*. Accessed October 22, 2015. http://securityassistance.org/africa

Chaudhury, Dipanjan Roy. 2014. "Global Strategic Move: India Increases Defense Trainings in Asia, Africa, and Latin America." *The Economic Times*. September 5. Accessed October 25, 2015. http://articles.economictimes.indiatimes.com/2014–09–05/news/53602190_1_defence-cooperation-african-countries-myanmar

Chazan, Naomi, Peter Lewis, Robert Mortimer, Donald Rothchild and Stephen John Stedman. 1999. *Politics and Society in Contemporary Africa*, 3rd ed. Boulder, CO: Lynne Rienner Publishers.

Chivvis, Christopher S. and Andrew Liepman. 2013. *North Africa's Menace: AQIM's Evolution and the U.S. Policy Response*. Santa Monica, CA: RAND Corporation.

Chothia, Farouk. 2011. "Could Somali Famine Deal a Fatal Blow to al-Shabab?" *BBC News*. August 9. Accessed October 19, 2015. www.bbc.com/news/world-africa-14373264

Clapham, Christopher, ed. 1998. *African Guerrillas*. Bloomington, IN: Indiana University Press.

Clapham, Christopher. 1998. "Degrees of Statehood." *Review of International Studies* 24, no. 2 (April): 143–157.

Cody, Edward. 2012. "In Mali, an Islamist Extremist Haven Takes Shape." *Washington Post*. June 7. Accessed October 25, 2015. www.washingtonpost.com/world/africa/in-mali-an-islamic-extremist-haven-takes-shape/2012/06/06/gJQAIKNlKV_story.html

Collier, Paul. 2000. "Doing Well Out of War: An Economic Perspective." In: *Greed and Grievance: Economic Agendas in Civil Wars*, edited by Mats Berdal and David M. Malone, 91–112. Boulder, CO: Lynne Rienner Publishers.

Collier, Paul. 2007. *The Bottom Billion: Why the Poorest Countries Are Failing and What Can Be Done about It*. Oxford, UK: Oxford University Press.

Combined Joint Task Force Horn of Africa. 2015. *CJTF-HOA Factsheet.* Accessed October 18, 2015. www.hoa.africom.mil

Copnall, James. 2012. "Sudan Mobilises Army over Seizure of Oilfield by South Sudan." *The Guardian.* April 11. Accessed October 25, 2015. www.theguardian.com/world/2012/apr/11/sudan-south-border-war-crisis

Copnall, James. 2013. "Darfur Conflict: Sudan's Bloody Stalemate." *BBC News.* April 29. Accessed October 25, 2015. www.bbc.com/news/world-africa-22336600

Cordesman, Anthony H. and Abdullah Toukan. 2014. *The Indian Ocean Region: A Strategic Net Assessment.* Washington, DC: Center for Strategic and International Studies.

Crocker, Chester A. 1992. *High Noon in Southern Africa: Making Peace in a Rough Neighborhood.* New York, NY: W. W. Norton & Company.

Cumming-Bruce, Nick. 2014. "UN Warns of Anti-Muslim Violence in Central African Republic." *New York Times.* March 20. Accessed October 18, 2015. www.nytimes.com/2014/03/21/world/africa/un-central-african-republic.html

Davenport, Coral. 2014. "Climate Change Deemed Growing Security Threat by Military Researchers." *New York Times.* May 13. Accessed October 25, 2015. www.nytimes.com/2014/05/14/us/politics/climate-change-deemed-growing-security-threat-by-military-researchers.html

De Soysa, Indra. 2000. "The Resource Curse: Are Civil Wars Driven by Rapacity or Paucity?" In: *Greed and Grievance: Economic Agendas in Civil Wars,* edited by Mats Berdal and David M. Malone, 113–135. Boulder, CO: Lynne Rienner Publishers.

De Wet, Phillip. 2012. "From Bully Boys to Wimps: The Decline of SA's Military." *Mail & Guardian.* May 04. Accessed October 15, 2015. http://mg.co.za/article/2012–05–04-lack-of-funds-leaves-sa-vulnerable

De Witte, Ludo. 2001. *The Assassination of Lumumba,* 2nd ed. London, UK: Verso.

Decalo, Samuel. 1990. *Coups and Army Rule in Africa,* 2nd ed. New Haven, CT: Yale University Press.

Desai, Raj M. and James Raymond Vreeland. 2014. "What the New Bank of BRICS Is All About." *Washington Post.* July 17. Accessed October 22, 2015. www.washingtonpost.com/blogs/monkey-cage/wp/2014/07/17/what-the-new-bank-of-brics-is-all-about/

DeSilva-Ranasinghe, Sergei. 2011. "Why the Indian Ocean Matters." *The Diplomat.* March 2. Accessed October 22, 2015. http://thediplomat.com/2011/03/why-the-indian-ocean-matters/

DeYoung, Karen. 2009. "Special Forces Raid in Somalia Killed Terrorist with al Qaeda Links, U.S. Says." *Washington Post.* September 15. Accessed October 25, 2015. www.washingtonpost.com/wp-dyn/content/article/2009/09/14/AR2009091403522.html

DeYoung, Karen, Adam Goldman, and Julie Tate. 2014. "U.S. Captures Benghazi Suspect in Secret Raid." *Washington Post.* June 17. Accessed October 25, 2015. www.washingtonpost.com/world/national-security/us-captured-benghazi-suspect-in-secret-raid/2014/06/17/7ef8746e-f5cf-11e3-a3a5–42be35962a52_story.html

Dobson, Alan P. and Steve Marsh. 2006. *U.S. Foreign Policy since 1945,* 2nd ed. New York, NY: Routledge.

Dokken, Karin. 2008. *African Security Politics Redefined.* New York, NY: Palgrave Macmillan.

Dutta, Arvind. 2008. "Indo-African Defense Cooperation: Need for Enhanced Trust." *Journal of Defense Studies* 2, no. 2: 170–177.

Economist. 2000. "The Hopeless Continent." May 13.

Economist. 2001. "Stoking Fires: Muslims in Africa." September 22.

Economist. 2012. "Surprising Somalia Nice Beaches and Good Shopping." June 16.

Economist. 2012. "The Gateway to Africa?" June 2.

Economist. 2013. "Beyond Blackwater." November 23.

Economist. 2013. "Pipeline Poker." May 25.

Economist. 2013. "Special Report: Emerging Africa—A Hopeful Continent." March 2.

Economist. 2013. "The Toll of a Tragedy." July 8.

Economist. 2014. "Arms and the African." November 22.

Economist. 2014. "Fertility Treatment." March 8.

Economist. 2015. "A Sub-Saharan Scramble." January 24.

Economist Intelligence Unit. 2015. "Democracy Index 2014." January 28.

Ellis, Stephen. 2004. "Briefing: The Pan-Sahel Initiative." *African Affairs* 103, no. 412 (July): 459–464.

Englebert, Pierre and Kevin C. Dunn. 2013. *Inside African Politics.* Boulder, CO: Lynne Rienner Publishers.

Enloe, Cynthia H. 1980. *Ethnic Soldiers: State Security in Divided Societies.* London, UK: Penguin Books.

Erickson, Andrew S. and Austin M. Strange. 2013. "No Substitute for Experience: Chinese Antipiracy Operations in the Gulf of Aden." *China Maritime Study* 10, November. Newport, RI: U.S. Naval War College.

Erthal Abdenur, Adriana and Danilo Marcondes de Souza Neto. 2014. "Brazil's Growing Relevance to Peace and Security in Africa." *NOREF Report.* March. Oslo, Norway: Norwegian Peacebuilding Resource Centre.

Euronews. 2012. "UNHCR: Mali Humanitarian Crisis 'Threatens Whole Region'." August 3. Accessed October 25, 2015. www.euronews.com/2012/08/03/unhcr-mali-humanitarian-crisis-threatens-whole-region/

European Commission. 2015. *Africa-EU Continental Cooperation.* Accessed October 20, 2015. https://ec.europa.eu/europeaid/regions/africa/africa-eu-continental-coopera tion_en

Eyal, Jonathan. 2014. "Commonality, Competition between China and India." *The Straits Times.* September 25. Accessed October 25, 2015. www.straitstimes.com/opinion/commonality-competition-between-china-and-india

Fabricius, Peter. 2015. "Standing By or Standing Up: Is the African Standby Force Nearly Ready for Action?" *Institute for Security Studies.* July 23. Accessed October 23, 2015. www.issafrica.org/iss-today/standing-by-or-standing-up-is-the-african-standby-force-nearly-ready-for-action

Farah, Douglas. 2002. "Report Says Africans Harbored Al Qaeda." *Washington Post.* December 29. Accessed October 25, 2015. www.washingtonpost.com/archive/politics/2002/12/29/report-says-africans-harbored-al-qaeda/54a83960–2ae4–46f8–9387-bedfde28d5f8/

Farah, Douglas. 2004. *Blood from Stones: The Secret Financial Network of Terror.* New York, NY: Broadway Books.

Farrell, Maureen and Jessica Lee. 2015. "Civil-Military Operations in East Africa: Coordinated Approaches." In: *The U.S. Military in Africa: Enhancing Security and Development?*, edited by Jessica Piombo, 103–120. Boulder, CO: FirstForum Press.

Feickert, Andrew. 2013. "The Unified Command Plan and Combatant Commands: Background and Issues for Congress." *CRS Report to Congress.* January 3. Washington, DC: Congressional Research Service.

Fettweis, Christopher J. 2004. "Militarizing Diplomacy: Warrior-Diplomats and the Foreign Policy Process." In: *America's Viceroys: The Military and U.S. Foreign Policy*, edited by Derek S. Reveron, 47–70. New York, NY: Palgrave Macmillan.

Field, Kimberly, James Learmont, and Jason Charland. 2013. "Regionally Aligned Forces: Business not as Usual." *Parameters* 43, no. 3 (Autumn): 55–63.

Filiu, Jean-Pierre. 2010. "Could Al-Qaeda Turn African in the Sahel." *Carnegie Papers* 112 (June). Washington, DC: Carnegie Endowment for International Peace.

Finer, Samuel. 1962. *The Man on Horseback*. London, UK: Penguin Books.

Fisher-Thompson, Jim. 2007. "New African Command to Have Unique Structure, Mission." *United States Library of Congress*. June 22.

FlorCruz, Michelle. 2015. "Prime Minister of Burkina Faso Yacouba Isaac Zida Resigns Following RSP Tension." *International Business Times*. July 5. Accessed October 15, 2015. www.ibtimes.com/prime-minister-burkina-faso-yacouba-izaac-zida-resigns-following-rsp-tension-1996211

Foreign Policy. 2005. "Africa's Second Front." no. 150 (September/October): 22.

Forest, James J. F. and Rebecca Crispin. 2009. "AFRICOM: Troubled Infancy, Promising Future." *Contemporary Security Policy* 30, no. 1: 5–27.

France 24. 2015. "Nigeria to Lead New Regional Force against Boko Haram." June 12. Accessed October 15, 2015. www.france24.com/en/20150611-nigeria-regional-force-boko-haram-MNJTF

Frazer, Jendayi E. 2010. "Reflections on U.S. Policy in Africa, 2001–2009." *Fletcher Forum of World Affairs* 34, no. 1 (Winter): 95–123.

French, Howard W. 2014. *China's Second Continent: How a Million Migrants Are Building a New Empire in Africa*. New York, NY: Knopf Doubleday.

Fund for Peace. 2014. *Fragile States Index 2014*. Accessed October 12, 2015. http://fsi.fundforpeace.org/rankings-2014

Fund for Peace. 2015. *Fragile States Index 2015*. Accessed October 22, 2015. http://fsi.fundforpeace.org/rankings-2015

Garbesi, Gregg. 2004. "U.S. Unified Command Plan." In: *America's Viceroys: The Military and U.S. Foreign Policy*, edited by Derek S. Reveron, 17–46. New York, NY: Palgrave Macmillan.

Gartenstein-Ross, Daveed and Seungwon Chung. 2010. "The African Union's Beleaguered Somalia Mission." *Long War Journal*. July 20. Accessed October 18, 2015. www.longwarjournal.org/archives/2010/07/the_african_unions_b.php

Gates, Robert M. 2010. "Helping Others Defend Themselves: The Future of U.S. Security Assistance." *Foreign Affairs* 89 (May/June): 2–6.

Gertler, Jeremiah. 2011. "Operation Odyssey Dawn (Libya): Background and Issues for Congress." *CRS Report to Congress*. March 30. Washington, DC: Congressional Research Service.

Gettleman, Jeffrey. 2011. "Opposition Leader Is Handed Reins in Zambia." *New York Times*. September 23. Accessed October 25, 2015. www.nytimes.com/2011/09/24/world/africa/zambias-presidency-changes-hands-after-election.html

Gettleman, Jeffrey. 2014. "Sudan Said to Revive Notorious Militias." *New York Times*. June 24. Accessed October 25, 2015. www.nytimes.com/2014/06/25/world/africa/sudan-darfur-janjaweed-militia-khartoum.html

Gettleman, Jeffrey, Mark Mazzetti, and Eric Schmitt. 2011. "U.S. Relies on Contractors in Somalia Conflict." *New York Times*. April 10. Accessed October 24, 2015. www.nytimes.com/2011/08/11/world/africa/11somalia.html?_r=0

Gettleman, Jeffrey and Eric Schmitt. 2009. "U.S. Aided a Failed Plan to Rout Ugandan Rebels." *New York Times*. February 6. Accessed October 25, 2015. www.nytimes.com/2009/02/07/world/africa/07congo.html

Giles, Keir. 2013. *Russian Interests in Sub-Saharan Africa*. Carlisle, PA: Strategic Studies Institute.

Gladstone, Rick. 2014. "Number of Darfur Displaced Surged in 2013." *New York Times*. January 23. Accessed October 16, 2015. www.nytimes.com/2014/01/24/world/africa/number-of-darfurs-displaced-surged-in-2013.html?_r=0

Global Witness. 2003. "For a Few Dollars More: How al Qaeda Moved into the Diamond Trade." *Global Witness Report*. Accessed October 18, 2015. www.globalwitness.org/sites/default/files/import/Few%20Dollars%20More%200–50.pdf

Global Witness. 2015. "Blood Timber: How Europe Helped Fund War in the Central African Republic." *Global Witness Report*. July 15. Accessed October 22, 2015. www.globalwitness.org/documents/18026/BLOOD_TIMBER_web.pdf

GlobalSecurity. 2012. *African Contingency Operations Training and Assistance (ACOTA)*. Accessed October 18, 2015. www.globalsecurity.org/military/ops/acota.htm

Goldstein, Joshua S. 2011. *Winning the War on War: The Decline of Armed Conflict Worldwide*. New York, NY: Dutton.

Goodman, Colby. 2015. "Post-Coup Leader in Burkina Faso Helped Steer U.S. Military Exercises." *Security Assistance Monitor*. September 18. Accessed October 25, 2015. www.securityassistance.org/blog/post-coup-leader-burkina-faso-helped-steer-us-military-exercises

Gordon, Michael R. 2002. "U.S. Turns Horn of Africa into a Military Hub." *New York Times*. November 17. Accessed October 18, 2015. www.nytimes.com/2002/11/17/international/africa/17HORN.html

Green, Michael J. and Andrew Shearer. 2012. "Defining U.S. Indian Ocean Strategy." *Washington Quarterly* 35, no. 2: 175–189.

Greig, Jonathan. 2013. "News Analysis: Fixing Mismatch between U.S. Aid Policy and Africa's Needs." *Business Day*. December 17. Accessed October 25, 2015. www.bdlive.co.za/africa/africannews/2013/12/17/news-analysis-fixing-mismatch-between-us-aid-policy-and-africas-needs

Guardian. 2015. "Nigeria Suffers Highest Number of Deaths in African War Zones." January 23. Accessed October 18, 2015. www.theguardian.com/global-development/2015/jan/23/boko-haram-nigeria-civilian-death-toll-highest-acled-african-war-zones

Haastrup, Toni. 2013. "Africa-EU Partnership on Peace and Security." In: *Africa and the European Union: A Strategic Partnership*, edited by Jack Mangala, 47–68. New York, NY: Palgrave Macmillan.

Ham, Carter. 2013. *Statement before the Senate Armed Services Committee*. March 7. Accessed October 12, 2015. www.africom.mil/Doc/10432

Hammes, Thomas X. 2005. "War Evolves into the Fourth Generation." *Contemporary Security Policy* 26, no. 2 (August): 189–221.

Hanauer, Larry and Lyle J. Morris. 2014. *Chinese Engagement in Africa: Drivers, Reactions, and Implications for U.S. Policy*. Santa Monica, CA: RAND Corporation.

Handy, Russell J. 2003. "African Contingency Operations Training Assistance: Developing Training Partnerships for the Future of Africa." *Air and Space Power Journal* 17, no. 3 (Fall), 57–64.

Heinecken, Lindy. 2001. "HIV/AIDS, the Military, and the Impact on National and International Security." *Society in Transition* 32, no. 1: 121–122.

Heinecken, Lindy. 2009. "The Potential Impact of HIV/AIDS on the South African Armed Forces: Some Evidence from Outside and Within." *African Security Review* 18, no. 2: 60–77.

Hesse, Brian J. 2005. "Celebrate or Hold Suspect? Bill Clinton and George W. Bush in Africa." *Journal of Contemporary African Studies* 23, no. 3 (September): 327–344.

Hirsch, Afua. 2013. "Niger Suicide Bombings Reported to be Work of Mokhtar Belmokhtar." *The Guardian.* May 24. Accessed October 24, 2015. www.theguardian. com/world/2013/may/24/niger-suicide-bombings-mokhtar-belmokhtar

Hoffman, Max and Conor Lane. 2013. "Guinea-Bissau and the South Atlantic Cocaine Trade." *Center for American Progress.* August 22. Accessed October 25, 2015. www.americanprogress.org/issues/security/report/2013/08/22/72557/guinea-bissau-and-the-south-atlantic-cocaine-trade/

Hough, Mike. 2001. "International Terrorism: Contemporary Manifestations in Africa." *Strategic Review for Southern Africa* 23, no. 2 (November).

Houngnikpo, Mathurin. 2010. *Guarding the Guardians.* Surrey, UK: Ashgate Publishing.

Houngnikpo, Mathurin. 2011. "Small Arms and Big Trouble." In: *African Security and the Africa Command: Viewpoints on the U.S. Role in Africa,* edited by Terry F. Buss, Joseph Adjaye, Donald Glodstein, and Louis A. Picard, 165–185. Sterling, VA: Kumarian Press.

Howe, Herbert M. 2001. *Ambiguous Order: Military Forces in African States.* Boulder, CO: Lynne Rienner Publishers.

Huang, Chin-Hao 2008. "China's Renewed Partnership with Africa: Implications for the United States." In: *China into Africa,* edited by Robert I. Rotberg, 296–312. Cambridge, UK: Brookings.

Human Rights Watch. 2007. *Darfur 2007: Chaos by Design.* September 9. Accessed October 17, 2015. www.hrw.org/node/10678/section/5

Human Security Baseline Assessment for Sudan and South Sudan. 2012. "The Sudan-Chad Proxy War." February 6. Accessed October 17, 2015. www.smallarms-surveysudan.org/facts-figures/sudan/darfur/sudan-chad-proxy-war-historical.html

Huntington, Samuel P. 1957. *The Soldier and the State.* Cambridge, MA: Belknap.

Huntington, Samuel P. 1968. *Political Order in Changing Societies.* New Haven, CT: Yale University Press.

Institute for Security Studies. 2004. "Al Qaeda Presence in South Africa?" *African Terrorism Bulletin* no. 1 (December). Accessed October 18, 2015. www.issafrica.org/futures/other-publications/newsletter-african-terrorism-bulletin-issue-1

International Chamber of Commerce. 2014. "Somali Pirate Clampdown Caused Drop in Global Piracy, IMB Reveals." *ICC Commercial Crime Services.* January 15. Accessed October 25, 2015. https://icc-ccs.org/news/904-somali-pirate-clampdown-caused-drop-in-global-piracy-imb-reveals

International Crisis Group. 2000. "Scramble for the Congo: Anatomy of an Ugly War." *Africa Report* 26. December 20.

International Crisis Group. 2010. "Guinea: Reforming the Army." *Africa Report* 164. September 23.

International Crisis Group. 2012. "The Gulf of Guinea: The New Danger Zone." *Africa Report* 195. December 12.

International Crisis Group. 2014. "Congo: Ending the Status Quo." *Africa Briefing* 107. December 17.

International Crisis Group. 2014. "Cote d'Ivoire's Great West: Key to Reconciliation." *Africa Report* 212. January 28.

International Crisis Group. 2014. "Curbing Violence in Nigeria (II)ı The Boko Haram Insurgency." *Africa Report* 216. April 3.

International Crisis Group. 2015. "Executive Summary. Sudan and South Sudan's Merging Conflicts." *Africa Report* 223. January 29.

IRIN News. 2012. "Guinea: Deadlock over Parliamentary Elections." August 29. Accessed October 18, 2015. www.irinnews.org/report/96199/guinea-deadlock-over-parliamentary-elections

Jackson, Paul. 2007. "Are Africa's Wars Part of a Fourth Generation of Warfare?" *Contemporary Security Policy* 28, no. 2 (August): 267–285.

Jackson, Robert H. 1990. *Quasi-States: Sovereignty, International Relations, and the Third World.* Cambridge, MA: Cambridge University Press.

Jackson, Robert H. and C. G. Rosberg. 1982. "Why Africa's Weak States Persist: The Empirical and the Juridical in Statehood." *World Politics* 35, no. 1: 1–24.

Jentleson, Bruce W. 2014. "Strategic Recalibration: Framework for a 21st Century National Security Strategy." *Washington Quarterly* 37, no. 1: 115–136.

Joscelyn, Thomas. 2015. "Jihadist Divisions Grow in Nigeria." *The Long War Journal.* February 23. Accessed October 19, 2015. www.longwarjournal.org/archives/2015/02/jihadist-divisions-grow-in-nigeria.php

Joselow, Gabe. 2014. "AU: Standby Force Needed to Respond to Conflicts." *Voice of America.* January 31. Accessed October 25, 2015. www.voanews.com/content/au-says-standby-force-needed-to-respond-to-conflicts/1841962.html

Kaiser Family Foundation. 2014. "The U.S. President's Emergency Plan for AIDS Relief (PEPFAR)." June 04. Accessed October 19, 2015. http://kff.org/hivaids/fact-sheet/the-u-s-presidents-emergency-plan-for/

Kaldor, Mary. 2006. *New and Old Wars,* 2nd ed. Stanford, CA: Stanford University Press.

Kaldor, Mary. 2007. *Human Security.* Malden, MA: Polity Press.

Kandeh, Jimmy D. 2004. "Civil-Military Relations." In: *West Africa's Security Challenges,* edited by Adekeye Adebajo and Ismail Rashid, 145–168. Boulder, CO: Lynne Rienner Publishers.

Kaplan, Fred. 2013. *The Insurgents: David Petraeus and the Plot to Change the American Way of War.* New York, NY: Simon and Schuster.

Keeler, Dan. 2014. "Africans See U.S. Trade Policy Hindering American Firms." *The Wall Street Journal.* August 11.

Kent, John. 2000. "The United States and the Decolonization of Black Africa, 1945–63." In: *The United States and Decolonization: Power and Freedom,* edited by David Ryan and Victor Pungong, 168–187. New York, NY: St. Martin's Press.

Klare, Michael T. 2012. *The Race for What's Left: The Global Scramble for the World's Last Resources.* New York, NY: Picador.

KPMG. 2013. "Oil and Gas in Africa: Africa's Reserves, Potential and Prospects." *Full Sector Report.* Accessed October 21, 2015. www.kpmg.com/Africa/en/IssuesAnd Insights/Articles-Publications/Documents/Oil%20and%20Gas%20in%20Africa.pdf

Kulish, Nicholas, Eric Schmitt, and Mark Mazzetti. 2013. "Target in U.S. Raid in Somalia Is Called Top Shabaab Planner of Attacks Abroad." *New York Times.* October 6. Accessed October 25, 2015. www.nytimes.com/2013/10/07/world/africa/target-in-us-raid-on-somalia-is-called-top-shabab-planner-of-attacks-abroad.html

Lacher, Wolfram. 2012. "Organized Crime and Conflict in the Sahel-Sahara Region." *Carnegie Papers.* Washington, DC: Carnegie Endowment for International Peace.

Laub, Zachary and Jonathan Masters. 2014. "Al Qaeda in the Islamic Maghreb." *Council on Foreign Relations Backgrounders*. January 8. Accessed October 19, 2015. www.cfr.org/terrorist-organizations-and-networks/al-qaeda-islamic-maghreb-aqim/p12717

Le Sage, Andre. 2010. "Africa's Irregular Security Threats." *Strategic Forum* 255. May.

Lee, Henry and Dan Shalmon. 2008. "Searching for Oil: China's Oil Strategies in Africa." In: *China into Africa*, edited by Robert I. Rotberg, 109–135. Cambridge, UK: Brookings.

Leffler, Melvyn P. 2011. "9/11 in Retrospect: George W. Bush's Grand Strategy, Reconsidered." *Foreign Affairs* 90 no. 5, 33–44.

Lerner, Mitch. 2011. "Climbing off the Back Burner: Lyndon Johnson's Soft Power Approach to Africa." *Diplomacy and Statecraft* 22, no. 4 (December): 578–607.

Londoño, Ernesto. 2013. "Study: Iraq, Afghan War Costs to Top $4 Trillion." *Washington Post*. March 28. Accessed October 26, 2015. www.washingtonpost.com/world/national-security/study-iraq-afghan-war-costs-to-top-4-trillion/2013/03/28/b82a5dce-97ed-11e2-814b-063623d80a60_story.html

Londoño, Ernesto. 2013. "U.S. Expands Aid to French Mission in Mali." *Washington Post*. January 26. Accessed October 20, 2015. www.washingtonpost.com/world/national-security/us-expands-aid-to-french-mission-in-mali/2013/01/26/3d56bb5c-6821-11e2-83c7-38d5fac94235_story.html

Louw-Vaudran, Liesl. 2014. "Africa: Who Will Foot the Bill for Africa's New Intervention Force?" *Institute for Security Studies*. July 7. Accessed October 18, 2015. http://allafrica.com/stories/201407081177.html

Luna, David M. 2014. "Trans-African Security: Combating Illicit Trafficking along the Crime-Terror Continuum." Remarks at AFSEC 14, West African Coastal Surveillance and Maritime Security Summit. February 26. Accessed October 22, 2015. www.state.gov/j/inl/rls/rm/2014/222591.htm

Lyman, Princeton. 2013. "The War on Terrorism in Africa." In: *Africa in World Politics: Engaging a Changing Global Order*, edited by John W. Harbeson and Donald Rothchild. Boulder, CO: Westview Press.

Lynch, Colum. 2012. "China's Arms Exports Flooding Sub-Saharan Africa." *Washington Post*, August 25. Accessed October 21, 2015. www.washingtonpost.com/world/national-security/chinas-arms-exports-flooding-sub-saharan-africa/2012/08/25/16267b68-e7f1-11e1-936a-b801f1abab19_story.html

Ma, Tiffany. 2009. "China and Congo's Coltan Connection." *Project 2049 Institute*. June 22. Accessed October 15, 2015. http://project2049.net/documents/china_and_congos_coltan_connection.pdf

Magyar, Karl P. 2000. "Introduction: Africa's Transitional Role in America's Post-Cold War Era Diplomacy." In: *United States Interests and Policies in Africa*, edited by Karl P. Magyar, 5–9. New York, NY: St. Martin's Press.

Mahajan, Vijay. 2009. *Africa Rising: How 900 Million African Consumers Offer More Than You Think*. Upper Saddle River, NJ: Prentice Hall.

Malan, Mark. 2008. "Prepared Statement of Mark Malan, Peacebuilding Program Officer, Refugees International." Unites States House of Representatives, Hearing before the Subcommittee on National Security and Foreign Affairs of the Committee on Oversight and Government Reform. July 23.

Mann, Gregory. 2012. "Foreign Policy: The Mess in Mali." *National Public Radio*. April 10. Accessed October 18, 2015. www.npr.org/2012/04/10/150343027

Marshall, Paul. 2002. "The Next Hotbed of Islamic Radicalism?" *Washington Post.* October 8. Accessed October 18, 2015. www.washingtonpost.com/archive/opinions/ 2002/10/08/the-next-hotbed-of-islamic-radicalism/c60c6d78-293e-4cad-a7de-fc69c3d409ba/

Matfess, Hilary. 2013. "Are We Pivoting to Africa rather than Asia?" *The Atlantic.* October 6.

Mauldin, William and Drew Hinshaw. 2014. "U.S., Africa Aim to Boost Trade." *The Wall Street Journal.* August 4.

McCormack, Ty. 2015. "Exclusive: U.S. Operates Drones from Secret Bases in Somalia." *Foreign Policy.* July 2.

Menkhaus, Ken. 2009. "Somalia. What Went Wrong?" *RUSI Journal* 154, no. 4 (August): 6–12.

Meyer, Angela. 2011. "Peace and Security Cooperation in Central Africa." *Discussion Paper* 56. Uppsala, Sweden: Nordic Africa Institute.

Michaels, Jeffrey H. 2012. "Breaking the Rules: The CIA and Counterinsurgency in the Congo 1964–1965." *International Journal of Intelligence and Counterintelligence* 25, no. 1: 130–159.

Miles, Donna. 2005. "New Counterterrorism Initiative to Focus on Saharan Africa." *U.S. Forces Press Service.* May 17.

Mills, Greg. 2004. "Africa's New Strategic Significance." *Washington Quarterly* 27, no. 4: 157–169.

Morrison, Stephen J. 2001. "Prepared Statement of J. Stephen Morrison." United States House of Representatives, Hearing before the Subcommittee on Africa of the Committee on International Relations on "Africa and the War on Global Terrorism." One Hundred Seventh Congress. November 15.

Mukum Mbaku, John. 2014. "Has Military Intervention Created a Constitutional Crisis in Burkina Faso?" *Brookings.* November 4. Accessed October 15, 2015. www.brookings.edu/blogs/africa-in-focus/posts/2014/11/04-military-intervention-constitutional-crisis-burkina-faso-mbaku

Munene, Macharia. 2005. "Mayi Mayi and Interahamwe Militias: Threats to Peace and Security in the Great Lakes Region." In: *Civil Militia: Africa's Intractable Security Menace?*, edited by David J. Francis, 231–250. Burlington, VT: Ashgate.

Musah, Abdel-Fatau. 2009. "West Africa: Governance and Security in a Changing Region." *Africa Program Working Paper Series.* Oslo, Norway: International Peace Institute.

N'Diaye, Boubacar and Sandy Africa. 2009. "AFRICOM and the Interests of Africans: Beyond Perceptions and Strategic Communication." *Contemporary Security Policy* 30, no. 1: 62–66.

Nagl, John A. 2002. *Learning to Eat Soup with a Knife: Counterinsurgency Lessons from Malaysia and Vietnam.* Chicago, IL: The University of Chicago Press.

Nathan, Laurie. 2009. "AFRICOM: A Threat to Africa's Security." *Contemporary Security Policy* 30, no. 1: 58–61.

National Consortium for the Study of Terrorism and Responses to Terrorism. 2015. *Global Terrorism Database.* Accessed October 12, 2015. www.start.umd.edu/gtd/

New York Times. 2014. "South Sudan: China to Send Troops for U.N. Mission." September 26. Accessed October 26, 2015. www.nytimes.com/2014/09/26/world/africa/ south-sudan-china-to-send-troops-for-un-mission.html

Newman, Edward. 2001. "Human Security and Constructivism." *International Studies Perspectives* 2, no. 3: 239–251.

Nissanbaum, Dion and Julian E. Barnes. 2015. "U.S. Military to End African Ebola Role." *The Wall Street Journal*. February 10, accessed January 29, 2016. www.wsj.com/articles/u-s-to-end-african-ebola-role-1423612366.

Nossiter, Adam, Eric Schmitt, and Mark Mazzetti. 2013. "French Strikes in Mali Supplant Caution of U.S." *New York Times*. January 13. Accessed October 26, 2015. www.nytimes.com/2013/01/14/world/africa/french-jets-strike-deep-inside-islamist-held-mali.html

Nugent, Paul. 2012. *Africa since Independence*, 2nd ed. New York, NY: Palgrave Macmillan.

Nzongola-Ntalaja, Georges. 2002. *The Congo from Leopold to Kabila: a People's History*. New York, NY: Zed Books.

O'Grady, Siobhan and Elias Groll. 2015. "Nigeria Taps South African Mercenaries in Fight against Boko Haram." *Foreign Policy*. March 12.

O'Regan, Davin. 2014. "The Evolving Drug Trade in Guinea-Bissau and West Africa." *The International Relations and Security Network*. July 28.

Obi, Cyrl I. 2010. "Oil Extraction, Dispossession, and Conflict in Nigeria's Oil-Rich Niger Delta." *Canadian Journal of Development Studies* 30, no. 1–2: 219–236.

Ohaegbulam, Ugboaja. 2004. *U.S. Policy in Postcolonial Africa: Four Case Studies in Conflict Resolution*. New York, NY: Peter Lang Publishing.

Okumu, Wafula. 2007. "Prepared Statement of Dr. Wafula Okumu, Head of the African Security Analysis Program Institute for Security Studies." United States House of Representatives, Hearing before the Subcommittee on Africa and Global Health of the Committee on Foreign Affairs. August 2.

Onuoha, Freedom C. 2012. "Oil Piracy in the Gulf of Guinea." *Conflict Trends* 4; 28–35.

Onwumechili, Chuka. 1998. *African Democratization and Military Coups*. Westport, CT: Praeger.

Paris, Roland. 2001. "Human Security: Paradigm Shift or Hot Air?" *International Security* 26, no. 2: 87–102.

Payne, Donald M. 2007. "Africa Command: Opportunity for Engagement or the Militarization of the U.S. Africa Relationship?" United States House of Representatives, Hearing before the Subcommittee on Africa and Global Health of the Committee on Foreign Affairs. August 2.

Pendleton, John H. 2010. "Prepared Statement of John H. Pendleton, Director of Defense Capabilities and Management, GAO." Unites States House of Representatives, Hearing before the Subcommittee on National Security and Foreign Affairs of the Committee on Oversight and Government Reform. July 28.

Pendleton, John H., Robert Repasky, Tim Burke, Leigh Caraher, Taylor Matheson, Amber Simco, Grace Coleman, Ron La Due Lake, and Lonnie McAllister. 2009. "Defense Management: Actions Needed to Address Stakeholder Concerns, Improve Interagency Collaboration, and Determine Full Costs Associated with the U.S. Africa Command." *Congressional Report*. February. Washington, DC: Government Accountability Office.

Perlmutter, Amos. 1977. *The Military and Politics in Modern Times*. New Haven, CT: Yale University Press.

Perlo-Freeman, Sam and Carina Solmirano. 2014. "Trends in World Military Expenditure, 2013." *SIPRI Fact Sheet*. April. Stockholm, Sweden: Stockholm International Peace Research Institute.

Pew Research Center. 2010. "Tolerance and Tension: Islam and Christianity in Sub-Saharan Africa." April 15. Accessed October 18, 2015. www.pewforum.org/2010/04/15/executive-summary-islam-and-christianity-in-sub-saharan-africa/

Pew Research Center. 2013. "America's Global Image Remains More Positive than China's." July 18. Accessed October 22, 2015. www.pewglobal.org/files/2013/07/Pew-Research-Global-Attitudes-Project-Balance-of-Power-Report-FINAL-July-18–2013.pdf

Pham, J. Peter. 2010. "Back to Africa: Russia's New African Engagement." In: *Africa and the New World Era: From Humanitarianism to a Strategic View*, edited by Jack Mangala, 71–83. New York, NY: Palgrave Macmillan.

Pham, J. Peter. 2010. "India's New Engagement of Africa." In: *Africa and the New World Era: From Humanitarianism to a Strategic View*, edited by Jack Mangala, 115–128. New York, NY: Palgrave Macmillan.

Piombo, Jessica. 2012. "U.S. Africa Policy: Rhetoric versus Reality." *Current History* 111, no. 745 (May): 194.

Piombo, Jessica. 2015. "Evolving Civilian and Military Missions." In: *The U.S. Military in Africa: Enhancing Security and Development?*, edited by Jessica Piombo, 37–64. Boulder, CO: FirstForum Press.

Piombo, Jessica. 2015. "Pursuing Multidimensional Security." In: *The U.S. Military in Africa: Enhancing Security and Development?*, edited by Jessica Piombo, 213–230. Boulder, CO: FirstForum Press.

Pizzi, Michael. 2014 "Nigeria's Undersized, Undertrained Military under Fire." *Al Jazeera America.* May 10. Accessed October 15, 2015. http://america.aljazeera.com/articles/2014/5/10/nigeria-militaryfailure.html

Ploch, Lauren. 2010. "Countering Terrorism in East Africa: The U.S. Response." *CRS Report to Congress.* November 3. Washington, DC: Congressional Research Service.

Ploch, Lauren. 2011. "Africa Command: U.S. Strategic Interests and the Role of the U.S. Military in Africa." *CRS Report to Congress.* July 22. Washington, DC: Congressional Research Service.

Polgreen, Lydia. 2013. "Mali Army, Riding U.S. Hopes, Is No Match for Militants." *New York Times.* January 24. Accessed October 19, 2015. www.nytimes.com/2013/01/25/world/africa/mali-army-riding-us-hopes-is-proving-no-match-for-militants.html?_r=0

Power, Samantha. 2002. *A Problem from Hell: America and the Age of Genocide.* New York, NY: Harper Collins.

Priest, Dana. 2004. *The Mission: Waging War and Keeping Peace with America's Military.* New York, NY: W. W. Norton & Company.

Project for a United and Strong America. 2013. *Setting Priorities for American Leadership.* March 7. Accessed October 22, 2015. http://nationalsecuritystrategy.org/pdf/pusa-report-march-2013.pdf

Prunier, Gérard. 2008. *Africa's World War: Congo, the Rwandan Genocide, and the Making of a Continental Catastrophe.* Oxford, UK: Oxford University Press.

Raghavan, Sudarsan. 2013. "Congo's M-23 Rebel Group Ends Its Insurgency." *Washington Post.* November 5. Accessed October 17, 2015. www.washingtonpost.com/world/africa/congos-m23-rebel-group-ends-its-insurgency/2013/11/05/fdbbf56e-462a-11e3-bf0c-cebf37c6f484_story.html

Ratnam, Gopal. 2014. "Africa Military Moves by U.S. Reflect Iraq, Afghan Wars." *Bloomberg.* August 1.

Rawlinson, Kevin. 2013. "U.S. Special Forces Raids Target Islamist Militants in Libya and Somalia." *The Guardian*. October 6. Accessed October 26, 2015. www.the guardian.com/world/2013/oct/06/us-special-forces-libya-somalia

Reno, William. 1999. *Warlord Politics and African States*. Boulder, CO: Lynne Rienner Publishers.

Reno, William. 2007. "Liberia: The LURDS of the New Church." In: *African Guerrillas: Raging against the Machine*, edited by Morten Bøås and Kevin C. Dunn, 69–80. Boulder, CO: Lynne Rienner Publishers.

Reno, William. 2012. "The Regionalization of African Security." *Current History* 111, no. 745 (May): 175–176.

Renwick, Danielle. 2015. "Peace Operations in Africa." *Council on Foreign Relations Backgrounders*. May 15. Accessed October 22, 2015. www.cfr.org/peacekeeping/peace-operations-africa/p9333

Reuters. 2013. "U.S. Resumes Aid to Mali after New President Takes Office." September 6. Accessed October 25, 2015. www.reuters.com/article/2013/09/06/us-usa-mali-idUSBRE98515Y20130906

Reveron, Derek S. and Kathleen A. Mahoney-Norris. 2011. *Human Security in a Borderless World*. Boulder, CO: Westview Press.

Rodrigues, Luis N. 2004. "Today's Terrorist Is Tomorrow's Statesman; The United States and Angolan Nationalism in the Early 1960s." *Portuguese Journal of Social Science* 3, no. 2: 115–140.

Rodriguez, David M. 2014. *Statement before the Senate Armed Services Committee*. March 6.

Roelf, Wendell. 2014. "Exclusive: South African Military in 'Critical Decline' Review Says." *Reuters*. March 25. Accessed October 15, 2015. www.reuters.com/article/2014/03/25/us-safrica-defence-exclusive-idUSBREA2O10U20140325

Rosen, Armin 2015. "Almost a Year After #BringBackOurGirls, They're Still Missing but the U.S. Has Pulled Its 80 Troops Looking for Boko Haram." *Business Insider*. March 11. Accessed October 26, 2015. http://uk.businessinsider.com/the-us-pulled-its-80-troops-that-were-in-chad-looking-for-boko-haram-2015-3?r=US&IR=T

Rotberg, Robert I. 2008. "China's Quest for Resources, Opportunities, and Influence in Africa." In: *China into Africa*, edited by Robert I. Rotberg, 1–20. Cambridge, UK: Brookings.

Rotberg, Robert I. 2014. "China's Trade with Africa at Record High." *The Christian Science Monitor*. March 19.

Saferworld. 2011. "China's Growing Role in African Peace and Security." January. www.saferworld.org.uk/resources/view-resource/500-chinas-growing-role-in-african-peace-and-security

Santora, Marc. 2015. "As South Sudan Crisis Worsens, 'There Is No More Country'." *New York Times*. June 22. Accessed October 26, 2015. www.nytimes.com/2015/06/23/world/africa/as-south-sudan-crisis-worsens-there-is-no-more-country.html

Sarjoh Bah, A. and Kwesi Aning. 2008. "U.S. Peace Operations Policy in Africa: From ACRI to AFRICOM." *International Peacekeeping* 15, no. 1 (March): 118–132.

Schmitt, Eric. 2002. "U.S. to Add Forces in Horn of Africa." *New York Times*. October 10. Accessed October 18, 2015. www.nytimes.com/2002/10/30/international/30MILI.html

Schmitt, Eric. 2011. "Libya Crisis Thrusts U.S. Africa Command into Leadership Role." *New York Times*. March 22. Accessed October 26, 2015. www.nytimes.com/2011/03/23/world/africa/23command.html

Schmitt, Eric. 2013. "Military Says Law Barring U.S. Aid to Rights Violators Hurts Training Mission." *New York Times*. June 20. Accessed October 26, 2015. www.nytimes.com/2013/06/21/us/politics/military-says-law-barring-us-aid-to-rights-violators-hurts-training-mission.html

Schogol, Jeff. 2006. "Africa Command Approved by Bush, DOD Officials Confirm." *Stars and Stripes*. December 30. Accessed October 19, 2015. www.stripes.com/news/africa-command-plans-approved-by-bush-dod-officials-confirm-1.58476

Schraeder, Peter J. 1994. *United States Foreign Policy toward Africa: Incrementalism, Crisis and Change*. Cambridge, UK: Cambridge University Press.

Serafino, Nina M. 2008. "The DOD Role in Foreign Assistance: Background, Major Issues, and Options for Congress." *CRS Report to Congress*. December 9. Washington, DC: Congressional Research Service.

Serafino, Nina M. 2014. "Security Assistance Reform: 'Section 1206' Background and Issues for Congress." *CRS Report to Congress*. December 8. Washington, DC: Congressional Research Service.

Sergie, Mohammed Aly and Toni Johnson. 2015. "Boko Haram." *Council on Foreign Relations Backgrounders*. March 5. Accessed October 18, 2015. www.cfr.org/nigeria/boko-haram/p25739

Sewall, Sarah. 2007. "Introduction: A Radical Field Manual." In: *The U.S. Army/Marine Corps Counterinsurgency Field Manual*, edited by John A. Nagl, David H. Petraeus, and James F. Amos, xxi–xliii. Chicago, IL: The University of Chicago Press.

Shanker, Thom and Rick Gladstone. 2011. "Armed U.S. Advisers to Help Fight African Renegade Group." *New York Times*. October 14. Accessed October 26, 2015. www.nytimes.com/2011/10/15/world/africa/barack-obama-sending-100-armed-advisers-to-africa-to-help-fight-lords-resistance-army.html

Shinn, David H. 2004. "Fighting Terrorism in East Africa and the Horn." *Foreign Service Journal* 81 (September): 36–42.

Shinn, David H. 2008. "Military and Security Relations: China, Africa, and the Rest of the World." In: *China into Africa*, edited by Robert I. Rotberg, 155–196. Cambridge, UK: Brookings.

Shinn, David H. 2009. "Africa: The United States and China Court the Continent." *Journal of International Affairs* 62, no. 2 (Spring/Summer): 37–53.

Shinn, David H. 2012. "Emerging Powers Expand Ties with Africa." *International Policy Digest*. September 17.

Shubin, Vladimir. 2010. "Russia and Africa: Coming Back?" *Russian Analytical Digest* 83: 4–7. September 24.

Singer, P. W. 2003. *Corporate Warriors: The Rise of the Privatized Military Industry*. Ithaca, NY: Cornell University Press.

Slater, Emma. 2012. "Somalia: Reported U.S. Covert Actions 2001–2015." *The Bureau of Investigative Journalism*. February 22. Accessed October 19, 2015. www.thebureauinvestigates.com/2012/02/22/get-the-data-somalias-hidden-war/

Smith, David. 2013. "U.S. Drone Strike in Somalia Kills Top al-Shabaab Explosives Expert." *The Guardian*. October 29. Accessed October 26, 2015. www.theguardian.com/world/2013/oct/29/us-drone-strike-somalia-al-shabaab-expert

Smith, David. 2014. "Christian Militias Take Bloody Revenge on Muslims in Central African Republic." *The Guardian*. March 10. Accessed October 25, 2015. www.theguardian.com/world/2014/mar/10/central-african-republic-christian-militias-revenge

South African Government. 1996. *National Defense White Paper*. May. Accessed October 18, 2015. www.gov.za/documents/national-defence-white-paper

Southern Africa Development Community. 2012. *Organ on Politics, Defense and Security*. Accessed October 18, 2015. www.sadc.int/sadc-secretariat/directorates/office-executive-secretary/organ-politics-defense-and-security/

Stearns, Jason. 2011. *Dancing in the Glory of Monsters*. New York, NY: PublicAffairs.

Stein, Harry, 2015. "Congress Passed a Budget Deal. Now What?" Center for American Progress, November 2, 2015. Accessed January 27, 2016. www.americanprogress.org/issues/budget/news/2015/11/02/124733/congress-passed-a-budget-deal-now-what

Stevenson, Jonathan. 2011. "AFRICOM's Libya Experience." *Foreign Affairs*. May 9.

Stolte, Christina. 2012. *Brazil in Africa: Just Another BRICS Country Seeking Resources?* London, UK: Chatham House.

Sun, Yun and Michael Rettig. 2014. "American and Chinese Trade with Africa: Rhetoric vs. Reality." *The Hill*. August 5. Accessed October 26, 2015. http://thehill.com/blogs/pundits-blog/international/214270-american-and-chinese-trade-with-africa-rhetoric-vs-reality

Sundberg, Ralph, Kristine Eck, and Joakim Kreutz. 2012. "Introducing the UCDP Non-State Conflict Database." *Journal of Peace Research* 49, no. 2: 351–362.

Tadjbakhsh, Shahrbanou and Anuradha Chenoy. 2007. *Human Security: Concepts and Implications*. New York, NY: Routledge.

Tan, Michelle. 2014. "Army Unveils New Plan to 'Win in a Complex World'." *Army Times*. October 13. Accessed October 26, 2015. http://archive.armytimes.com/article/20141013/NEWS/310130024/Army-unveils-new-plan-win-complex-world-

Taylor, Ian. 2012. "India's Rise in Africa." *International Affairs* 88, no. 4: 779–798.

Thomson, Alex. 2008. *U.S. Foreign Policy towards South Africa, 1948–1994: Conflict of Interests*. New York, NY: Palgrave Macmillan.

Tieku, Thomas K. 2007. "African Union Promotion of Human Security In Africa." *African Security Review* 16, no. 2: 26–37.

Tran, Mark. 2014. "Africa's Economic Growth Failing to Stimulate Development and Jobs." *The Guardian*. January 20. Accessed October 12, 2015. www.theguardian.com/global-development/2014/jan/20/africa-economic-growth-failing-development-jobs

Tremlett, Giles. 2004. "U.S. Sends Special Forces into North Africa." *The Guardian*. March 15. Accessed October 18, 2015. www.theguardian.com/world/2004/mar/15/alqaida.terrorism

Tuck, Christopher. 2000. "'Every Car or Moving Object Gone'—The ECOMOG Intervention in Liberia." *African Studies Quarterly* 4, no. 1 (Spring): 1–16.

Tukur, Sani. 2014. "Nigeria Cancels U.S. Military Training as Relations Between Both Nations Worsen." *The Premium Times, Nigeria*. December 1. Accessed October 25, 2015. www.premiumtimesng.com/news/headlines/172178-nigeria-cancels-u-s-military-training-relations-nations-worsen.html

Tull, Denis M. 2007. "The Democratic Republic of Congo: Militarized Politics in a 'Failed State'." In: *African Guerrillas: Raging against the Machine*, edited by Morten Bøås and Kevin C. Dunn, 113–130. Boulder, CO: Lynne Rienner Publishers.

Turse, Nick. 2015. "Tomgram: Nothing Succeeds like Failure." *TomDispatch* (blog). September 10. Accessed October 22, 2015. www.tomdispatch.com/blog/176042/tomgram%3A_nick_turse,_nothing_succeeds_like_failure/

Turse, Nick. 2015. *Tomorrow's Battlefield: U.S. Proxy Wars and Secret Ops in Africa*. Chicago, IL: Haymarket Books.

Ulfelder, Jay. 2014. "Coup Forecasts for 2014." *Dart-Throwing Chimp* (blog). January 25. Accessed October 15, 2015. https://dartthrowingchimp.wordpress.com/2014/01/25/coup-forecasts-for-2014/

United Nations Department of Public Information. 2005. *Sierra Leone—UNMAMSIL— Background.* Accessed October 17, 2015. www.un.org/en/peacekeeping/missions/past/unamsil/background.html

United Nations Development Program. 1994. *Human Development Report 1994.* Accessed October 16, 2015. http://hdr.undp.org/en/content/human-development-report-1994

United Nations Development Program. 2010. *Human Development Report 2010.* November. Accessed October 17, 2015. http://hdr.undp.org/sites/default/files/reports/270/hdr_2010_en_complete_reprint.pdf

United Nations Development Program. 2014. *Human Development Index 2014.* Accessed October 17, 2015. http://hdr.undp.org/en/content/human-development-index-hdi-table

United Nations Economic Commission for Africa. 2011. *Minerals and Africa's Development.* Accessed October 21, 2015. www.uneca.org/sites/default/files/Publication Files/mineral_africa_development_report_eng.pdf

United Nations High Commissioner for Refugees. 2013. *Regional Bureau for Africa— Fact Sheet.* October. Accessed October 12, 2015. www.unhcr.org/526934e89.html

United Nations High Commissioner for Refugees. 2015. *2015 UNHCR Regional Operations Profile—Africa.* Accessed October 12, 2015. www.unhcr.org/pages/4a02d7fd6.html

United Nations International Children's Emergency Fund. 2014. *Generation 2030 Africa.* August. New York, NY: UNICEF Division of Data, Research and Policy. Accessed October 26, 2015. www.unicef.org/publications/index_74751.html

United Nations News Centre. 2015. "Leaders' Personal Rivalry Has Undermined South Sudan's Hard-Won Independence—Security Council." July 9. Accessed October 26, 2015. www.un.org/apps/news/story.asp?NewsID=51375#.Vi4YDCtzu14

United Nations Office on Drugs and Crime. 2013a. *Transnational Organized Crime in West Africa: A Threat Assessment.* February 26. Accessed October 16, 2015. www.unodc.org/documents/data-and-analysis/tocta/West_Africa_TOCTA_2013_EN.pdf

United Nations Office on Drugs and Crime. 2013b. *Transnational Organized Crime in Eastern Africa: A Threat Assessment.* Vienna, Austria: UNODC. Accessed October 26, 2015. www.unodc.org/documents/data-and-analysis/Studies/TOC_East_Africa_2013.pdf

United Nations Peacekeeping Operations, "Current Peacekeeping Operations Facts and Figures," United Nations Peacekeeping Operations. Accessed January 29, 2016. www.un.org/en/peacekeeping/operations/current.shtml

United States. 1990. *The National Security Strategy of the United States.* March. Accessed October 18, 2015. https://bush41library.tamu.edu/files/select-documents/national_security_strategy_90.pdf

United States. 1994. *A National Security Strategy of Engagement and Enlargement.* July. Accessed October 18, 2015. http://nssarchive.us/NSSR/1994.pdf

United States. 1998. *A National Security Strategy for a New Century.* October. Accessed October 18, 2015. http://nssarchive.us/NSSR/1998.pdf

United States. 2002. *The National Security Strategy of the United States of America.* September. Accessed October 18, 2015. www.state.gov/documents/organization/63562.pdf

United States. 2006. *The National Security Strategy of the United States of America.* March 16. Accessed October 9, 2015. http://nssarchive.us/NSSR/2006.pdf

United States. 2010. *National Security Strategy.* May. Accessed October 9, 2015. www.whitehouse.gov/sites/default/files/rss_viewer/national-security-strategy.pdf

United States. 2012. "U.S. Strategy toward Sub-Saharan Africa." June. Accessed October 22, 2015. www.state.gov/documents/organization/209377.pdf

United States. 2014. *Fact Sheet: U.S. Support for Peacekeeping in Africa.* August 6. Accessed October 23, 2015. www.whitehouse.gov/the-press-office/2014/08/06/fact-sheet-us-support-peacekeeping-africa

United States Africa Command. 2012. "African Contingency Training Operations and Assistance." *U.S. Africa Command Fact Sheet.* October. Accessed October 18, 2015. www.africom.mil/Doc/9836

United States Africa Command. 2015. *Interagency.* Accessed October 19, 2015. www.africom.mil/about-the-command/interagency

United States Africa Command. 2015. *Mission Statement.* Accessed October 9, 2015. www.africom.mil/what-we-do

United States Africa Command. 2015. *Posture Statement 2015.* Accessed October 22, 2015. www.africom.mil/newsroom/document/25285/usafricom-posture-statement-2015

United States Census Bureau. "Trade in Goods with Africa." Accessed January 27, 2016. www.census.gov/foreign-trade/balance/c0013.htm/#204

United States Department of Defense. 2009. "Stability Operations." *Department of Defense Instruction* 3000.05. September 16. Accessed October 19, 2015. www.dtic.mil/whs/directives/corres/pdf/300005p.pdf

United States Department of Defense. 2010. *Joint Publication 1–02, Department of Defense Dictionary of Military and Associated Terms.* November 8. Accessed October 9, 2015. www.dtic.mil/doctrine/new_pubs/jp1_02.pdf

United States Department of Defense. 2012. *Sustaining U.S. Global Leadership: Priorities for 21st Century Defense.* January. Accessed October 22, 2015. www.defense.gov/news/defense_strategic_guidance.pdf

United States Department of Defense. 2014. *Quadrennial Defense Review 2014.* March 4. Accessed October 22, 2015. http://archive.defense.gov/pubs/2014_Quadrennial_Defense_Review.pdf

United States Department of Energy. 2015. "Nigeria. International Energy Data and Analysis." February 27. Accessed October 22, 2015. www.eia.gov/beta/international/country.cfm?iso=NGA

United States Department of Health and Human Services. 2014. "The Global HIV/AIDS Epidemic." *Global Statistics.* November 13. Accessed October 18, 2015. www.aids.gov/hiv-aids-basics/hiv-aids-101/global-statistics/

Unites States Department of State. 2003. *Patterns of Global Terrorism 2002.* April. Accessed October 18, 2015. www.state.gov/j/ct/rls/crt/2002/

United States Energy Information Administration. 2013. "Oil and Natural Gas in Sub-Saharan Africa." August 1. Accessed October 21, 2015. www.eia.gov/pressroom/presentations/howard_08012013.pdf

United States Government Accountability Office. 2010. "DOD Needs to Determine the Future of Its Horn of Africa Task Force." Report to the Subcommittee on National Security and Foreign Affairs, Committee on Oversight and Government Reform, House of Representatives. April. Accessed October 19, 2015. www.gao.gov/assets/310/303408.pdf

United States Government Accountability Office. 2012. "Humanitarian and Development Assistance. Project Evaluations and Better Information Sharing Needed to Manage the Military's Efforts." Report to Congressional Committees. February. Accessed October 19, 2015. www.gao.gov/assets/590/588334.pdf

United States Government Accountability Office. 2013. "DOD Needs to Reassess Options for Permanent Location of U.S. Africa Command." Report to Congressional Committees. September. Accessed October 19, 2015. www.gao.gov/assets/660/657492.pdf

Uppsala Conflict Data Program. 2012. *The Number of Conflicts Increased Strongly in 2011—Press release*. July 13. Accessed October 17, 2015. www.uu.se/en/media/news/article/?id=1724&area=2,3,16&typ=pm&na=&lang=en

Uppsala Conflict Data Program. 2015. *Global Instances of Political Violence*. Accessed October 17, 2015. www.ucdp.uu.se/ged/

Van Creveld, Martin. 2005. "It Will Continue to Conquer and Spread." *Contemporary Security Policy* 26, no. 2: 229–232.

Van De Walle, Nicolas. 2009. "U.S. Policy towards Africa: The Bush Legacy and the Obama Administration." *African Affairs* 109, no. 434: 1–21.

Vandiver, John. 2015. "Staging Sites Enable AFRICOM to Reach Hot Spots 'Within 4 Hours,' Leader Says." *Stars and Stripes*. May 8. Accessed October 26, 2015. www.stripes.com/news/africa/staging-sites-enable-africom-to-reach-hot-spots-within-4-hours-leader-says-1.345120

Voice of America. 2009. "Defining Sudan-Chad Relations." October 27. Accessed October 16, 2015. www.voanews.com/content/a-13-chad2007–01–14-voa17–66511042/553219.html

Wald, Charles F. 2006. "The Phase Zero Campaign." *Joint Forces Quarterly* 43, no. 4 (October): 72–75.

Wall Street Journal. 2002. "Spreading Influence: In South Africa, Mounting Evidence of al Qaeda Links." December 10.

Ward, William. 2007. *Statement before the House Armed Services Committee*. November 14.

Warner, Jason. 2015. "Complements or Competitors: The African Standby Force, the African Capacity for Immediate Response to Crises, and the Future of Rapid Reaction Forces in Africa." *African Security* 8: 56–73.

Welch, Claude E., ed. 1970. *Soldier and State in Africa*. Evanston, IL: Northwestern University Press.

Wezeman, Pieter D., Siemon T. Wezeman, and Lucie Béraud-Sudreau. 2011. "Arms Flows to Sub-Saharan Africa." *SIPRI Policy Paper* 30. December. Stockholm, Sweden: Stockholm International Peace Research Institute.

Whelan, Theresa. 2008. "Prepared Statement of Theresa Whelan, Deputy Assistant Secretary African Affairs, DOD." United States House of Representatives, Hearing before the Subcommittee on National Security and Foreign Affairs of the Committee on Oversight and Government Reform. July 16.

Whiteman, Kay and Douglas Yates. 2004. "France, Britain, and the United States." In: *West Africa's Security Challenges*, edited by Adekeye Adebajo and Ismail Rashid, 373–374. Boulder, CO: Lynne Rienner Publishers.

Whitlock, Craig. 2012. "Contractors Run U.S. Spying Missions in Africa." *Washington Post*. June 14. Accessed October 25, 2015. www.washingtonpost.com/world/national-security/contractors-run-us-spying-missions-in-africa/2012/06/14/gJQAvC4RdV_story.html

Whitlock, Craig. 2012. "Remote U.S. Base at Core of Secret Operations." *Washington Post*. October 25. Accessed October 26, 2015. www.washingtonpost.com/world/national-security/remote-us-base-at-core-of-secret-operations/2012/10/25/a26a9392–197a-11e2-bd10–5ff056538b7c_story.html

Whitlock, Craig. 2012. "U.S. Expands Secret Intelligence Operations in Africa." *Washington Post*. June 13. Accessed October 20, 2015. www.washingtonpost.com/world/national-security/us-expands-secret-intelligence-operations-in-africa/2012/06/13/gJQAHyvAbV_story.html

Whitlock, Craig. 2013. "Pentagon Deploys Small Number of Troops to War-Torn Mali." *Washington Post*. April 30. Accessed October 20, 2015. www.washingtonpost.com/world/national-security/pentagon-deploys-small-number-of-troops-to-war-torn-mali/2013/04/30/2b02c928-b1a0-11e2-bc39-65b0a67147df_story.html

Whitlock, Craig. 2013. "U.S. Trains African Soldiers for Somalia Mission." *Washington Post*. May 13. Accessed October 26, 2015. www.washingtonpost.com/world/national-security/us-trains-african-soldiers-for-somalia-mission/2012/05/13/gIQA-JhsPNU_story.html

Whitlock, Craig. 2014. "Coup Leader in Burkina Faso Received U.S. Military Training." *Washington Post*. November 3. Accessed October 26, 2015. www.washingtonpost.com/world/national-security/coup-leader-in-burkina-faso-received-us-military-training/2014/11/03/3e9acaf8-6392-11e4-836c-83bc4f26eb67_story.html

Wike, Richard. 2015. "5 Charts on America's (Very Positive) Image in Africa." *FactTank News in the Numbers*. July 23. Washington, DC: Pew Research Center. Accessed October 26, 2015. www.pewresearch.org/fact-tank/2015/07/23/5-charts-on-americas-very-positive-image-in-africa/

Williams, Paul. 2007. "Thinking about Security in Africa." *International Affairs* 83, no. 6: 1021–1038.

Wong, Colleen. 2013. "China Embraces Peacekeeping Missions." *The Diplomat*. August 9. Accessed October 26, 2015. http://thediplomat.com/2013/08/china-embraces-peacekeeping-missions/

Woodward, Peter. 2006. *U.S. Foreign Policy and the Horn of Africa*. Burlington, VT: Ashgate.

World Bank. 2012. *Bridging the Atlantic: Brazil and Sub-Saharan Africa. South-South Partnering for Growth*. Washington, DC: World Bank. Accessed October 22, 2015. http://documents.worldbank.org/curated/en/2012/01/16279478/bridging-atlantic-brazil-sub-saharan-africa-south-south-partnering-growth

World Bank. 2013. *Africa's Pulse: An Analysis of Issues Shaping Africa's Economic Future*. Volume 8 (October). Washington, DC: World Bank. Accessed October 25, 2015. www.worldbank.org/content/dam/Worldbank/document/Africa/Report/Africas-Pulse-brochure_Vol9.pdf

World Bank. 2015. *Despite the End of the Commodities Boom, African Countries Can Sustain their Economic Rise*. April 21. Accessed October 17, 2015. www.worldbank.org/en/news/feature/2015/04/21/despite-the-end-of-the-commodity-boom-african-countries-can-sustain-their-economic-rise

World Bank. 2015. *Ebola: Most African Countries Avoid Major Economic Cost but Impact on Guinea, Liberia, and Sierra Leone Remains Crippling*. January 20. Accessed October 18, 2015. www.worldbank.org/en/news/press-release/2015/01/20/ebola-most-african-countries-avoid-major-economic-loss-but-impact-on-guinea-liberia-sierra-leone-remains-crippling

World Bank. 2015. *South Sudan Overview*. Accessed October 17, 2015. www.worldbank.org/en/country/southsudan/overview

World Bank. 2015. "Sub-Saharan Africa." *Global Economic Prospects*. January. Washington, DC: World Bank. Accessed October 9, 2015. www.worldbank.org/content/

dam/Worldbank/GEP/GEP2015a/pdfs/GEP2015a_chapter2_regionaloutlook_SSA. pdf

World Trade Organization. 2012. *International Trade Statistics 2012*. Geneva, Switzerland: WTO. Accessed October 22, 2015. www.wto.org/English/res_e/statis_e/ its2012_e/its12_merch_trade_product_e.pdf

World Trade Organization and Confederation of Indian Industry. 2013. *India-Africa: South-South Trade and Investment for Development*. Accessed October 22, 2015. www.wto.org/english/tratop_e/devel_e/a4t_e/global_review13prog_e/india_africa_ report.pdf

Wrage, Stephen D. 2004. "U.S. Combatant Commander: The Man in the Middle." In: *America's Viceroys: The Military and U.S. Foreign Policy*, edited by Derek S. Reveron, 185–202. New York, NY: Palgrave Macmillan.

Wrong, Michela. 2001. *In the Footsteps of Mr. Kurtz*. New York, NY: HarperCollins.

Yamamoto, Don. 2011. "Prepared Statement of Don Yamamoto, Principal Deputy Assistant Secretary, Bureau of African Affairs." United States House of Representatives. Testimony before the Foreign Affairs Committee. October 25.

Youde, Jeremy. 2010. "Confronting Africa's Health Challenges." In: *New Security Threats and Crises in Africa*, edited by Jack Mangala. New York, NY: Palgrave Macmillan, 129–148.

Zacarias, Agostinho. 2003. "Redefining Security." In: *From Cape to Congo: Southern Africa's Evolving Security Challenges*, edited by Mwesiga Baregu and Christopher Landsberg, 31–52. Boulder, CO: Lynne Rienner Publishers.

Zakaria, Fareed. 2009. *The Post-American World*. New York, NY: W. W. Norton and Company.

Zeleza, Paul Tiyambe. 2008. "Introduction: the Causes and Costs of War in Africa." In: *The Roots of African Conflicts. The Causes and Costs*, edited by Alfred Nhema and Paul Tiyambe Zeleza, 1–35. Oxford, UK: James Currey.

Index

Made in the USA
Middletown, DE
27 August 2021